Lecture Notes in Computer Science   12481

More information about this subseries at http://www.springer.com/series/7408

Regina Bernhaupt · Carmelo Ardito ·
Stefan Sauer (Eds.)

Human-Centered Software Engineering

8th IFIP WG 13.2 International Working Conference, HCSE 2020
Eindhoven, The Netherlands, November 30 – December 2, 2020
Proceedings

 Springer

Editors
Regina Bernhaupt ⓘ
Eindhoven University of Technology
Eindhoven, The Netherlands

Carmelo Ardito ⓘ
Politecnico di Bari
Bari, Italy

Stefan Sauer ⓘ
University of Paderborn
Paderborn, Germany

ISSN 0302-9743   ISSN 1611-3349   (electronic)
Lecture Notes in Computer Science
ISBN 978-3-030-64265-5   ISBN 978-3-030-64266-2   (eBook)
https://doi.org/10.1007/978-3-030-64266-2

LNCS Sublibrary: SL2 – Programming and Software Engineering

This Springer imprint is published by the registered company Springer Nature Switzerland AG
The registered company address is: Gewerbestrasse 11, 6330 Cham, Switzerland

Foreword

The 8th International Working Conference on Human-Centered Software Engineering (HCSE 2020) was intended to be held physically at Eindhoven University of Technology, The Netherlands, during November 30 – December 2, 2020, but was held virtually due to the COVID-19 pandemic. HCSE is a bi-annual, single-track, working conference organized by the IFIP Working Group (WG) 13.2 on Methodology for User-Centred System Design. It aims at bringing together researchers and practitioners interested in strengthening the scientific foundations of user interface design, examining the relationship between software engineering and human–computer interaction and on how to strengthen human-centered design as an essential part of software engineering processes. Previous events were held in Salamanca, Spain (2007); Pisa, Italy (2008); Reykjavik, Iceland (2010); Toulouse, France (2012); Paderborn, Germany (2014); Stockholm, Sweden (2016); and Sophia Antipolis, France (2018).

The organization of the HCSE 2020 conference reflected how research in general, and conference organization in particular, is changing. Starting in August 2019, preparing the conference announcement and details to be distributed during INTER-ACT 2019's still physically held workshop, HCSE 2020 was organized not only once but three times: To be held physically in August 2020, to be held possibly in hybrid mode November 2020, and finally to be run fully as a virtual event due to the second wave of COVID-19 in The Netherlands envisaged for this time frame. It has now been the first edition run virtually, a milestone for our research field, demonstrating how publication models and associated conferences will change in our field. As organizers of HCSE, we are grateful to our community and loyal members of IFIP WG 13.2 from research and industry for virtually following us through this labyrinth of organizational changes, still submitting their recent work, and actively participating in our working conference online.

HCSE 2020 was focused on the interdependencies (overlapping and possibly conflicting dependencies that might occur) between user interface properties (such as usability, ux, privacy, trust, security, reliability, among others). We were also concerned by how stakeholders and developers value diverse user interface properties and how they manage conflicts between them (when a property might degrade the value of another). Our aim was to cover a large set of user interface properties and try to reveal their inner dependencies. The ultimate goal was to contribute to the development of theories, methods, tools, and approaches for dealing with multiple properties that should be taken into account when developing interactive systems.

The HCSE 2020 program included contributions from Belgium, Finland, France, Germany, Italy, The Netherlands, Norway, Spain, Sweden, and the UK. All contributions were peer-reviewed and received at least three reviews. In total, HCSE 2020 accepted six full research papers and four late-breaking results, with an acceptance rate of 35%. Five posters and demos were also accepted for inclusion in the conference program. Our sincere gratitude goes to the members of our Program Committee who devoted countless hours to providing valuable feedback to authors, ensuring the high quality of HCSE 2020's technical program.

The program was organized in three technical sessions and a demonstration and poster session. The conference program is available at http://www.hcse-conference.org/.

HCSE 2020 was supported by Eindhoven University of Technology, the Software Innovation Campus Paderborn (SICP) at Paderborn University, Springer, and IFIP's Technical Committee on Human–Computer Interaction (IFIP TC13) whose generous support was essential for making HCSE 2020 special and successful! Finally, our thanks go to all the authors who actually did the research work and especially to the presenters who sparked inspiring discussions with all the participants at HCSE 2020.

For further information about past and future events organized by IFIP WG 13.2, its members and activities, please visit the website http://ifip-tc13.org/working-groups/working-group-13-2/.

We thank all contributors and participants for making HCSE 2020 a special and fruitful conference!

Stay safe and healthy.

November 2020

Regina Bernhaupt
Carmelo Ardito
Stefan Sauer

IFIP TC13 - http://ifip-tc13.org/

Established in 1989, the International Federation for Information Processing Technical Committee on Human–Computer Interaction (IFIP TC 13) is an international committee of 32 member national societies and 10 Working Groups (WG), representing specialists of the various disciplines contributing to the field of human–computer interaction. This includes (among others) human factors, ergonomics, cognitive science, computer science, and design.

IFIP TC 13 aims to develop the science, technology, and societal aspects of human–computer interaction (HCI) by: encouraging empirical research; promoting the use of knowledge and methods from the human sciences in design and evaluation of computer systems; promoting better understanding of the relation between formal design methods and system usability and acceptability; developing guidelines, models, and methods by which designers may provide better human-oriented computer systems; and, cooperating with other groups, inside and outside IFIP, to promote user-orientation and humanization in system design. Thus, TC 13 seeks to improve interactions between people and computers, to encourage the growth of HCI research and its practice in industry and to disseminate these benefits worldwide.

The main orientation is to place the users at the center of the development process. Areas of study include: the problems people face when interacting with computers; the impact of technology deployment on people in individual and organizational contexts; the determinants of utility, usability, acceptability, and user experience; the appropriate allocation of tasks between computers and users especially in the case of automation; modeling the user, their tasks, and the interactive system to aid better system design; and harmonizing the computer to user characteristics and needs.

While the scope is thus set wide, with a tendency toward general principles rather than particular systems, it is recognized that progress will only be achieved through both general studies to advance theoretical understanding and specific studies on practical issues (e.g., interface design standards, software system resilience, documentation, training material, appropriateness of alternative interaction technologies, guidelines, the problems of integrating multimedia systems to match system needs and organizational practices, etc.).

IFIP TC 13 stimulates working events and activities through its WGs. WGs consist of HCI experts from many countries, who seek to expand knowledge and find solutions to HCI issues and concerns within their domains. The list of WGs and their area of interest is given below.

WG13.1 (Education in HCI and HCI Curricula) aims to improve HCI education at all levels of higher education, coordinate and unite efforts to develop HCI curricula and promote HCI teaching.

WG13.2 (Methodology for User-Centred System Design) aims to foster research, dissemination of information, and good practice in the methodical application of HCI to software engineering.

WG13.3 (HCI and Disability) aims to make HCI designers aware of the needs of people with disabilities and encourage development of information systems and tools permitting adaptation of interfaces to specific users.

WG13.4 (also WG2.7) (User Interface Engineering) investigates the nature, concepts, and construction of user interfaces for software systems, using a framework for reasoning about interactive systems and an engineering model for developing user interfaces.

WG 13.5 (Resilience, Reliability, Safety, and Human Error in System Development) seeks a framework for studying human factors relating to systems failure, develops leading edge techniques in hazard analysis and safety engineering of computer-based systems, and guides international accreditation activities for safety-critical systems.

WG13.6 (Human-Work Interaction Design) aims at establishing relationships between extensive empirical work-domain studies and HCI design. It will promote the use of knowledge, concepts, methods, and techniques that enable user studies to procure a better apprehension of the complex interplay between individual, social, and organizational contexts and thereby a better understanding of how and why people work in the ways that they do.

WG13.7 (Human–Computer Interaction and Visualization) aims to establish a study and research program that will combine both scientific work and practical applications in the fields of human–computer interaction and visualization. It will integrate several additional aspects of further research areas, such as scientific visualization, data mining, information design, computer graphics, cognition sciences, perception theory, or psychology, into this approach.

WG13.8 (Interaction Design and International Development) is currently working to reformulate their aims and scope.

WG13.9 (Interaction Design and Children) aims to support practitioners, regulators, and researchers to develop the study of interaction design and children across international contexts.

WG13.10 (Human-Centred Technology for Sustainability) aims to promote research, design, development, evaluation, and deployment of human-centered technology to encourage sustainable use of resources in various domains.

New WGs are formed as areas of significance in HCI arise. Further information is available at the IFIP TC13 website: http://ifip-tc13.org/.

IFIP WG 13.2 Members

Officers

Chair

Regina Bernhaupt   Eindhoven University of Technology, The Netherlands

Vice-chair

Carmelo Ardito   Politecnico di Bari, Italy

Secretary

Stefan Sauer   Paderborn University, Germany

Members

Balbir Barn	Middlesex University, UK
Cristian Bogdan	KTH Royal Institute of Technology, Sweden
Birgit Bomsdorf	Fulda University of Applied Sciences, Germany
Jan Borchers	RWTH Aachen University, Germany
Anders Bruun	Aalborg University, Denmark
John Carroll	Penn State University, USA
Bertrand David	École Centrale de Lyon, France
Anke Dittmar	University of Rostock, Germany
Xavier Ferre	Universidad Politécnica de Madrid, Spain
Holger Fischer	eresult, Germany
Peter Forbrig	University of Rostock, Germany
Tom Gross	University of Bamberg, Germany
Jan Gulliksen	KTH Royal Institute of Technology, Sweden
Anirudha Joshi	IIT Bombay, India
Kati Kuusinen	Technical University of Denmark, Denmark
Rosa Lanzilotti	University of Bari Aldo Moro, Italy
Marta Lárusdóttir	Reykjavik University, Iceland
Célia Martinie	Paul Sabatier University, France
Syed Bilal Naqvi	Lappeenranta University of Technology (LUT), Finland
Philippe Palanque	Paul Sabatier University, France
Fabio Paternò	ISTI-CNR, Italy
Michael Pirker	Hellobank BNP Paribas S.A., Austria
Ahmed Seffah	Lappeenranta University of Technology (LUT), Finland
Jan Hårvard Skjetne	SINTEF Digital, Norway
Alistair Sutcliffe	The University of Manchester, UK

Ricardo Tesoriero   University of Castilla-La Mancha, Spain
Jan Van den Bergh   Hasselt University, Belgium
Janet Wesson   Nelson Mandela University, South Africa
Marco Winckler   Université Nice Sophia Antipolis, France
Enes Yigitbas   Paderborn University, Germany

Observers

Selem Charfi   HD Technology, France
Shamal Faily   Bournemouth University, UK
Antonio Piccinno   University of Bari Aldo Moro, Italy
José Luís Silva   Instituto Universitário de Lisboa (ISCTE), Portugal
Jonathan Tolle   Thales Alenia Space, France

Organization

General Conference Chairs

Regina Bernhaupt   Eindhoven University of Technology, The Netherlands
Carmelo Ardito   Politecnico di Bari, Italy
Stefan Sauer   Paderborn University, Germany

Demos and Posters Chairs

Rosa Lanzilotti   University of Bari Aldo Moro, Italy
Jan Van den Bergh   Hasselt University, Belgium

Program Committee

Balbir Barn   Middlesex University, UK
John Carroll   Penn State University, USA
Bertrand David   École Centrale de Lyon, France
Anke Dittmar   University of Rostock, Germany
Shamal Faily   Bournemouth University, UK
Xavier Ferre   Universidad Politécnica de Madrid, Spain
Peter Forbrig   University of Rostock, Germany
Eduardo Garcia   CANSO, Belgium
Chris Johnson   Queen's University Belfast, UK
Anirudha Joshi   IIT Bombay, India
Jil Klünder   Leibniz Universität Hannover, Germany
Célia Martinie   Paul Sabatier University, France
Randall Mumaw   NASA, San José State University, USA
Syed Bilal Naqvi   Lappeenranta University of Technology (LUT), Finland
Philippe Palanque   Paul Sabatier University, France
Fabio Paternò   ISTI-CNR, Italy
Regina Peldszus   German Aerospace Center, Germany
Antonio Piccinno   University of Bari Aldo Moro, Italy
José Luís Silva   Instituto Universitário de Lisboa (ISCTE), Portugal
Alistair Sutcliffe   The University of Manchester, UK
Ricardo Tesoriero   University of Castilla-La Mancha, Spain
Janet Wesson   Nelson Mandela University, South Africa
Marco Winckler   Université Nice Sophia Antipolis, France
Enes Yigitbas   Paderborn University, Germany

Local and Online Organizing Committee

Raphael Reimann   Paderborn University, Germany
Nicole Weitzenbürger   Paderborn University, Germany
Enes Yigitbas   Paderborn University, Germany

Supporters and Partners

Supporters

Partners

International Federation for Information Processing

Contents

Poster and Demos

User-Centred Design Approaches

An Agile Framework Towards Inclusion

Supporting Teachers Working in an Inclusive Learning Environment

Dena Hussain[1]([⊠]) [iD], Jan Gulliksen[1] [iD], Olga Viberg[1] [iD], and Rebekah Cupitt[2] [iD]

[1] Media Technology and Interaction Design, School of Electrical Engineering and Computer Science, KTH Royal Institute of Technology, Stockholm, Sweden
{denah,gulliksen,oviberg}@kth.se

[2] Department of Film, Media and Cultural Studies, Birkbeck, University of London, London, UK
r.cupitt@bbk.ac.uk

Abstract. This paper reviews a user-centered agile systems design process, in the context of facilitating an educational environment. It focuses on the design of an ICT tool to support teachers in building an inclusive learning environment for children with Special Educational Needs (SEN), applying the "Index of Inclusion" (IoI) as a framework that directs the development process. The IoI is a set of guidelines that offers schools a supportive process of self-review and development when it comes to SEN; it draws on the views of staff in the educational sector. Extracting a requirements specification from a theoretical framework can be challenging. This study investigates how end-users, clients and stakeholders' involvement in the development process can be used with the aim of establishing design implications. The outcomes suggest that integration of user experience in the development processes, design ideas, and/or framework can be useful for software developers, specifically when working with diverging needs and perspectives.

Keywords: Information and communication technologies · User-centered design · HCI design and evaluation methods · Special Educational Needs · Index of inclusion · User-centered agile design

1 Introduction

Working towards providing an inclusive, high quality education for all pupils contributes towards the Sustainable Development Goals of the United Nations in 2018 [1]. Not only this, but high-quality learning environments, "can be particularly beneficial for children with disabilities" [2] and particularly, children with Special Educational Needs (SEN). There are different aspects when it comes to measuring quality of education. One of these measures is equal access to educational opportunity, such as mutual learning and sharing of best practices, with the aim to enable learning for everyone, including children with SEN. SEN is an umbrella term used to cover many kinds of difficulties in learning, and can be interpreted differently depending on the country [3]. For example, the Network of

© IFIP International Federation for Information Processing 2020
Published by Springer Nature Switzerland AG 2020
R. Bernhaupt et al. (Eds.): HCSE 2020, LNCS 12481, pp. 3–23, 2020.
https://doi.org/10.1007/978-3-030-64266-2_1

Experts in Social Sciences of Education and Training distinguishes between normative and non-normative difficulties. Whereas normative difficulties refer to physical and sensory difficulties, non-normative difficulties include social, emotional and behavioural difficulties, as well as learning difficulties, such as dyslexia [4]. Kaulina et al. [5] stress that children with SEN are children that require additional medical, educational or social support due to "disorders caused by illness, trauma or hereditary disease, regardless of whether the child has been defined as disabled in accordance with the procedure defined by the law" [5]. According to the Salamanca Statement and Framework for Action on Special Needs Education [6], inclusive education is based on the principles of social justice and provides everyone with equal access to education, suggesting that all children have equal rights to be included in the general education system to learn. This perspective can be considered as the core in defining an inclusive education. In most cases to achieve an inclusive education for children with SEN, additional information is required. This information is documented in an individual 'Action Plan'. An Action Plan is thus a tool that documents individual requirements and is a part of the assessment processes for children with SEN. It is therefore central to the process of creating an inclusive education. Teachers play a significant role and rely heavily on each student's action plan, and is essential to derive in consultation with the pupils themselves, their parents and specialist support teachers [7]. This action plan is continuously updated, evaluated, monitored for progress and can be altered if necessary. Within Sweden, action plans can contain: a) goals and learning objectives for the child, b) resources to be used, c) time-plans and methods of evaluation. Further to its core value of equal access, inclusive education planning is often guided by an Index of Inclusion (IoI) framework. This ICT tool is designed to fit into the existing processes and to aid teachers working to establish and maintain equal access in the education of children with SEN. As far back as the early 1990s, HCI characterized itself as a field concerned a human-needs driven process that developed alongside technological innovation [8]. As such, it can include various design approaches as well as cognitive or empirical approaches [9]. The version used in this study was a user-centred agile design approach that focused on the practices, organizational mechanisms, and relationships between each stakeholder group. During this study it was important to gain in-depth knowledge regarding different stakeholders' opinions on inclusion and how ICT tools could support their needs. The design process was motivated by the goal to develop supportive communication approaches between teachers in the educational sector in keeping with the IoI philosophy of collaboration [10]. It was also designed specifically for teachers that focus on supporting children with SEN. With the aim to examine the viewpoints and experiences of teachers in how ICT can support the process of creating an inclusive environment for children with SEN. The study aim is to examine and answer the following questions using an agile user centred development method:

1. What are the viewpoints held by teachers in regards to the link between the index of inclusion and SEN?
2. What are the viewpoints held by teachers in regards to ICT as a supportive tool in regards to inclusion?

2 Background

The purpose of this study was to utilize a User-Centered Agile development method and reflect on the important role of the teacher in identifying what forms of information can support the inclusion process of children with SEN. Applying the IoI in a number of different countries helped identify a common framework which can support creating an inclusive learning environment. In addition, to create optimized action plans that can lead towards sustainable processes. Hence, create a better understanding of how to create an inclusive school for all children. According to UNESCO policy guidelines on inclusion in education, it has been established that people's participation in so-called knowledge and information societies is contingent on the availability and affordability of ICTs, the relevance of ICT-based content and services, but also on their accessibility [11]. "Users must be able to perceive, understand and act upon ICT interfaces" [11]. Research often focuses on technical solutions designed to compensate for specific special educational needs in the form of a pedagogical tool. With an emphasis on "building collaborative relationships" [12] in educational settings, the IoI focuses on three factors, which are: 1) the child, 2) the environment, and 3) associated activities, with the aim of creating a guide that can support educators towards an inclusive way of thinking. Given the IoI frameworks focus on the importance of collaboration and communication in establishing an inclusive educational environment, this study focuses on the teachers' informational and communication needs and take into consideration their perspective on inclusive education for children with SEN.

2.1 The Index of Inclusion (IoI)

The index of inclusion is a set of guidelines that offers schools a supportive process of self-review and development when it comes to SEN. It draws on the views of staff in the educational sector. The emphasis is on factors affecting the development of thought and practice within schools, as well as broader contextual influences that that limit these changes, an exploration of overlooked possibilities for moving practice forward. [13–15]. The IoI support educators reflect and review the current structures, and create an inclusive development structure with the recognition and sharing of good practices, while at the same time drawing attention to ways of working which may pose obstacles to certain students' involvement and learning. The IoI creates a unified guide for educators to effectively support children with SEN [14]. The IoI is a set of guidelines, good practices and activities that can be adapted by schools to develop inclusive learning environments, including creating inclusive values, developing a school for all, and organizing support for diversity [14]. Originally deployed in 22 UK schools, the framework has since been tested in a number of schools in Australia [12–16], New Zealand [17] and some developing countries [18]. Studies have shown that the IoI framework can be applied to diverse educational settings ranging from schools to higher education in a number of different countries [19]. Together with existing mechanisms like Action Plans, the IoI guides teachers in their efforts to create an inclusive learning environment for children with SEN.

2.2 The Dimensions of Inclusion

Inclusion is context-bound and can therefore be interpreted in different ways. Previous research has identified 'inclusion' as a process of addressing and responding to the diversity of needs for all children, youth and adults through increasing participation in learning, cultures and communities aiming to eliminate exclusion within the educational system [20]. Qvortrup argues that the definition of an inclusive education must be according to the following three dimensions: 1) different levels of inclusion, identifying if the child is "recognized member of the community". 2) different arenas of inclusion, identifying "different types of social communities, in or from which a child may be included or excluded," and finally and 3) different degrees of inclusion, identifying "different degrees of being included in and/or excluded from social communities" [20]. Qvortrup concludes that to achieve an inclusive educational environment one must create a balance between the described dimensions and this is achieved by acknowledging these dimensions [20]. Skoglund identifies three factors: 1) Equivalence: the capability to see, recognize and understand the Childs' preconditions and needs; 2) Accessibility: the capability to adapt teaching, localities and social community from a diversity of needs, and 3) Participation: the capability to stimulate children to 'take part'; learning to be led, to lead oneself and learning to lead others [21]. These perspectives by Skoglund were considered as main requirements in this study.

2.3 Information and Communication Technologies and SEN

The impact of using ICTs has been investigated and studied over the years with different perspectives, including how ICT has offered new possibilities for improving different aspects of the educational sector, i.e. educational delivery and management processes, changing processes of teaching and learning environments, such as virtual environments. Designing ICT tools can be considered as a user' needs driven process used in complementing suitable technological innovation. Recent studies have shown some of the benefits of using information communication technologies (ICTs) in a SEN context, including a significant number of studies that examine how ICTs are being used in practice and what impact they have on the life of children with SEN [22, 23]. The results of these studies highlight such benefits as alternative communication, assistive and enabling technologies, virtual environments, technology integration, as well as saving time and labour [23]. Moreover, during the last decade, the design and development of software that provides children with SEN equal access to education has progressed significantly [24]. This paper draws on these instances of implementation of the IoI framework and its role in creating an inclusive educational environment and presents a case study that demonstrates how the IoI can also be applied in the development of an ICT tool.

3   Method

This study was built from a collaborative research project with three municipalities in Sweden, Iceland and Germany, in a project called the "iDea" (inclusion, Diversity and equity for all children) project. With the idea of inclusion taken to primarily mean recognizing the Childs' right to equal access to high-quality education and to be part of the social environment of a school. Behind this was an understanding of the need to strengthen an organizations' ability to work with and share all necessary information. Achieving this meant including both teachers and school administration i.e. headmasters in this part of the study. The project included participants such as teachers, pedagogical specialists, educational and administrators; and was conducted over a two-year period. The project's focus was to work with teachers on formalizing and identifying features and guidelines included in the IoI that they considered useful when supporting children with SEN. These features and guidelines were then used as requirements in the development of an ICT tool named "Digi-flow". To achieve this, the project consisted of three main milestones, each milestone focused on different aspects such as formalizing requirements, reviewing prototypes, etc. The participants participated in workshops, discussions, field visits and took part in a tailored education. The aim of these activities was for all members to gain better insights and understanding regarding different aspects associated with inclusion practices, i.e. the dimensions of inclusion, school systems and methods used by schools to support inclusion. Thus, gaining a better understanding of the educational environment of children and how they can develop skills to meet diversity.

3.1 User-Centered Agile Method (UCA)

A common challenge when developing a product involves understanding and identifying requirements that fit into context with the user's needs. User-Centered Agile (UCA) incorporates the user by bringing them into the various stages of an agile design approach. UCA is an iterative design process in which designers focus on the users and their needs in each phase of the design process. During this study the UCA process included the following stages: 1) understanding context of use; 2) specifying user requirements; 3) design solutions, and 4) evaluating against requirements [25]. In UCA, design teams involve users throughout the design process via a variety of research and design techniques, including user interviews, persona definition and prototype creation. [26, 27]. Hence, using an UCA method was key in gaining a better understanding of teachers' opinions and needs, adding an advantage in defining and confirming user needs and usability requirements. In addition to collecting data to gain a better understanding of the ICT tool requirements and system structure, with the objective to provide better insight into the potential benefits and limitations of the users' needs. This was achieved during different stages that are referred to as the 1) exploratory phase, 2) the development phase and the 3) evaluation phase. Each stage helped in determining if the design requirements accumulated were to be modified, eliminated and/or merged with others.

1. **Exploratory/Awareness stage**; the first stage included an exploratory study to verify the problem scope and evaluate the research problem. Starting with a general problem statement and initial awareness, which helped in collecting information about the problem domain, constraints, and environment. Investigating existing solutions via unstructured interviews with teachers. All the information gathered during this stage were combined to generate initial designs, which were then prototyped focusing on generating an overview of the main ICT tool. During the exploratory stage information was also gained via conducting workshops and discussion sessions, with the focus on process analysis and design. Identifying the status and challenges related

to children in need of special assistance and how teachers could identify and meet these needs.

2. **Development stage**; since user involvement can be critical in domains where user reflections are used to capture design feedback and can be more beneficial for specialized tools aimed for a particular context of use than for tools with a broader target user group [28]. In addition, since ICT tools can include various understandings, which influence the requirements, therefore during this study it was important to capture the different participants' views, the second stage consisted of several increments, which consisted of suggestions using prototypes, with the aim to capture user requirements in regards to the ICT design process. Which led to gaining a better understanding of the ICT tool being developed.

3. Finally, an **Evaluation stage,** which included evaluating various prototypes via surveys. The evaluation of technologies, i.e. ICT tools are often performed to learn how a new tool is being used, accepted and perceived. Another purpose of conducting evaluations is to gain knowledge about the effects of introducing new technologies into an organization. To achieve this, various approaches can be used including i.e. workshops and surveys.

Figure 1 represents a general overview of the design method used during this study, as illustrated; the study used a mix method approach, including workshops, surveys and prototyping that acted as development increments. Gathering requirements, over different stages in an incremental approach. Prototyping was used during this research study to obtain user feedback, confirming and/or generate requirements, which were then analyzed, prioritized and implemented into upcoming stages. Which were further refined during the development and evaluation phases, with the objective to answer questions and investigate unclear aspects of the problem.

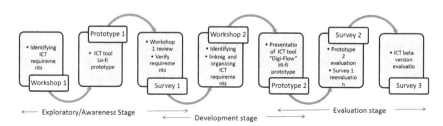

Fig. 1. Design method milestones including main activities driven by stakeholders

As Fig. 1 illustrates, since the user is the centre of the design process a number of workshops were conducted including the majority of project members to get feedback and drive the design process. Building design specifications in sets, each set of requirements collected was reviewed and confirmed by the study group using surveys and/or prototypes.

4   Results and Discussion

Several outcomes have been achieved during this study, which included benchmarking the concept of "dimensions of inclusion" between all European partners, and thus creating a unified framework that can be adapted to all countries. The development of the ICT tool "Digi-Flow" was influenced by gathering different reflections and information over three main milestones, giving a clearer objective for the tool and the information from the IoI needed to be included.

4.1   Exploratory/Awareness Stage

4.1.1   Workshop 1: Identifying ICT Requirements

The aim of the digital tool was to help users i.e. teachers in schools to structure their work when meeting with children with special needs. The first workshop was part of the exploratory methods and was conducted over a period of two days. The aim of the workshop was to identify and create a unified understanding between participants regarding the term the "Index of Inclusion". The goal of the workshop was to create a logical structure of questions generated from the specified index. To achieve this, a workshop including 18 participants from Sweden and Iceland, creating three teams each representing a country partner in the project. Each team consisted of six members, including teachers, educational administrators and special needs educators. The objective of the workshop was for each group to discuss and summarize their opinions and reflect on the concept of inclusion, leading further on to group discussions and finalizing a unified perspective that all project members could agree upon. The following is a list of general questions used for the workshop:

1. What is the status and challenges related to children in need of special assistance?
2. How can an ICT tool help the teachers in the school to structure the work in the meeting with children with SEN?

The participants reflected on the dimensions of inclusion and adapted them into three factors that could be explored and used as requirements to achieve inclusion for children with SEN. Which are: a) see and recognize; b) understand the need; and finally, c) adapt and support. The data collected from each of these questions is key to building inclusion in educational settings for children with SEN. As a result, the following list of associated factors and relevant information needed based on the requirements:

1. The first requirement was to include the viewpoint "See and recognize the problem and how it reveals itself". This means that the ICT tool should support the user in identifying issues in association to inclusion and frame these problems. To achieve this the participant's questions focused on the child, identifying the Childs' school history, social relations and communication and information regarding diagnoses and formal evaluations of the child, and other observations.
2. A second requirement was that the ICT tool should support the user in reflecting on current state by "Understand the need"; in other words that after recognizing

the problem an evaluation, the tool should support by mapping the problem and gathering information. To support the requirements, the participants agreed that the following questions are necessary to answer; including reflections regarding the Childs' experience of its school environment. What challenges does the child experience? What barriers does the child experience? How does the child describe its own lifestyle? Finally, what does the Childs' parents, teachers and others say about the Childs' lifestyle.

3. The third requirement was to include the viewpoint "Adapt and support", the participants noted that to support a child with SEN, user of the tool need to understand what the Childs' needs are, to be able to adapt the learning environment. Therefore, this requirement included questions, such as a) Are there leisure activities the child can participate in? b) What possibilities of change are in the environment? c) What opportunities are in the teacher's abilities? d) What specialized professional assistance can we use? e) And what opportunities do we see in the resources of the municipality?

This list of questions was driven and provided by the participants based on the IoI and were identified by the participants as important factors in creating an inclusive education for children with SEN, which they considered had a direct influence on further stages of the project. Figure 2 illustrates the first sketches produced representing the participants conception of the concepts introduced in the workshop.

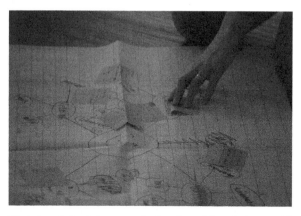

Fig. 2. Workshop 1, Participants early sketches of the mind map of inclusion

To give more depth to these concepts the study also needed to gather information relating to the Childs' education and care, such as, information on their school history, diagnoses and formal evaluations, and their experience of schooling.

The outcomes of this workshop were used to create a framework, which comprised a combined overview of the dimensions of inclusion in relation to the IoI. This translated into a unified process map for the design flow of the ICT tool that was to be developed (See Fig. 3).

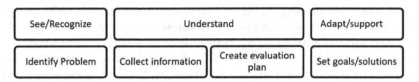

Fig. 3. Workshop 1, Participants first unified process map for the design flow of the ICT tool that was to be developed.

4.1.2   Survey 1: Verifying ICT Requirements

As part of the first milestone (the explorative phase) and after the first workshop, an initial questionnaire including 16 participants was conducted with the aim of gathering more detailed requirements and to verify the initial requirements previously identified and gathered. A survey was used to help; 1) verify potential users and their communication needs and perspectives; 2) what details are considered necessary as "basic information" and finally 3) identify if the developed tool should store all data or not. The question include in the survey were:

1. "Who do you see is the potential user?" – This question was framed to identify who will be the main user of the tool, to help identify in later stages what specific user's requirements could be needed. Three different users were presented; teacher, special education teacher and/or head of the school
2. "What background information should be included?" – This question was framed to help identify what information should be gathered, categorized and prioritized. Including information regarding the child, for example what are the Childs' interests such as music, painting, etc. In addition, contact information that the teacher could need, including other caregivers that support the child in other sectors, i.e. healthcare sector, including for example the Childs' name, caregivers name and role. In addition to noting the Childs' strong points/weak points, the Childs' perspective, and related social background and finally, background information such as telephone number, name of person/company, helpful websites.
3. "Is not saving data acceptable?" – This question was framed to verify if further design requirements regarding general data protection regulations were needed. In addition to considering the safety and wellbeing of the individual and others who may be affected.

Most of the questions in the survey included simple "yes", "no" feedback, with the aim to create a focus viewpoint from the different participants. The survey confirmed with 75% identifying the teacher as the target user group and 50% claiming the Special education teacher while only 25% identified the Head of the school as the main user. What was interesting during this survey was that all participants agreed that there was a lack of helpful information regarding both information regarding previous action plans and programs, with 100% defining the need for previous plans. In addition, 60% requested details regarding the Childs' strengths and weakness. In addition, 100% indicated the need for supportive information and guidance in the form of helpful websites and contact information of caregivers in other sectors. The feedback also indicates that the majority agreed that saving information was not acceptable, with 93% response to not saving information due the sensitivity of the data. Therefore, the ICT tool was designed to produce results that could not be stored. Even though this survey helped formalizing early design requirements, more in-depth details were required before development of the tool could begin. Therefore, a second iteration was conducted, and it included a second workshop and a second survey in addition to creating the first digital prototype.

4.1.3 Prototype 1: ICT Tool Lo-Fi Prototype

The results from the first workshop were used in creating a mind map as illustrated in Fig. 3. (Workshop 1, Participants first unified process map for the design flow of the ICT tool that was to be developed). This was used in planning a second workshop, and as a source for the main requirements for the ICT prototype. However, before setting up the second workshop, confirmation of the first set of requirements was needed. Therefore, based on the main requirements derived from the first workshop, a lo-fi prototype was produced (See Fig. 4) and presented to the project participants. It illustrated a structured requirement overview for the ICT prototype in the form of a flowchart that became part of the ICT-tool, Digi-Flow.

Fig. 4. Confirmation of requirements, illustrated in an overview of the first Digi-Flow Lo-fi prototype

The purpose of Digi-Flow is that when a teacher meets a child who is in need of support, they use the ICT tool Digi-Flow, starting with the first step in Fig. 4, "basic information" (details included in survey 1), then depending on how the child responds to the framing of the questions in step two. This stage consisted of a set of "questions" formulated by the participants (details included in workshop 2) that helps teachers reflect on the IoI and finally the tool will assess the information and the results of the questions generating an assessment. Moreover, reach the "resources" step, which offers teachers advice on how they should proceed. Presenting this lo-fi prototype at the end of workshop 1 was to confirm our understanding of the intended tool that would be developed and to verify our understanding of the main project scope associated.

4.2   Development Stage

4.2.1   Workshop 2: Identifying ICT Requirements

As part of milestone two (the development stage) workshop 2 was organized based on the results from the survey 1. Preparations for this workshop included that the participants provided a new version of the mind map sketch created in workshop 1. This resulted with the participants providing an in-depth design of the min map. As illustrated in Fig. 5 the mind map now included a clearer perspective from the participants regarding the dimensions of inclusion, identifying three main factors that must be included in the assessment phase of the tool, which are 1) the environment, 2) the activities and 3) the child. This modified mind map helped all participants in preparations for workshop 2. The workshop was conducted with 25 participants, dividing all participants into five groups; each group included two children between the ages of 12 to 15 that had agreed to participate with the consent of their parents.

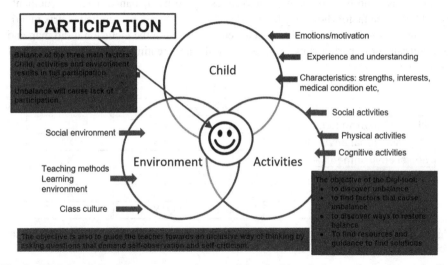

Fig. 5.   Workshop 2, Participants presented a second sketch of the mind map of inclusion originally designed in workshop1 (see Fig. 2)

Based on the workshop layout the following information was produced by the participants and includes three main discussion categories in relation to the dimension of inclusion mind map created in workshop 1, which are a) barriers; b) child participation and c) learning opportunities. Participants reflected on associated factors that could affect participation: a) children's understanding, b) acceptance of children by peers and c) atmosphere in both the classroom and in school, as illustrated in Fig. 6.

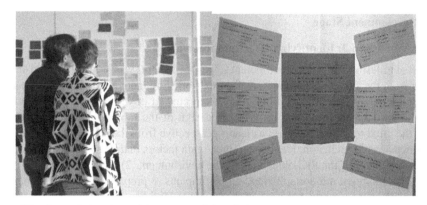

Fig. 6. Workshop 2, participants organizing, linking and formalizing requirements.

This was done by providing colored notes to the participants, where participants would link these factors how they felt needed. Figure 7 represent a unified matrix identifying the relation between the different aspects included in the inclusion mind map and the main categories participants considered to influence creating an inclusive educational environment.

	Barriers	Participation	Opportunities
Physical environment	X	X	
Organizational environment		X	X
Social environment	X	X	X
Class/school culture	X	X	X
Teaching environment	X	X	X
Child	X	X	

Fig. 7. Workshop2, Participants perspectives identifying the relation between the different aspects included in the inclusion mind map

The outcomes of workshop2 resulted in an updated mind map of inclusion. This update included creating inclusion qualities (see Fig. 8). After reflections from the participants regarding the workshop, participants presented their views. This in terms led to the identification of what was termed, "full participation" [40] and was defined as the 'actions and resources required in helping the teacher in creating an inclusive environment for children with SEN'. This included:

1. Environmental needs – details provided by the participants included: Childs' social background; Childs' social relations; Teaching and evaluation methods; Teacher's and other staff's perception of child and it's family; Organization of classroom and other surroundings in school; Transportation; Technical support, use of support devices; School/classroom culture regarding diversity and inclusion.

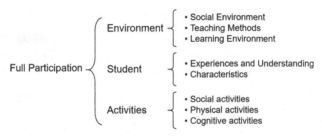

Fig. 8. A unified perspective created by the participants, identifying factors associated with creating a balanced learning environment

2. Childs' needs – this category included information such as; Childs' experience of school; Childs' understanding of school demands; Child's self-efficacy; Childs' success and achievements; Childs' strengths; Childs' interests; Existing medical and cognitive conditions and diagnoses teachers need to know.
3. Associated activities – everything the child does in school and other surroundings that matter; Childs' participation; Childs' communication; Childs' skills regarding school related and social activities, i.e. reading, writing, communicating with others, physical activities, cognitive activities, etc.

This unified perspective was an important result in this project, since it created a unified model of the IoI that all participants agreed to use and which was utilized in the development of Prototype 2. Digitalizing the concept "full participation" as a core system requirement (details in prototype 2) [29]. As a result, the ICT tool "Digi flow" needed to support the users in investigating and determining the factors associated with creating a balanced learning environment by assessing the level of 'full participation'.

4.2.2   Prototype: 2: Teachers ICT Tool "Digi-Flow"

As part of milestone three (the evaluation stage) the following model illustrated in Fig. 9 was provided by participants including their thoughts on the main design requirements to be included in the ICT tool "Digi-flow". Based on this model, the ICT tool was designed in two segments; the first segment consisted of general background information form, this decision was based on the requirements gathered and confirmed in survey 1 (Identifying ICT requirements) and prototype 1 (ICT tool lo-fi prototype). The second segment of questions totally depended on the answers received from stage one; in this stage the user, i.e. teacher, goes through a series of logical questions that help in the filtering process. This was based on survey 1 and included details form the updated mind map in workshop 2 (Identifying ICT requirements).

In addition to including base question; which were generated from the inclusion mind map, details were required in order to digitalize the concept of "full participation". Therefore, a subset of participants were asked to fill in a customized datasheet provided by the developers, which included the following columns:

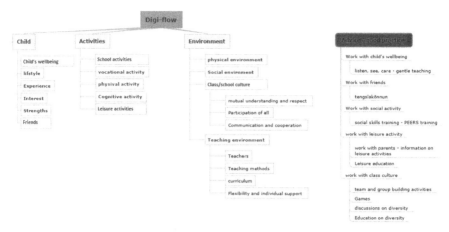

Fig. 9. Prototype sketch provided by the participants including main ICT tool features

1. Column one included each question and a sub list of answer options. Participants were required to provide each question with a set of related answers in the form of multiple choices.
2. Column two included a numeric scale, a 'weight values' associated with each answer that was used and represented by a numerical scale from 1 to 5. Participants were asked to determine 'weight values' where 1 represented less critical/low priority and 5 representing highly critical, thus giving the associated answer a high priority.
3. Column three included the main categories based on the inclusion mind map, which are: a) child; b) activities and c) environment, where the participants needed to link each question in the list to one or more of these categories.
4. Colum four included additional subcategories, which were based on the inclusion mind map, i.e. for the main category environment, subcategories could be social environment, learning environment or other subcategories. This association between main and sub categories was determined by the participants.
5. Finally, column five included follow-up questions; the objective was to crosslink and associate questions to others that could be related.

Identifying these 'weights' helped create additional attributes to the questions being asked, and helped determine the data navigation process. Thus, using the base question to represent the main distribution of the weight scheme in the designed prototype was to create an interactive questionnaire system that can respond according to the answers provided by the users of the tool. As the ICT platform fetches a question, examining and depending on the answer provided, the tool will identify any sub-questions linked to it. The 'weights' in this platform are used to determine the importance of the questions. Weights are stored for every answer and affect the questions in a 'positive' or 'negative' way. Linking every question and resources to a category. Each question answered by the user will determine the next set of questions, creating a customized map/path for each child, the final result of the ICT tool would help illustrate to the user i.e. teacher what can be prioritized and/or what to take into consideration as a first step towards inclusion for the child in hand. Based on the weight analysis (accumulated values). The main categories were organized with the aim of creating a ranking dependency based on the associated values. Results of the ICT tool are illustrated in a graphical representation for the user (See Fig. 14) in a simple layout. This included that users could only print the full details since storing information was not an option to be used based on the feedback from survey 1 (Identifying ICT requirements).

4.3 Evaluation Stage

4.3.1 Survey 2: Prototype 2 Evaluation

As part of milestone three (the evaluation stage) and after collecting in-depth details from the participants in both workshop 2 and hands-on involvement from participants in designing the second prototype, the development team was able to produce a second digitalized hi-fi prototype. To receive feedback from the participants regarding the presented prototype, an online survey was distributed. The aim of the survey was as follows:

1. **Verify requirements** – the following questions were asked to understand what type of platforms and internet browsers teachers' use on a daily basis. With the aim of creating a tool that could support teachers with everyday technology and not impose new needs. Therefore, the survey included questions such as, what type of device are you using? In addition, which browser are you using?
2. **Validate and evaluate the prototype** – the following questions aimed on understanding the teacher's general acceptance of the tool's layout and information navigation. Collecting information regarding how the teachers used the tool and if they thought that the tool included and conveyed all the information from earlier stages. In addition to verifying that there were no unnecessary stages or details in the tool, with the aim of creating an easy to use tool that was not time consuming but useful for teachers to use. Since it was important to create a tool that would not require additional efforts and time, which could lead to the teacher not using the tool, i.e. did you have any problems when filling in the Childs' basic information. Did you have any problems showing the result page? Did you find any problems downloading the PDF? Were there too many questions? etc.

The survey included questions with a rating scale from 1 to 5 (where 1 represents the lowest value and 5 the highest). Figure 10 and Fig. 11 illustrates a general acceptance from participants regarding the use of the ICT tool "Digi-flow", in addition to giving feedback on what could be improved for the upcoming sprints [29]. During 16 participants responded out of the original 30 participants.

As illustrated 80% gave feedback which indicated a general satisfaction with the presented tool, with a percentage of 63% in total expressing a higher level of content with the general performance of the tool and 75% finding the tool easy to understand. Feedback from the survey identified that 65.5% of the teachers use Internet Explorer, while 25% use Safari and the remaining 12.5% used Edge. In addition, 100% of all participants use either desktops or laptop, therefore the development team did not need to consider touch

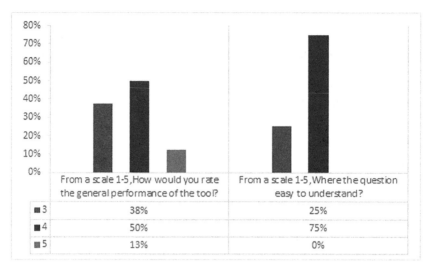

Fig. 10. Survey 2 feedback

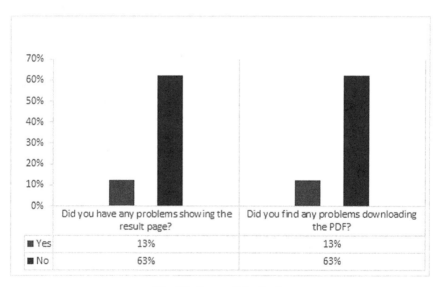

Fig. 11. Survey 2 feedback

screens features in their development requirements. In addition, 50% thought that some questions could be removed and that there was 35% similarity between some questions, which lead to 75% indicating that they would prefer to skip some question. Based on the feedback revisions were made to the tool [29]. As a result, developers were able to produce the first ICT BETA tool. This version of the tool was shared with the participants, and were provided with a third evaluation survey.

4.3.2 Survey 3: ICT Beta Version Evaluation

Since the project was conducted in an UCA approach and based on the feedback in the previous survey 2 (Prototype evaluation), modifications were made to the prototype leading to an ICT beta version. After the release of the ICT beta version a new survey was conducted; the objective was to validate the prototype that was built according to the specified requirements.

Participants were asked to use the tool and reflect on their experience (See Fig. 12, 13). The results would then be taken into consideration before the final deployment of the ICT tool. By utilizing the tool, the teacher initiates the first step in the flowchart then depending on how the child responds to the framing of a question/issues they will continue in the flowchart and will ultimately get a form of advice on how they should proceed. Figure 12 is an example based on the questionnaire results and illustrates that the main issue that the teacher needs to focus on, which is associated with the activities as a main focus point, since it received the higher priority and the learning environment with a lower priority.

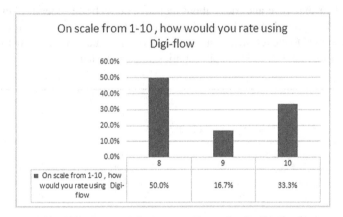

Fig. 12. Survey 3, ICT beta version evaluation feedback

By answering questions divided into different categories, the tool can determine which resources that are applicable. Depending on what category and subcategory gets the most weight (i.e. Environment - social environment) the user will be provided with a collection of information material and tips on where to seek for more information.

The tool was design with simple design elements to create a common and easy to use everyday tool, as illustrated in Fig. 14 and Fig. 15. The user also will get information on good practice examples. including a draft Action plan containing; 1) Goals and objectives for working with the child; 2) Resources, ways to reach goals and cooperation partners in other sectors, i.e. healthcare sectors for working with the child; 3) Methods to be used, including the Childs' strengths and interests, adaptation of environment, working on inclusive attitude, etc. On an overall level, this represents the initial dimensions of inclusion stages presented in Fig. 4 and Fig. 7. By using a user-centered agile design approach that incorporates workshops, surveys and iterative prototyping, the Digi-Flow design process offered an example of how to involve teachers in the design process and

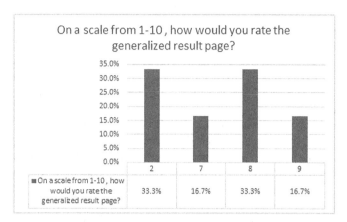

Fig. 13. Survey 3, ICT beta version evaluation feedback

how to use their expertise and ideas about inclusive education to identify key requirements. Digi-Flow provided teachers with essential information in the form of a digital
map that responded to the teachers' categorizations of information according to the three
dimensions of inclusion (barriers, opportunities and atmosphere).

DigiFlow
Here you answer questions about the student divided into the existing categories. Use the plus-button (+) to expand the containers. Below each question you can see which category it belongs to. If a question have a sub-question it will be shown when an answer is selected. When you have answered all the questions in all containers you will be able to press the submit button. If nothing happens when clicking submit, make sure that you really have answered all questions and try again.
Child category   **+**
Activity category   **+**
Environment category   **+**
Submit

Fig. 14. Digi-Flow first page

In addition, the focus on teachers in class, who are responsible for providing an
inclusive environment for children with SEN. The study's findings have a number of
implications concerning creating an inclusive environment for children with SEN from
the teachers' perspective. One issue is the teacher's role in identifying the SEN required
for each child as a process that requires detailed information from a number of sources
that is presented in a structured way that aligns with their views on inclusion. The IoI

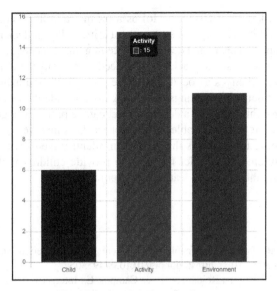

Fig. 15. The Digi-Flow result page

proved to be a logical framework that mapped neatly onto the teachers' perspectives and acted, as a communicative device that made it possible for both teachers' and developers to identify the correct resources required, supporting a child with SEN in the Swedish educational context. When it comes to UCD activities, there is no size fits all. The specific context will often include certain unique aspects that require some form of tailored UCD activities. Therefore, during this study the use of UCA activities shows that some questions in the survey were design driven, identifying from a user's point of view what information is needed and if the presented solution was easy to use and thus support users working with SEN on a daily basis.

5 Conclusion and Contribution

During a two years research and development period, we realized how using an UCA method supported both developers and stakeholders in formalizing ideas, forming and organization information, which lead to creating requirements that stakeholders could recognize and relate to. This helped stakeholders reflect on previous requirements gathered and provide them with the knowledge needed to formulate ideas, which supported modifying any requirements in further stages. We realized that to support user participation working in an agile framework, it was important to include them in creating objectives and prioritize requirements based on a joint perspective. Thus, the participants helped derive the development process, which also led to a clearer understanding of the users' needs. In conclusion, this study offers an example of how the various aspects of how utilizing a UCA method and including various stakeholders throughout the design process, for example, by obtaining domain specific knowledge from users that can support and categorize requirements. In other words, how potential users', i.e. teacher's, perspective plays a key role. Using the IoI as a means to collect input from various teachers representing the educational sector was a critical design decision. In addition, this framework helped teachers and designers alike in gaining a better understanding of user requirements as well as the teachers' own needs, and lead to the identification of some of the major challenges associated with the process of establishing an inclusive educational environment. The findings that emerged alongside the development of the ICT tool are key insights into how a design project can be part of a larger effort toward inclusion. Moreover, it offers valuable support for teachers involved in the design process, through creating focus points that help them identify their own core values and informational requirements in order for them to provide children with SEN with an inclusive and sustainable balanced learning environment.

References

1. Griggs, D., et al.: Policy: sustainable development goals for people and planet. Nature **495**(7441), 305–307 (2013). https://doi.org/10.1038/495305a
2. García-Carrión, R., Molina Roldán, S., Roca Campos, E.: Interactive learning environments for the educational improvement of students with disabilities in special schools. Front. Psychol. **9**, 1744 (2018). https://doi.org/10.3389/fpsyg.2018.01744
3. Meijer, C., et al.: Inclusive education across Europe: reflections upon 10 years of work from the European agency for development in special needs education. Child. Educ. **83**(6), 361–365 (2007)
4. Drabble, S.: Support for children with special educational needs (SEN) (2013)
5. Kauliņa, A., et al.: Children with special educational needs and their inclusion in the educational system: pedagogical and psychological aspects. J. Pedagogy Psychol. "Signum Temporis" **8**(1), 37–42 (2016)
6. UNESCO Basic Education: The Salamanca statement and framework for action on special needs education. UNESCO, Paris (1994)
7. Bartolo, P., Björck-Åkesson, E., Giné, C., Kyriazopoulou, M.: Inclusive early childhood education: an analysis of 32 European examples. European Agency for Special Needs and Inclusive Education (2016)
8. Marchionini, G., Sibert, J.: An agenda for human-computer interaction: science and engineering serving human needs. ACM SIGCHI Bull. **23**(4), 17–32 (1991)
9. Braund, P., Schwittay, A.: The missing piece: human-driven design and research in ICT and development. In: 2006 International Conference on Information and Communication Technologies and Development. IEEE (2006)
10. Hansen, J.H., Carrington, S., Jensen, C.R., Molbæk, M., Secher Schmidt, M.C.: The collaborative practice of inclusion and exclusion. Nordic J. Stud. Educ. Policy **6**(1), 47–57 (2020)
11. UNESCO, P.U.: Policy guidelines on inclusion in education (2009)
12. Deppeler, J., Harvey, D.: Validating the British index for inclusion for the Australian context: stage one. Int. J. Incl. Educ. **8**(2), 155–184 (2004)
13. Ainscow, M.: Developing inclusive education systems: what are the levers for change? J. Educ. Change **6**(2), 109–124 (2005). https://doi.org/10.1007/s10833-005-1298-4
14. Booth, T. Ainscow, M.: Index for inclusion (2002)
15. Ainscow, M., Sandill, A.: Developing inclusive education systems: the role of organisational cultures and leadership. Int. J. Incl. Educ. **14**(4), 401–416 (2010)
16. Vaughan, M.: An index for inclusion. Eur. J. Spec. Needs Educ. **17**(2), 197–201 (2002)

17. Carrington, S., Bourke, R., Dharan, V.: Using the index for inclusion to develop inclusive school communities. In: Teaching in Inclusive School Communities, pp. 341–366 (2012)
18. Carrington, S., Duke, J.: Learning about inclusion from developing countries: using the index for inclusion. Meas. Incl. Educ. **3**, 189–203 (2014)
19. Cabral, L., Mendes, E., Anna, L., Ebersold, S.: Academic and professional guidance for tertiary students with disabilities: gathering best practices throughout European universities (2015)
20. Qvortrup, A., Qvortrup, L.: Inclusion: dimensions of inclusion in education. Int. J. Incl. Educ. **22**(7), 803–817 (2018)
21. Skoglund, P.: Fundamental challenges and dimensions of inclusion in Sweden and Europe. La nouvelle revue de l'adaptation et de la scolarisation **1**, 207–221 (2014)
22. Drigas, A., Kokkalia, G.: ICTs and special education in kindergarten. Int. J. Emerg. Technol. Learn. (iJET) **9**(4), 35–42 (2014)
23. Abed, M.G.: Teachers' perspectives surrounding ICT Use amongst SEN students in the mainstream educational setting. World J. Educ. **8**(1), 6–16 (2018)
24. Adam, T., Tatnall, A.: Using ICT to Improve the Education of Students with Learning Disabilities. In: Kendall, M., Samways, B. (eds.) Learning to Live in the Knowledge Society. ITIFIP, vol. 281, pp. 63–70. Springer, Boston, MA (2008). https://doi.org/10.1007/978-0-387-09729-9_8
25. ISO B and B. STANDARD: Ergonomics of human-system interaction (2010)
26. Vinekar, V., Slinkman, C.W., Nerur, S.: Can agile and traditional systems development approaches coexist? An ambidextrous view. Inf. Syst. Manag. **23**(3), 31–42 (2006)
27. Williams, H., Ferguson, A.: The UCD perspective: before and after agile. In: Agile 2007, AGILE 2007. IEEE (2007)
28. Jurca, G., Hellmann, T.D., Maurer, F.: Integrating agile and user-centered design: a systematic mapping and review of evaluation and validation studies of Agile-UX. In: 2014 Agile Conference, pp. 24–32 (2014)
29. Hussain, D.: The development of ICT tools for E-inclusion qualities. In: Auer, M., Zutin, D. (eds.) Online Engineering & Internet of Things. LNNS, vol. 22, pp. 645–651. Springer, Cham (2018). https://doi.org/10.1007/978-3-319-64352-6_60

A Generic Visualization Approach Supporting Task-Based Evaluation of Usability and User Experience

Regina Bernhaupt[1], Célia Martinie[2(✉)], Philippe Palanque[2(✉)], and Günter Wallner[1]

[1] Department of Industrial Design, Eindhoven University of Technology, Eindhoven, The Netherlands
{r.benrhaupt,g.wallner}@tue.nl
[2] ICS-IRIT, Université Paul Sabatier Toulouse III, Toulouse, France
{martinie,palanque}@irit.fr

Abstract. Analyzing evaluation results of usability and user experience studies has its limitations when it comes to personalized user interfaces, highly complex and connected systems, or internationally used services involving millions of users. To support the analysis of the evaluation results of usability and user experience, a task-based evaluation approach is proposed. This approach uses multiple visualization views to support the analysis of evaluation results. The visualization offers different temporal views ranging from individual to more cumulative data views in order to combine results from evaluations and task models. The applicability of this approach is presented on a simple but demonstrative case study from television and entertainment.

Keywords: Visualization · User experience · Usability · Task modelling · Evaluation · User studies

1 Introduction

Traditional approaches, processes, and methods of user-centered design and development have recently been challenged by a variety of technological shifts and changes in users' behaviors and expectations. The introduction and usage of artificial intelligence (AI) technologies, the challenges of the internet of things with its plethora of connected devices, and the phenomena of internet-based services and companies with millions of users push these methods, processes, and approaches to their boundaries. Especially when it comes to usability and user experience (UX) evaluation.

While evaluation methods have partly evolved and changed, some main challenges remain. It is unclear how to evaluate and deal with systems where every individual user will get a personalized recommendation that evolves each time

R. Bernhaupt et al. (Eds.): HCSE 2020, LNCS 12481, pp. 24–44, 2020.
https://doi.org/10.1007/978-3-030-64266-2_2

another user is interacting with the system (cf. [27]). Due to such personalized recommendations every experience for one user will be different, leading to incomparable different user experiences for a user and between users in terms of evaluation findings.

The challenge when performing an evaluation related to connected devices, like in a household today, is the multitude and plethora of available devices and services that people use (alongside the product that might be available) making it difficult to understand the technological context of usage that can affect the outcomes of the evaluation. When looking at web services and companies like Facebook, the number of evaluation participants must be extremely high to represent characteristics of the world-wide user base. This brings the challenge of comparing millions of data points and the key question is how to make such data points comparable, when the same or similar user activities are performed.

Finally, research in human-computer interaction (and other domains such as software engineering) faces the same challenges when it comes to research evaluation methods. It becomes more and more difficult to make sense of gathered data, as the contextual information when it was gathered is merely not recorded/represented. And it is challenging to compare evaluation data that was gathered over time or in different studies. When it comes to empirical and artefact research contributions, evaluation methods [15] have to be adapted.

A common problem of these challenges is the non-comparability of the results for different user experiences when performing the same activity (within user) and for different user experiences (between users). Key challenge is the missing ability to understand what people have been doing and which task or tasks people were performing, and how this relates to the evaluation data that was gathered. The proposed approach to address these challenges is to design visualization techniques for evaluation data in order to support evaluators' activities. More precisely, these techniques enable to (a) compare unique personal user experiences for a user or between users, (b) understand the impact of contextual influences on the evaluation data, (c) compare evaluation data over longer periods of time or time spans – or over different user studies, and (d) compare multiple software qualities like usability and UX and their effects on one another.

More precisely, we developed a novel visualization approach that supports evaluators (when conducting evaluations) that use as a basis user activities that can at least be loosely described. This includes usability and UX studies or tests and experiments with given user activities the participants have to perform. The visualization approach is combined with a task-based evaluation approach using task models as key component for extracting scenarios for experiments and for presenting evaluation results. As task models are able to cope with complex work, the approach is intended for large-scale and complex interactive systems such as command and control systems.

2   Related Work

Evaluation methods and research evaluation methods in human computer interaction focusing on usability and user experience can be classified in (a) methods involving users such as observations, field studies, surveys, usability studies, interviews or focus groups [15], (b) methods performed by experts, and (c) automated methods [2]. Today evaluations, like user studies, are performed either in person (in the laboratory or in the field) or remotely (asynchronous or synchronous; independently by the users including users self-observations or guided by evaluators;...) [14].

When it comes to research focusing on UX and trying to understand UX, a broad range of evaluation methods has been developed, adapted, and adopted [29] to address the temporal aspect of UX, typically classified as before, during, and after interaction with a product, as well as the overall episodic UX.

Performing a usability or UX evaluation involving users requires activities beyond conducting the study per se [15]. Evaluation starts with the identification of evaluation goals and the selection (or even adaptation or development) of a set of evaluation methods. This is followed by the preparation of the necessary material, like usability study protocols or guidelines that will be used to perform the study, recruiting and selection of participants, and pre-testing of the evaluation methods. After conducting the study, various other tasks such as data collection and data pre-processing and the analysis of data are performed. Key to every evaluation is the interpretation of the data and what the evaluation results mean for the iterative (re-) design of the system and the required changes to the software or product. As Bernhaupt et al. [2] indicated, this step typically fails in many projects.

Limitations of current methods in usability and UX evaluation and research are [14, 15]:

- missing validation of results (typically evaluation studies are not re-done in research nor confirmed when applied in industry)
- sharing of evaluation results between researchers or beyond
- analysis phase of results, not done in relation with activities or tasks, influences of context (temporal, physical, social, technological, and societal), ability to analyze cross-over studies
- support for long-term studies or comparison of studies.

2.1   Task Driven User Interface Design and Evaluation

User tasks are analyzed since the early phases of the design of interactive systems and their analysis provides support to various stages of User-Centered Design and of interactive system development, from first prototype assessment to interactive system deployment. Beyond the identification and description of required functions for an interactive system [10, 23], this includes the identification and description of knowledge required to perform a task [6, 13, 18, 26], as well as different roles users can have in groupware systems [24, 31], and how users collaborate [24, 31]. Central for understanding evaluation results is the understanding of the application domain [22], the ability to produce scenarios for user evaluation [33], and the identification and generation of models describing user errors [8].

PRENTAM is a process model describing how to integrate usability and UX evaluation results into task models [4]. Key for such an approach is the integration of functionalities like data import and export alongside the ability to report evaluation data alongside the task models [3].

2.2 Visualization as a Tool for Evaluation

Especially for the evaluation of complex environments such as games [32], visualizations have become a vital aspect for the interpretation of user behaviour and subsequent reporting thereof. For instance, heat maps and gaze plots have also become popular in gaze-based usability evaluation [9] of not only games but also websites and applications. These visualizations are, however, usually tailored towards specific analysis goals and the virtual environment itself can be used as reference for the visualization. Many evaluations, however, take a more abstract, task-based, perspective where usability and UX measures are evaluated over time. In this regard, several existing tools aim to support the design and implementation of experiments.

The *Touchstone2* tool aims to facilitate the exploration of alternative sample sizes and counterbalancing strategies for experiment design. It provides support to weigh the cost of additional participants against the benefit of detecting smaller effects [7]. It is hence focused on the statistical settings of experiments. It provides support for visualizing the possible combinations of devices and interaction techniques but does not provide support for visualizing the results of the experiment itself. *NexP* [20] aims to facilitate the preparation and implementation of experimentation for persons with limited knowledge in experimental design. The results of the experiment are collected by a running platform and are saved in csv files. However, it does not provide support for visualizing the results. These tools were demonstrated with examples of measuring temporal performance and motor accuracy, they thus focus on usability measures and do not provide explicit support for dealing with UX measures.

What is currently missing in evaluation as well as task modeling tools is the ability to combine both worlds. Such a combination would allow to present evaluation data in the task, to provide the possibility to visualize data, and to support the analysis of evaluation results with values, depictions, or visualizations beyond basic statistical values (such as average time spent on a task [3]).

3 Task-Based Evaluation of Interactive Systems

3.1 Problem Description and Background

Task-based evaluation of usability and UX as key software qualities involves several components. First, the user activity has to be analyzed, described in terms of goals to reach, and tasks to be performed in order to reach those goals. Often, these tasks are described, in its simplest form as free text or using Excel files ending up in long lists of activities. As pointed out by Peter Johnson in his keynote at TAMODIA 2004 [12] starting with: *"What is the point of modelling anything. . . "*, for complex systems, it is advisable to use dedicated software tools for task modelling in order to deal with large and complex task models. The detail of the task model typically is heavily influenced by the expressive power of the tool.

Usability and UX as key software qualities benefit differently from a task-based evaluation approach. Usability evaluation is still in the majority of cases performed as a laboratory study, often only once within the overall user-centered development process. One of the reasons might be that usability, as a quality, is seen as rather static (after a training/learning period) and not easily influenced by small changes in the work environment. On the contrary, user experience is diverse along several dimensions:

1. temporal aspect: UX is changing over time, the user experience before, during, and after the interaction with a product and the cumulative user experience need different measures over time. This results in the need for a tool that allows to show these different measures in one place and to enable the understanding of influencing factors like contextual changes during the analysis.
2. multi-dimensional: UX per se is multi-faceted and typically a construct of different dimensions [25] that are evaluated, thus the (sub-) dimensions of UX have to be visualized and made accessible during the analysis phase in 'one image'.
3. inter-dependability: The interplay between usability and UX (and other software qualities) is dynamic and complex. To enable improved evaluation results, the comparison of usability and UX must be supported by such a system, as well as the investigation how different software qualities impact each other.

In the following we use UX as a more general term for all possible software qualities that can be evaluated, including usability.

To enable task-based evaluation of usability and UX a system must support the above mentioned aspects. To accomplish this it is necessary to have task representations and task models that support user studies, providing the ability not only to describe tasks, but also to define scenarios. Scenarios represent activities that users perform when conducting standard usability evaluation studies. Key for the success of such a system is the degree to which the task model notation and the support tool are able to represent and store evaluation results from user activities.

The central problem is how to help evaluators make the most out of evaluation results. Our proposed solution is the combination of task models that incorporate scenarios to represent user activities performed with a system and to visualize the usability and UX evaluation results accordingly. The goal is to solve and support evaluators when they face the challenge of comparability of personalized user interfaces, when the technological usage context is difficult to describe, as well as when large amounts of data points have to be compared.

3.2   Tasks Representation and Task Models to Support User Studies

Task modelling and task models support task analysis activities and are a means to represent the outcomes of the task analysis. Task models consist of an abstract description of user activities structured in terms of goals, sub-goals, and actions [22]. The models that result from task analysis will differ according to the features of the selected modelling language or notation. These modelling differences are likely to illuminate (or suppress) different aspects of the interaction. It is, therefore, important to choose the most suitable task modelling technique, i.e. the notation with the most suitable expressiveness, which highlights the aspects that are relevant to the goals of the analysis.

As highlighted in Bernhaupt et al. [4], task analysis and modelling provides support to check for completeness of the sets of tasks used for user studies. Moreover, if the task modelling notation is exhaustive enough, it provides support to identify the types of data that has to be collected (e.g., motor/reaction time to be monitored, input data to be recorded in the system,...). Bernhaupt et al. [4] also show that task models can be used to record the results of user evaluation to inform re-design.

3.3   Scenarios

As defined by Rosson and Carroll [28], scenarios *"consist of a setting, or situation state, one or more actors with personal motivations, knowledge, and capabilities, and various tools and objects that the actors encounter and manipulate. The scenario describes a sequence of actions and events that lead to an outcome. These actions and events are related in a usage context that includes the goals, plans, and reactions of the people taking part in the episode"*. The main differences between scenarios and task models are that scenarios contain concrete data (e.g., user name and characteristics) whereas task models are abstract. A scenario is a sequence of actions (like a story line) whereas task models are hierarchical (from more abstract to more concrete) and can describe several possible actions for the user in different temporal orders. At last, scenarios may be borderline (e.g., represent cases at the limit) whereas task models are mainline as they represent the standard, usual, and prescribed activities.

Although they differ, task models and scenarios are complementary. Scenarios can be produced by the execution of task models [21] and they are also a means to verify task models. Most of the task modelling tools provide a simulator which allows to analyze the possible sequences of actions for a task model. These possible sequences can be recorded as scenarios. Scenarios produced from task models can be used as input for driving the execution of the system [21] and the execution of training sessions [19]. They can also be used as input to prepare empirical studies [33], as it is the case in this paper. Furthermore, when tool-supported, task models can also provide support to produce scenarios that will be used for conducting the study and in which the various types of measures will be recorded (according to the type of task) [3].

3.4 Importance of the Expressiveness of Modeling Notation and Tool

The systematic identification of possible user actions and the analysis of effects of the study setup on user tasks requires to exhaustively and precisely describe:

1. user actions and their type (e.g., perceptive, motor, cognitive) in order to identify where a usability or UX issue can come from,
2. their temporal ordering and/or temporal constraints to compare the impact of the possible temporal ordering of user actions on usability and UX,
3. the information, knowledge and devices being manipulated during these actions in order to identify the information, knowledge, and devices required to perform the evaluation, as well as to compare the impact of the possible alternatives on usability and on UX.

4 The Visualization Approach

To enable the usage of task models and support a systemic view on the design and development of interactive systems, we used the previously defined PRENTAM model to integrate usability study results into task models [4]. The HAMSTERS-XL notation [17] embeds all these elements that are important to support user evaluation. We complement the tool HAMSTERS-XLE with a novel visualization approach.

The visualization was built with the overarching goal to support evaluation by visually highlighting potential issues and to inform redesign of the evaluated system. To support this, the visualization addresses the following three sub-goals:

1. provide an overview of temporal aspects of UX and usability for scenario-based evaluations
2. allow to compare different conditions (e.g., design variants) and scenarios against each other
3. provide a summary of UX/usability measures while also allowing to view details with regard to individual users and the underlying task model

To help assist with evaluating UX and usability based on task models of user activity and the above mentioned goals we devised an interactive visualization consisting of three different views. The main view provides an aggregated overview of all the collected UX data across multiple scenarios and conditions over time (Goal 1 and 2). This view also acts as a hub to add views of more detailed data for selected scenarios and conditions (thus following the established visual information seeking mantra *Overview first, zoom and filter, then details-on-demand* postulated by Shneiderman [30]). These views – supporting Goal 3 – provide a) an aggregated summary of user-selected UX measures on a per-activity basis and b) an overview of individual activity-execution times and UX measures for each participant, and c) also allow to visually compare results across conditions and scenarios. All views offer tooltips showing detailed data of the color-coded measures. In the following, these views will be explained in detail. Views can be combined freely to match analysis goals and preferences of the user.

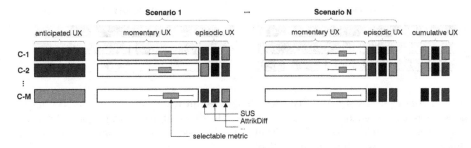

Fig. 1. Overview: Columns represent different scenarios while rows indicate different conditions for the individual scenarios. The visualization follows the *UX over time* concept, covering anticipated, momentary, episodic, and cumulative UX. Colors reflect the values of the UX values (in this case a red-to-green gradient was chosen). (Color figure online)

4.1 Overview

The overview, as illustrated in Fig. 1, follows the *UX over Time* [16,29] scheme, showing from left to right, the anticipated UX, momentary and episodic UX for different scenarios, and finally cumulative (or sometimes also referred to as remembered) UX across all scenarios.

Each UX measure is represented using a block. For instance, anticipated UX could be measured using five seconds UX impressions in interviews, while standard questionnaires like the *SUS* [5] or *AttrakDiff* [11] can be used to assess episodic or cumulative UX. Momentary UX could be assessed through metrics such as time taken, ease of use, or aesthetic appeal. Except in case of momentary UX, these blocks are also color-coded to ease comparison of the measures. The color scheme can be defined for each UX measure separately, for example, a unipolar color gradient for a unipolar scale such as the *SUS* can be used or a bipolar color scheme for diverging measures such as the *AttrakDiff*. The momentary UX block contains a box plot to offer more details about the distribution of a selected metric at a glance.

In terms of overall layout, the overview follows a grid-based approach with rows representing different conditions and columns representing the scenarios. This can either be different scenarios or the same scenario at different points in time. In the latter case, these are sorted based on recency with the most recent one depicted in the right-most column to reflect the progression over time.

4.2 Aggregated User Activity View

This view (see Fig. 2) depicts the activities in a simplified tree structure, with the different activities represented as color-coded blocks, where the color indicates the mean of a momentary UX measure (e.g., average time or average difficulty rating). Multiple trees can be viewed side-by-side to allow for comparisons between different conditions or between scenarios (useful, for instance, when the

Fig. 2. Aggregated User Activity View: This view provides on overview of UX measures (here time needed: min ▬▬▬ max) for the different activities performed within a scenario. Multiple trees can be visualized side-by-side to ease comparisons across different conditions. (Color figure online)

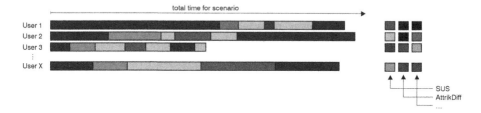

Fig. 3. Individual User View: Visualization of activity times together with UX measures such as *SUS* or *AttrakDiff* on a per-user basis for a selected scenario and condition. Colors indicate the number of tasks within an activity (in this particular case: 1 ▬▬▬ 4). (Color figure online)

same scenario has been assessed at multiple points in time). Figure 2 illustrates this concept by comparing two different conditions. Assuming the colors encode time, with more reddish values indicating higher required times, one can see that Activity A on overall required more time in Condition 1 than in Condition 2, which is mainly caused by the sub-activities C_2 and C_3 within Activity C.

4.3 Individual User View

In order to allow the evaluator to inspect individual participant data in more detail, this view summarizes activity execution order on a per-user basis (cf. Fig. 3). Each row represents a single user and each block represents a single activity with the color indicating the number of tasks within it. The width of each block indicates the time the user has needed to perform the respective activity. The color-coded blocks to the right indicate the different episodic UX values as provided by the user. For example, in the example in Fig. 3 the first user took a comparatively very long time for the first activity (dark blue) compared to the others which may explain the lower UX ratings (red blocks). The last user – User X, to give another example, required a comparatively long time for the third activity which only includes one task, indicating potential struggles. As is the case with the *Aggregated User Activity View*, the data of multiple conditions and/or scenarios can be represented side-by-side to help with comparisons.

5   Case Study

As case study, we opted to use *Netflix* and compare different scenarios on two different conditions (PC and Smartphone). In the following we will first present the task models of the case study, explain the data collection procedure, and finally present how the collected data can be analyzed with the visualization outlined above.

5.1   Tasks Models and Relation to Task-Based Evaluation

As explained earlier, we used the HAMSTERS-XLE environment [17] to model the main tasks that users have to perform in order to consume content with *Netflix*. Figure 4 shows the main user tasks to perform in order to reach the goal "Consume content on Netflix" (located at the top of the task model). As the name indicates, it corresponds to a broad and loosely defined activity the user wants to perform. That task model must be read as follows: The user first opens Netflix and log-in into the service. Opening Netflix and log-in are interactive tasks, as indicated by the symbol for an interactive input/output tasks on the left-hand side of Fig. 4. Then, the main sub-goal of the user is to consume movies or content, this can be repetitive (indicated by a blue repetition arrow on the task symbol), until the user decides to quit Netflix (represented with the temporal ordering operator DISABLE, labelled "[>" upon the interactive input task "Leave Netflix").

The "Consume content" sub-goal is decomposed into several tasks described at the bottom of the task model (read from left to right). First, the Netflix application filters content and then processes the profile of the user. This is represented as tasks from the system labelled "Filter content" and "Process profile". Then it displays the welcome page (interactive output task named "Display a welcome (landing) page"). Then, the user can choose (represented by the temporal ordering operator OR labelled "[]") to select either content from the current Top 10 (abstract task named "Select a content from the Top 10") or to search for content (abstract task named "Search for content"). The detailed actions for the sub-goals "Select a content from the Top 10" and "Search for content" are presented in Fig. 5.

What is important is to understand the expressiveness of the task model notation, as this lays the basis to understand and interpret related evaluation results. Activities such as the sub-goal "Select a content from the Top 10" are represented as an abstract task. Such an abstract task allows, during the interpretation of the evaluation tasks, to look at summative values like task times or overall ratings on user experience like aesthetics values, to understand how users in general perform selection.

These abstract tasks can then be refined (if needed) into concrete tasks. Indeed, Fig. 5 (left-hand side) shows that "Select a content from Top 10" is decomposed into three actions that happen sequentially (represented by the temporal ordering operator SEQUENCE, labelled ">>"): "go to the Top 10" (interactive input/output task), "select a number" (interactive input task) and "go

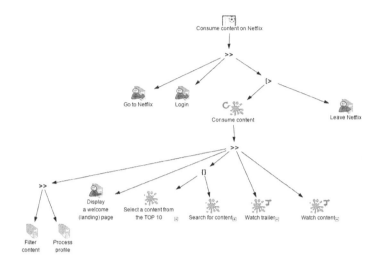

Fig. 4. Overview of the task model describing user actions to consume content. (Color figure online)

to the detail page" (interactive input/output task). The interactive input task "Select a number" modifies the value of the software object labelled "selected content" (represented by an orange rectangle with an incoming arrow from the "Select a number" interactive input task). This representation allows, for example, to investigate if any latency of the system in value modification or representation has an impact on the evaluation results.

The sub-goal "Search for content" (represented with an abstract task) is also decomposed into a sequence (">>") of two abstract tasks: "Use search function" and "Select target content". The "Use search function" abstract task is refined into the following sequence of tasks: "Locate search function" perceptive task, "Enter in search field" interactive input/output task, "Type the first characters" interactive input/output task (which modifies the content of the software object "characters"), and "Search content which name starts with input characters" system task (which uses the value of the software object "characters" and modifies the value of the software object "List of movies starting with characters"). This task is performed by Netflix and returns a list of movies matching the filter defined by the user while typing characters.

Computing the number of interactive tasks supports the evaluator to understand the quantity of interaction that the users will have to perform with the system (Netflix) before being able to watch the desired content.

In the task models of Fig. 4 and Fig. 5 we have not represented (due to space constraints) the cognitive activities of users. However, in this case, looking at cognitive activities can help the evaluator understand how long people on average need to decide, but more importantly how quick (minimum time) or how long (maximum time) users take to make up their mind. Such details can be important when redesigning the system to enhance user experience and, in this case, the

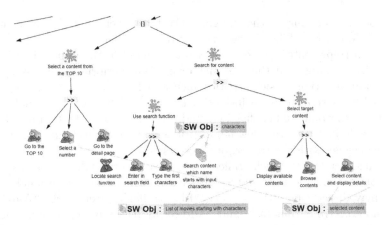

Fig. 5. Focus on the sub-goals "Select a content from the Top 10" and "Search for content" of the task model "Consume content on Netflix". (Color figure online)

long term perception of the user to, for example, *"never find the right content for me"*.

The "Select target content" abstract task is refined into the following sequence of tasks: "Display available contents" interactive output task (which uses the value of the software object "List of movies starting with characters"), "Browse contents" interactive input/output task, and "Select content and display details" interactive input/output task (which modifies the value of the software object "selected content").

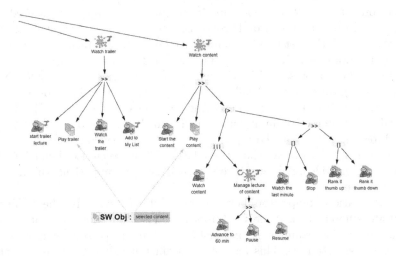

Fig. 6. Focus on the sub-goals "Watch trailer" and "Watch content" of the task model "Consume content on Netflix".

The detailed actions for the sub-goals "Watch trailer" and "Watch content" are presented in Fig. 6. The abstract tasks "Watch trailer" and "Watch content" are optional (represented by the blue arrows symbol in the upper right corner of the task), meaning that the user may or may not perform these tasks.

For the evaluation, basic statistics such as which percentage of users performed which activity can be insightful to decide if further data analysis on usage statistics would be beneficial for understanding the evaluation results. An example could be that a very low number of people are not watching the content once they engage with the trailer, or vice versa.

The abstract task "Watch trailer" is refined into the following sequence of tasks: "Start trailer lecture" interactive input task (which is optional as the system may directly play the trailer), "Play trailer" system task, "Watch the trailer" interactive output task, and "Add to my list" interactive input/output task (which is optional). Here a comparison if asking the user to engage in an activity is beneficial compared to the automation (trailer starts directly) can be insightful for the evaluation. Especially when user interfaces on different devices show different behaviors such comparisons can be helpful to understand the effect of automation on user experience aspects, for instance, users' perception of the ability to control the user interface.

The abstract task "Watch content" is refined into the following sequence of tasks: "Start the content" interactive input task, "Play content" system task and then, the execution of tasks that occur concurrently (represented by the temporal ordering operator CONCURRENCY, labelled "|||"), "Watch content" interactive output task and "Manage lecture of content" abstract task. The "Manage lecture of content" abstract task is optional. It is further broken down into the following sequence of tasks: "Advance to 60 min", "Pause", and "Resume", with all of them being interactive input tasks. The concurrent execution of the "Watch content" and "Manage lecture of content" tasks stops (represented with the temporal ordering operator DISABLE, labelled "[>") when the user performs the "Watch the last minute" interactive input/output task or (represented with the temporal ordering operator OR, labelled "[]") the "Stop" interactive input task. Then (represented by the temporal ordering operator SEQUENCE, labelled ">>"), the user can "Rank it thumb up" (interactive input/output task) or (represented with the temporal ordering operator OR, labelled "[]") "Rank it thumb down" (interactive input/output task). In the evaluation activity of such media browsing activities, the representation of data beyond the visualization might be beneficial, as it can show the relationship between user behaviors, like overshooting the video, repetitive presses when users are impatient with a slowly reacting system, etc.

For evaluation comparison between two different systems, the ability to instantiate different task models is important. The "Consume content on Netflix" task model, for example, is once instantiated for the personal computer and once for the smartphone. This instantiation aims at exhaustively representing which user action can be performed on each specific device. Figure 7 and Fig. 8 present excerpts of the "Consume content on Netflix" task model instantiated for the task to be performed with a Personal Computer (PC) and with a Smartphone. In this task model, we see that interactive tasks are connected to devices. For example, the interactive input/output task "Go to the Top 10" requires the use of the output device display (represented with a stroke between the task and the blue rectangle labelled "out D: Display") and of the input device mouse (represented with a stroke between the task and the blue rectangle labelled "in D: Mouse"). For the evaluation such indicated connections can allow the investigation of special cases, for example, by taking into account logging of system data like mouse movements and which device is used for which task.

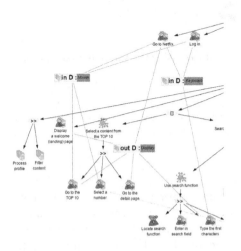 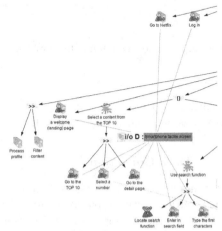

Fig. 7. Extract from the task model "Consume content on Netflix" instantiated for PC devices.

Fig. 8. Extract from the task model "Consume content on Netflix" instantiated for a Smartphone device.

5.2   Scenarios of the Case Study

Once the user tasks are described, we produce the scenarios that are required for the user study. For that purpose, we use the HAMSTERS-XLE simulator to execute the task model and generate several possible scenarios for the study. An example of output of such a simulation is the scenario presented in Fig. 9. This scenario contains a sequence of actions that the user has to perform to watch the 7th item of the Top 10 list of content on Netflix.

For each generated scenario, we identify the actions for which the time should be measured during the study. In Fig. 9, they are represented with the black heptagons labelled "T1", "T2", "T3", and "T4". A scenario that is selected to be performed during the study is modified to remove the description of the system tasks (e.g., system task labelled "3-Process profile" in Fig. 9) from the

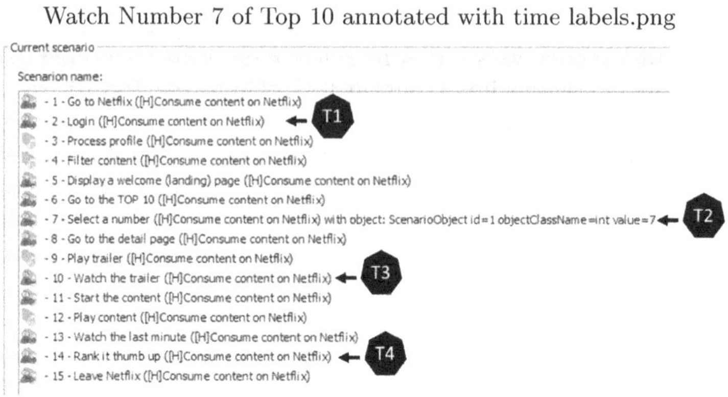

Watch Number 7 of Top 10 annotated with time labels.png

Fig. 9. Scenario "Watch number 7 of Top 10" produced using the task model simulator.

sequence of tasks. The final sequence of task we refer to as user activity as it contains only the actions that will be concretely performed by the user.

5.3 Data Collection

A remote user study was conducted to collect data for our case study. For that purpose, we prepared a guide for users how to perform such a remote study themselves, including descriptions of the activities to be performed, i.e. it included step-by-step instruction to be followed by the participants. Each step was linked with usability and user experience measures participants had to report as detailed in the following. Participants were also instructed to self-record themselves while performing the scenarios and extract the timings for different activities from it. In addition to the time taken for the different activities, participants had to report the following for each scenario: perceived difficulty of the scenario on a 5-point scale (1 = *very easy* to 5 = *very difficult*); aesthetic appearance of the interface, also on a 5-point scale (1 = *very beautiful* to 5 = *very displeasing*). Before commencing the scenarios, participants had to rate their anticipated UX on a scale from 0 (worst experience in your life) to 100 (heavenly experience). Once they were finished with all tasks, a *SUS* and *AttrakDiff* were used to measure cumulative UX. Participants were provided with a spreadsheet which they had to fill-in with the above mentioned requested data. The returned spreadsheets were checked for mistakes before processing them further.

Participants where free to choose one of two conditions (PC or Smartphone). Of the ten complete responses we received, seven performed the scenarios on a PC. These were imported into the visualization with exemplary results shown in Fig. 10.

5.4 The Visualization Approach Applied to the Use Case

Let us assume we are interested in getting an overview of how the different scenarios compare across the PC and Smartphone *Netflix* application. We thus take a look at the overview representation (Fig. 10, top) and can see that the aesthetics (A, ❶) on the smartphone were rated lower for each of the three scenarios it was assessed (more reddish values). In case of difficulty (D, ❶) there are no pronounced differences, except for the login which was rated to be easier on the PC, and which also shows in the much lower time needed for completing the activity. Generally, the scenarios were faster to solve on the PC than on the smartphone, where the times needed also exhibit more variation (box plots, ❷). We can also immediately see that users expect the same, rather high, user experience on both devices (dark green boxes, ❸). Cumulative UX measures were similar in general, suggesting that overall users had the same experience on both devices. However, the hedonic quality stimulation subscale of the *AttrakDiff* scored lower on the smartphone ❹.

Next, we are interested in taking a closer look at individual user experience and thus add the individual user views for each scenario (except the first, which only consisted of a single activity) and condition and arrange them like shown in Fig. 10 (middle). For instance, in case of the "Watch Number 7" scenario we can witness that users on the smartphone needed almost the same time for the "go to the details page and watch the trailer" activity (2nd to last box, ❺) while on the PC the timings are more varied. Its also apparent that one PC user was extremely fast (fourth user from the top) which could have been an expert user (or due to the user reporting wrong values). Lower timings in the other two scenarios confirm this impression to some extent. We can also notice that the time needed to complete the scenario was not necessarily a decisive factor for the perceived difficulty, with some people rating it more difficult while taking less time than others ❻. As another example, consider the individual timings for the "Watch Trailer" scenario where PC users usually required less time than smartphone users, except two. Of these two the first ❼ required relatively long for logging into Netflix (first box) and selecting the series (fourth box), pointing to some potential struggles of the user with navigating within Netflix. The other ❽ mainly did watch the trailer for a longer period of time (second to last box).

Suppose we would like to investigate overall differences in time needed for the different conditions in more detail. We thus add the *Aggregated User Activity View* for the "Watch Trailer" scenario for both the PC and smartphone and arrange them side-by-side (Fig. 10, bottom). Please note, that the color-coding is not based on individual trees but based on all displayed activity trees and thus can also be compared across them. For instance, we can observe that on average the whole scenario took longer to complete on the PC. However, it is also noticeable that users on the smartphone required longer to log into Netflix than PC users ❾. Searching for content (including the two sub-activities "locate search function" and "Type HYM") took about the some time in both conditions. Other noticeable differences arise for the "Watch Trailer" part of the scenario. Users on the smartphone spent more time on this activity, but this was not

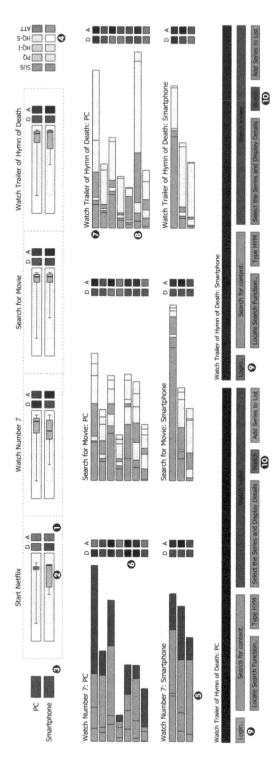

Fig. 10. Results of the evaluation visualized using the proposed approach. Overview (top) with added detail views of individual user data (middle) for all scenarios except the first and for both conditions. In addition, activity trees (bottom) for the "Watch Trailer" scenario for both conditions were added. Anticipated UX and cumulative UX (*SUS* and *AttrakDiff*) values are encoded using a white-green gradient (⬜⬛), episodic UX values in terms of difficulty (D) and attractiveness (A) with a green-red gradient (⬜⬛), with green corresponding to 'better' values. Time, as shown in the activity trees, also uses a red-green gradient with 2.3 ⬛ 94.7 s. Activities in the individual user views are color-coded based on the number of contained tasks, with ⬛ = 1, ⬛ = 2, and ⬛ = 3. (Color figure online)

actually caused – as one might assume – by users requiring more time to select the series and display the details but rather by users spending more time on average to watch the trailer ❿.

6   Conclusion and Perspectives

A generic visualization approach for task-based evaluation is a first building block for a more systemic view on interactive system development. Today it is not enough any more to only look at the user(s)/system(s). Instead, we need a view on how organizations and regulations change the requirements of such systems and how the environment overall affects usability and UX (POISE model [1]).

The majority of systems developed today, has some form of task descriptions or basic models describing user activities. The usage of detailed task models is more common for large-scale systems that are either safety-critical or economically-critical. Nevertheless, the task model approach combined with this type of evaluation result visualization does not need detailed or elaborate task models, but can also be performed with rather abstract models. The ability to show evaluation data not only from generic to individual user activity and their relation to the task model, but to also enable the presentation of different software qualities in one visualization is a key advantage of this approach. Especially with recent worldwide developments such an approach will also help to support evaluation of societal impact (e.g., an evaluation of a tracking app for diseases vs privacy). In terms of research the key advantage of this approach is the ability to counteract the lack of longitudinal studies [15], by supporting the comparison and visualization of data also over different studies (and years), for example, by showing averaged usability scores for key activities.

Our proposed approach clearly has limitations and limits its functionality on purpose. It is not intended to replace and support all activities during an evaluation and excludes activities like recruiting processes for participants or extensive data analysis (that can be ideally performed using standard statistics programs). Nor is it intended for the ideation phase or early (sketch) design phases, or artefact research where the task performed by users with the artefact can not be foreseen.

We demonstrated the feasibility of the application of the visualization approach through a use case of comparing UX of consuming content on *Netflix* for two different conditions (PC and Smartphone). In the future, this visualization approach needs to be assessed with evaluators, who are the target users of this approach, to ascertain its usefulness and efficiency for them. There are also opportunities for future extensions to the visualization itself such as including more ways to interact with the data (e.g., filtering of the data based on different criteria) and representation of human errors made. Here, we also focused on the visualization itself and less on the integration into an existing toolchain which should deserve further attention as well.

References

1. Bernhaupt, R., Palanque, P.: POISE - a framework for systemic change analysis (2020, in preparation)
2. Bernhaupt, R., Navarre, D., Palanque, P., Winckler, M.: Model-based evaluation: a new way to support usability evaluation of multimodal interactive applications. In: Law, E.L.C., Hvannberg, E.T., Cockton, G. (eds.) Maturing Usability: Quality in Software, Interaction and Value. HCIS, pp. 96–119. Springer, London (2008). https://doi.org/10.1007/978-1-84628-941-5_5
3. Bernhaupt, R., Palanque, P., Drouet, D., Martinie, C.: Enriching task models with usability and user experience evaluation data. In: Bogdan, C., Kuusinen, K., Lárusdóttir, M.K., Palanque, P., Winckler, M. (eds.) HCSE 2018. LNCS, vol. 11262, pp. 146–163. Springer, Cham (2019). https://doi.org/10.1007/978-3-030-05909-5_9
4. Bernhaupt, R., Palanque, P., Manciet, F., Martinie, C.: User-test results injection into task-based design process for the assessment and improvement of both usability and user experience. In: Bogdan, C., et al. (eds.) HESSD/HCSE -2016. LNCS, vol. 9856, pp. 56–72. Springer, Cham (2016). https://doi.org/10.1007/978-3-319-44902-9_5
5. Brooke, J., et al.: SUS-a quick and dirty usability scale. In: Jordan, P.W., Thomas, B., McClelland, I.L., Weerdmeester, B. (eds.) Usability Evaluation in Industry, pp. 189–194. Taylor & Francis, Abingdon (1996)
6. Diaper, D.: Task analysis for knowledge descriptions (TAKD): the method and an example. In: Task Analysis for Human-Computer Interaction, pp. 108–159. Lawrence Erlbaum Associates (1990)
7. Eiselmayer, A., Wacharamanotham, C., Beaudouin-Lafon, M., Mackay, W.E.: Touchstone2: an interactive environment for exploring trade-offs in HCI experiment design. In: Proceedings of the 2019 CHI Conference on Human Factors in Computing Systems. ACM, New York (2019)
8. Fahssi, R., Martinie, C., Palanque, P.: Enhanced task modelling for systematic identification and explicit representation of human errors. In: Abascal, J., Barbosa, S., Fetter, M., Gross, T., Palanque, P., Winckler, M. (eds.) INTERACT 2015. LNCS, vol. 9299, pp. 192–212. Springer, Cham (2015). https://doi.org/10.1007/978-3-319-22723-8_16
9. Goldberg, J.H., Wichansky, A.M.: Eye tracking in usability evaluation: a practitioner's guide. In: The Mind's Eye, pp. 493–516. Elsevier (2003)
10. Greenberg, S.: Working through task-centered system design. In: Diaper, D., Stanton, N. (eds.) The Handbook of Task Analysis for Human-Computer Interaction, pp. 49–66. Lawrence Erlbaum Associates, Hillsdale (2004)
11. Hassenzahl, M., Burmester, M., Koller, F.: AttrakDiff: Ein Fragebogen zur Messung wahrgenommener hedonischer und pragmatischer Qualität. In: Szwillus, G., Ziegler, J. (eds) Mensch & Computer 2003. Berichte des German Chapter of the ACM, vol. 57, pp. 187–196. Springer, Heidelberg (2003). https://doi.org/10.1007/978-3-322-80058-9_19
12. Johnson, P.: Interactions, collaborations and breakdowns. In: Proceedings of the 3rd Annual Conference on Task Models and Diagrams, pp. 1–3. ACM, New York (2004)
13. Johnson, P., Johnson, H., Hamilton, F.: Getting the knowledge into HCI: theoretical and practical aspects of task knowledge structures. In: Cognitive Task Analysis. Lawrence Erlbaum Associates (2000)

14. Lallemand, C., Gronier, G.: Méthodes de design UX: 30 méthodes fondamentales pour concevoir et évaluer les systèmes interactifs. Editions Eyrolles (2015)
15. Lazar, J., Feng, J.H., Hochheiser, H.: Research Methods in Human-Computer Interaction. Morgan Kaufmann, Burlington (2017)
16. Marti, P., Iacono, I.: Anticipated, momentary, episodic, remembered: the many facets of user experience. In: 2016 Federated Conference on Computer Science and Information Systems (FedCSIS), pp. 1647–1655 (2016)
17. Martinie, C., Palanque, P., Bouzekri, E., Cockburn, A., Canny, A., Barboni, E.: Analysing and demonstrating tool-supported customizable task notations, vol. 3. Association for Computing Machinery, New York, June 2019. https://doi.org/10.1145/3331154
18. Martinie, C., Palanque, P., Ragosta, M., Barboni, E.: Extending procedural task models by systematic explicit integration of objects, knowledge and information. In: Proceedings of the of the 31st European Conference on Cognitive Ergonomics, ECCE 2013. ACM, New York (2013)
19. Martinie, C., Palanque, P., Navarre, D., Winckler, M., Poupart, E.: Model-based training: an approach supporting operability of critical interactive systems. In: Proceedings of the 3rd ACM SIGCHI Symposium on Engineering Interactive Computing Systems, EICS 2011, pp. 53–62. ACM, New York (2011)
20. Meng, X., Foong, P.S., Perrault, S., Zhao, S.: NexP: a beginner friendly toolkit for designing and conducting controlled experiments. In: Bernhaupt, R., Dalvi, G., Joshi, A., K. Balkrishan, D., O'Neill, J., Winckler, M. (eds.) INTERACT 2017. LNCS, vol. 10515, pp. 132–141. Springer, Cham (2017). https://doi.org/10.1007/978-3-319-67687-6_10
21. Navarre, D., Palanque, P., Paternò, F., Santoro, C., Bastide, R.: A tool suite for integrating task and system models through scenarios. In: Johnson, C. (ed.) DSV-IS 2001. LNCS, vol. 2220, pp. 88–113. Springer, Heidelberg (2001). https://doi.org/10.1007/3-540-45522-1_6
22. Paterno, F.: Task models in interactive software systems. In: Handbook of Software Engineering and Knowledge Engineering. World Scientific (2000)
23. Paternó, F., Mancini, C., Meniconi, S.: ConcurTaskTrees: a diagrammatic notation for specifying task models. In: Proceedings of IFIP INTERACT 1997, pp. 362–369. Lawrence Erlbaum Associates (1997)
24. Pinelle, D., Gutwin, C., Greenberg, S.: Task analysis for groupware usability evaluation: modelling shared-workspace tasks with the mechanics of collaboration. In: ACM Transactions on Computer-Human Interaction, vol. 10, no. 4. pp. 281–311. ACM, New York (2003)
25. Pirker, M.M., Bernhaupt, R.: Measuring user experience in the living room: results from an ethnographically oriented field study indicating major evaluation factors. In: Proceedings of the 9th European Conference on Interactive TV and Video, pp. 79–82. ACM, New York (2011)
26. Ragosta, M., Martinie, C., Palanque, P., Navarre, D., Sujan, M.A.: Concept maps for integrating modelling techniques for the analysis and re-design of partly-autonomous interactive systems. In: Proceedings of the 5th International Conference on Application and Theory of Automation in Command and Control Systems, ATACCS 2015, pp. 41–52. ACM, New York (2015)
27. Resnick, P., Iacovou, N., Suchak, M., Bergstrom, P., Riedl, J.: GroupLens: an open architecture for collaborative filtering of netnews. In: Smith, J.B., Smith, F.D., Malone, T.W. (eds.) Proceedings of the Conference on Computer Supported Cooperative Work, pp. 175–186. ACM (1994)

28. Rosson, M.B., Carroll, J.M.: Usability Engineering: Scenario-Based Development of Human-computer Interaction. Elsevier, Amsterdam (2001)
29. Roto, V., Law, E., Vermeeren, A., Hoonhout, J.: User experience white paper: bringing clarity to the concept of user experience. In: Dagstuhl Seminar on Demarcating User Experience, pp. 1–12 (2011)
30. Shneiderman, B.: The eyes have it: a task by data type taxonomy for information visualizations. In: Proceedings of the 1996 IEEE Symposium on Visual Languages, pp. 336–343 (1996)
31. Van der Veer, G., Lenting, B., Bergevoet, A.: GTA: groupware task analysis - modelling complexity. In: Acta Psychologica, New York, NY, vol. 91, no. 3, pp. 297–322 (1996)
32. Wallner, G., Kriglstein, S.: Visualization-based analysis of gameplay data - a review of literature. Entertain. Comput. 4(3), 143–155 (2013)
33. Winckler, M., Palanque, P., Freitas, C.: Tasks and scenario-based evaluation of information visualization techniques. In: Proceedings of the 3rd Annual Conference on Task Models and Diagrams, TAMODIA 2004, pp. 165–172. ACM, New York (2004)

Digitalization of Training Tasks and Specification of the Behaviour of a Social Humanoid Robot as Coach

Peter Forbrig[1]([✉]) [iD], Alexandru Bundea[1] [iD], Ann Pedersen[3] [iD], and Thomas Platz[2,3] [iD]

[1] University of Rostock, Department of Computer Science, Albert-Einstein-Str. 22, 18055 Rostock, Germany
{Peter.Forbrig,Alexandru-Nicolae.Bundea}@uni-rostock.de

[2] Institut für Neurorehabilitation und Evidenzbasierung, An-Institut der Universität Greifswald, BDH-Klinik Greifswald, Karl-Liebknecht-Ring 26a, 17491 Greifswald, Germany
Thomas.Platz@uni-greifswald.de

[3] Neurorehabilitation Research Group, Universitätsmedizin Greifswald, Fleischmannstraße 44, 17491 Greifswald, Germany

Abstract. The number of physiotherapists and occupational therapists is not sufficient to cope with the demands of the increasing number of stroke survivors worldwide. These patients need specific training to promote recovery and prevent stroke-related disability. The paper discusses aspects how a social humanoid robots might serve as therapeutic assistant. It is not intended to replace human therapists, but to provide them with therapeutic assistance once therapeutic decisions are taken and the therapy has been introduced to the patient by the human therapists and the day to day practice needs to be supervised. The paper provides a case study of an HCD approach and exemplifies the strategy of digitalizing training tasks, the identification of exceptions, and ways of modelling the dynamic behaviour of the humanoid robot. This is demonstrated by task models. Some extensions of task models are suggested.

Keywords: Social humanoid robot · Human factors · Interaction design · Robot assistance · Arm rehabilitation for stroke patients · Task models

1 Introduction

Within the project E-BRAiN (Evidence-based Robot-Assistance in Neurorehabilitation; www.ebrain-science.de) we want to develop software that allows a humanoid robot to observe carefully selected training exercises. The project has the goal to support therapists by a new companion in the training of patients after a stroke. It was decided to follow a Human-Centered Design (HCD) approach that was adapted from Harte et al. [9]. To study the tasks and contexts is one of the first things one has to do.

A stroke is a leading cause of disability [8]. Brain lesions caused by stroke affect various body functions and lead to activity limitations and participations restrictions.

© IFIP International Federation for Information Processing 2020
Published by Springer Nature Switzerland AG 2020
R. Bernhaupt et al. (Eds.): HCSE 2020, LNCS 12481, pp. 45–57, 2020.
https://doi.org/10.1007/978-3-030-64266-2_3

Frequently, intensive specific training schedules are necessary to promote the recovery of body functions and reduce disability thereby. Platz and Lotze report in [16] about the clinical effectiveness of specific exercises in cases when stroke survivors suffer from mild to moderate arm paresis causing focal disability, i.e. limitations of dexterity. A specific group of such exercises is called Arm-Ability Training (AAT)

First, we will provide an overview of some of these exercises for post-stroke patients. Afterwards, the social humanoid robot Pepper is shortly introduced. This is followed by a discussion of digitalizing three of the training tasks with paper and paper. Models for specifying the collaboration between patients and therapists are discussed in the fourth section. In the fifth section we focus on modelling the collaboration of patients and therapists resp. humanoid robots. Some lessons learned from methodological and technological aspect are discussed in the six section before a summary with outlook follows.

2 Arm-Ability Training (AAT)

Arm-Ability Training has been especially designed to promote manual dexterity recovery for stroke patients who have mild to moderate arm paresis. Platz and Lotze report in [16] about its design, clinical effectiveness, and the neurobiology of the actions. The idea of AAT goes back to the identification of sensor motoric deficits of stroke survivors in [17]. Figure 1 provides an overview of the suggested training activities that are a result of previous research in [14] and [15].

1. AIMING: hitting targets with a stylus (distance 18 – 23cm, target width 3 – 50mm, on table surface and 30cm above table surface) requires fast and accurate goal-oriented arm movements

5. MAZE TRACKING: involves precision of slow, continuous, visually guided movements

2. TAPPING: fast, repetitive alternating selective movements of thumb, index and middle finger

6. BOLT and NUT: picking up bolts (diameter, 3, 5, 12mm) (non-affected arm) and nuts (affected arm) and screwing nuts on bolts (affected arm) requires finger dexterity, aiming, and steadiness

3. CANCELLATION: circles of various sizes are indicated with a pen which involves small and precise finger/hand movements while stabilizing the upper arm

7. PLACING SMALL OBJECTS: small wooden objects have to be placed on top of each other at different positions in the workspace involving finger dexterity, aiming, steadiness, and partially forearm pro- and supination

4. TURNING COINS: diameter, 18 and 23mm; requires finger dexterity and forearm pro- and supination

8. PLACING LARGER OBJECTS: plastic jars of different volumes and weights have to be transported to different positions across the workspace and put on top of each other

Fig. 1. Training tasks of AAT (from [16]).

The clinical effectiveness of the arm ability training was discussed in [16] on the basis of two single-blind randomized controlled studies that included 74 patients. Platz et al. (2009) were able to show is superior clinical effect on focal disability compared to therapeutic time-equivalent "best conventional" therapy.

However, the training is resource intensive because one therapist is necessary to observe and support the exercises of a patient. The idea arose to use a robot for assisting the patients. The robot is intended to provide instructions, provides feedback, be a motivator and suggest alternatives if something does not work well. It was analysed which existing kind of robot fits to the requirements of the arm ability training. As a result, the humanoid robot Pepper was selected for first experiments. A more detailed discussion related to humanoid robots can be found in Forbrig et al. [5] and [6].

3   The Humanoid Robot Pepper

SoftBank Robotics [20] offers an interesting social humanoid robot and call it Pepper. It is already in use for different domains. Pepper welcomes customers at banks or shopping centers. It gives advices in railway stations or airports. Sometimes it is also used to educate children or to entertain and support elderly people like in [10] (Fig. 2).

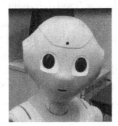

Fig. 2. Humanoid robot Pepper from SoftBanks Robotics [20].

Pepper looks a little bit like child and has a very nice appearance. Most people like Pepper and smile while they are looking at the robot. Pepper can talk, listen, move the head and focus on people that he interacts with. His eye blinking simulates the blink of an eye of humans in a nice way. The robot can also blink with shoulders and ears. Additionally, Pepper can move its arms and fingers and is gesturing while talking. Even that he does not have real legs the robot can move around.

It is our assumption that patients can establish a good relationship with the robot. We assume that this is very helpful for the training tasks that are intended to support the functional recovery of patients. We want to use Pepper mainly to supervise highly standardized training sessions as instructor and motivator and like in [10] or [13] and try to find the appropriate feedback. Therefore, within our E-BRAiN project we are cooperating with psychologists and Professionals from health care management. They will analyse whether a humanoid robot as therapy assistant can acceptable for patients. It is, however, well possible that the approach is only helpful for specific sub-groups of stroke survivors and specific types of functional training. It is one goal of our project to identify such groups and forms of training.

4 Robot-Supported Training Tasks

The goal of the project E-BRAiN is a combined therapy of human experts und humanoid robots. Background for any robot-supported training tasks are the assessment, goal-determination, selection of appropriate therapy, information and consent about any findings and plans with the patient and equally the introduction of the training tasks to the patients by a human therapist.

Accordingly, (human) therapists need to assess patients, explore the individual treatment goals, select, suggest and agree on the appropriate training, and introduce the training exercises to patients. They also need to supervise the first cycles of training performance. Once, this level of therapeutic care is achieved, there might be a role for a social robot to support additional largely standardized training sessions.

However, before this can be done, the therapist has to specify personal data and medical training specifications in detail. Additionally, personal goals of the patients have to be identified. Such a goal could be: "I want to play chess with my grandchildren again". Later in the therapy, these goals are used to motivate patients. Pepper can say: "Today your performance was very good. Soon you will be able to move pieces on the chessboard".

We learned from psychologist that individualized therapeutic goals are best expressed in a positive way, e.g. "I want to open a door by myself" instead of: "I do not want to ask for help if I to open a door." It is also known that training achieves the best results, when people are motivated. Psychological experiments showed for musicians who all trained the same exercise that training-related differences in changes of brain activation could be observed depending on whether the musicians were motivated or only forced to perform the exercises. Therefore, motivation seems to be one important aspect for training-related learning and hence presumably also for functional recovery post stroke. This is especially important, because success of the training tasks is only very slowly apparent after a large number of repetitions over a series of training sessions. Hence, there might be role for robot-supported training tasks once the level of routine day-to-day practice is achieved during therapy and the humanoid robot can help to assist training while supporting a patient's motivation at the same time.

Pepper has a lot of sensors. Nevertheless, it is sometimes very difficult to analyse manual tasks when performed with paper and pencil. Therefore, a digitalization of training tasks might help a lot. It was our idea to replace paper by tablets. Applications had to be implemented to allow the exercises to be done on those tablets. We will shortly present this approach for the three training tasks AIMING, CANCELLATION and MAZE TRACKING.

4.1 Digitalization of Training Task AIMING

A patient has to hit circles of different size from left to right and afterwards from right to left (see left part of Fig. 3) that are placed perpendicularly. Next, circles located horizontally on the table have to be hit (see right part of Fig. 3. Circle at the button). This can also be seen from the digitalized version with two tablets represented in Fig. 4.

After ten perpendicularly presented circles are hit, connection lines between the circle at the button of the left part of Fig. 3 to all other horizontally presented circles have to be drawn. Once this is done a patient has to start hitting the perpendicular circles again.

A patient has one minute for this exercise. When a circle is missed the patient has to try to hit it again. The task AIMING has to be repeated four times (e.g. for times repeated practice over approximately one minute).

The goal of becoming faster while always meeting the precision demand of hitting both the smaller (more difficult to hit) and larger (easier to hit) targets affords continuously the adjustment of the motor behaviour, will only gradually be reached, and implies an underlying improvement of performance, i.e. motor learning.

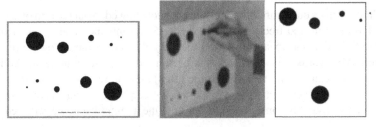

Fig. 3. Manual training task AIMING.

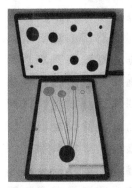

Fig. 4. Digitalized training task AIMING.

To implement the conventional AAT therapy manual procedure straight away would have triggered a verbal comment from Pepper that a circle was not hit in a correct way, if such an error occurred. However, we felt that it would be better since more direct, if the application on the tablet itself provides an appropriate feedback. In this way the robot is not considered as a kind of "opponent" because it has to provide corrective feedback. Negative aspects are related to the tablet.

We considered the following types of feedback for the task "hit the circle" on the tablet:

- The circle that has to be hit is blinking
- Properly targeted circle becomes green
- A specific acoustic sound will be provided for correct and incorrect hits

Some of the suggested feedback are redundant. It will be evaluated in the future which kind of patients would like to have which feedback.

We are also yet not able to answer the question: "When should the robot take corrective actions?" Experiments with different versions of our application will show, which solution is appreciated by patients and which solution does not assist, but puts more pressure on the patients. Psychologists will help us to find the right solutions.

4.2 Digitalization of the Training Task CANCELLATION

Patients have to cross out symbols of O's. They are not allowed to put the arm on the table. The arm has to be moved freely in the air. Figure 5 presents the tablet implementation for CROSSING. One has to start from left to right followed by the following line from right to left. Afterwards, crossing out has to be done from left to right again. At the top of the tablet one can see the remaining time (10 s) and the reached points (80). If the crossing out was done correctly the symbol gets a green background. If something was wrong, the background becomes read. In this case the attempt has to be repeated.

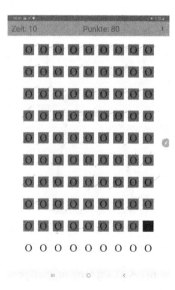

Fig. 5. Screenshot from the tablet application. (Color figure online)

Again, the robot itself does not comment on errors as a first instance. It only comments on exceptions like unexpected stop of the activities. Additionally, Pepper informs about the result and relates it to previous exercises. This is combined with some motivational sentences.

4.3   Digitalization of the Training Task MACE TRACKING

For the MACE TRACKING exercise patients have to follow the mace as far as possible in one minute without hitting its boundaries. The result is captured as the percentage of the correctly followed mace. 100% are the complete mace.

In case there is time left, a patient can start to follow a second labyrinth, but this time s/he starts with the opposite direction. In this case more than 100% can be reached.

Each mistake, touching or crossing the border, results in one second penalty (Fig. 6).

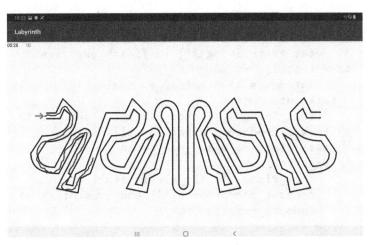

Fig. 6. Example of a training task of MACE TRACKING on a tablet.

We discussed the preconditions for the observation of three specific training tasks. The support for further training tasks is under development. Some videos can be found on the website of [3].

5   Modelling Collaboration

In this paragraph we want to model the task model for Pepper, the patient in DSL-CoTaL [4], that is based on features of Buchholz et al. [2]. The DSL supports the specification of a team model that reflects the collaborative activities of the participants.

```
team coop {
  root training = greeting >> train >> finish
    task greeting = pepper.greet |=| patient.greet
    task train = pepper.introduce >>
      patient.perfoms_exercises{*} [> patient.finishes_exercises
    task finish = pepper.finish_exercise ||| patient.bye
}
```

Fig. 7. Specification of a simplified Training collaborative model.

The specification of Fig. 7 expresses that a training consists of a greeting part that is followed by the training (≫-enabling). Afterwards some ending activities have to be performed. In the greeting part pepper and the patient have to perform the task greet in any order (|=|-order independence). The role model of pepper and patient must have a task greet each. For the training pepper provides an introduction that is followed by the performance of the patient, which is an iteration that is finished by finishing the exercises. At the end pepper finishes exercises and in parallel (|||) the patient says bye (Fig. 8).

```
role pepper {
  root roo1 =
      greet >> training {*} [> finish_exercise
    task training =
        introduce >> starting >> train
      task introduce =
        tell_introd ||| show_pict1 ||| show_pict2
      task introduce pre patient.allInstances.greet
      task starting = say_can_we_tart
      task train =
        show_video ||| say_please_start |||
        comment_performance{*}[>end_commenting >>
        comment_results
}
```

Fig. 8. Role model of Pepper.

After greeting the training pepper has to wait until all patients (most of the time there is only one) greeted. First a short introduction is provided. In parallel to the talk two pictures are shown on the tablet of the robot that demonstrate important elements of the training task. Afterwards the patient is asked, whether the training can start. If ready, the robot says: "Please start" and later comments regarding the performance are provided. Finally, the robot comments on the results of the training.

Fig. 9. Training Task CANCELLATION with presenting previous results by Pepper.

Figure 9 presents the captured situation at the end of a task while Pepper says the number of reached points and presents a graph with recently reached results.

Currently, from our language DSL-CoTaL code can be generated to CoTaSE [2], to CTTE [12] and to HAMSTERS [11].

Figure 10 shows the generated CTTE model of the specification of Fig. 7.

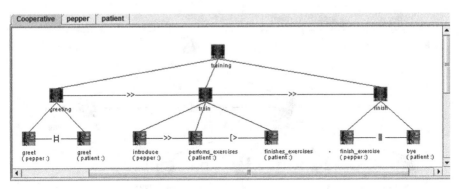

Fig. 10. Generated cooperative model for CTTE.

It would also be good to generate code directly for Pepper. To be able to do that some more specific language constructs like **say**(text) would be necessary. In [7] we provide a little bit mor extended discussion about this aspect.

Additionally, we recognised a further problem: in the specification of the role model of Pepper. Sometimes Pepper has to ask: "Can we proceed?". This has to be repeated until a positive answer is given. Even for the case of maximal three repetitions, the task model becomes quite complex.

It would be nice to have iterations that can end with a certain condition like a repeat until statement in programming languages. Our language DSL-CoTaL will be extended in this way.

Figure 11 gives an impression how the language could look like. The task asking is repeated until the task yes is performed.

```
object answer { attribute: String value }
component askingForStart [text, seconds]{
  root roottask =  asking{until answer.value == "Y"}
    task asking = say(text) >> yes [] no [] wait(seconds)
        task yes = input(yes) action answer.setValue("Y")
        task no  = input(no)  action answer.setValue("N")
}
```

Fig. 11. Object specification and component with iteration.

A modified version of the component (without the new language constructs) was used to generate the CTTE model for an instance of the generic component askingForStart with the two instance parameters "Can we" and "180". tThe instance is created by *askingForStart[Can we, 180]*.

The result is presented by Fig. 12

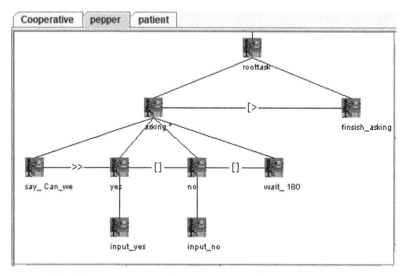

Fig. 12. CTTE model for instance *askingForStart[Can we, 180]*.

6 Lessons Learned

6.1 Methodology

Following the HCD approach worked quite well. Therapists were interviewed, the artefacts they work with were analysed and videos of their work with patients were taped. Textual transcriptions were produced and evaluated. Specific events were extracted and highlighted. In this way, exceptions for our applications were identified. As example we can mention the exception that patients did stop the crossing out at the end of a line even when the instructions said that they should continue in the following line and all these lines were visible. We did not expect such a behaviour.

The therapist said in the case: "There is still time left. You should continue in the following line." We do the same now with our application. The tablet app throws an exception when no activities can be identified at the end of a line within three seconds and informs the robot. The robot says the sentences of the therapist.

Modelling the behaviour of the therapist, patient and the robot was useful to understand the domain. It also supported the communication with experts. Especially, the animation of specifications helped a lot to establish a common ground between all participants.

As we know already from requirements engineering, we recognized that communication between psychologists, sociologists, expert from medicine and people form computer science in natural language is very problematic. Requirements are sometimes very vague like: "The robot has always to say some motivational words". Neither is clear what the robot should say nor when. Modelling helped us a lot to be more precise and to understand the ideas of other people. Some ideas for further extending task model features were identified. Interaction will be the challenge for success [1].

6.2 Technology

We started to implement applets in java on the robot and on the tablets. Connection was realized directly via wireless local area network. Connection was often lost and applications had to start again.

Therefore, we used the Message Queuing Telemetry Transport (MQTT) technology [18]. It was designed as an extremely lightweight publish/subscribe messaging transport opportunity for the "Internet of Things". MQTT was designed for low-bandwidth, high-latency and unreliable networks. Messages are sent via a server and it can be checked whether a message was received by recipient. If something went wrong, a message is sent again.

Using MQTT made our applications much more stable. We really recommend it for similar applications.

Having a stable message exchange established in our applications, we discussed the idea of implementing the behaviour of the robot externally. In this way, the robot has only an interpreter of messages that delivers the execution of commands. As a consequence, available technologies like knowledge management, machine learning or behaviour specification can be used without limitations.

The robot becomes something like a thin client. We have the impression that this software architecture facilitates digital implementation. However, we will investigate these aspects in more detail in the future. Alternative designs will be evaluated.

7 Summary and Outlook

The paper provides a case study of digitalizing Arm-Ability Training (AAT) for patients with mild to moderate arm paresis after a stroke causing focal disability. It was discussed how a social humanoid robot like Pepper can assist patients during AAT. Such a robot will play the role of a supervisor providing instructions and feedback, a motivator and supporter. Its application is restricted to highly standardized training schedules and excludes clinical decision making.

AAT training tasks need a digitalization to allow a smooth observation by humanoid robot. For three training tasks it was shown how training can be supported based on tablets and corresponding applications. It was shortly demonstrated how collaboration of patients and robot can be modelled by task models. Using a textual domain-specific language allows the generation of code for other tools that visualize the task models and allow their animation. A comprehensive domain-specific language (DSL) for robot actions will be a challenge for the future.

Currently, a data base is under development that contains user models of the patients. Beside general personal data and any individual details regarding the prescribed training, the data base has to store goals of the patients they want to reach. Such goals can be: "I want to be able to hold playing cards in my hands to be able to play with my grandchildren". The robot will refer to these goals in order to motivate a patient. In addition, medical data will be stored that characterize the ability of a person like data characterizing the degree of (lack of) dexterity as assessed with the Box-and-Block-Test or the Nine-Hole-Peg-Test (Platz et al. 2005). From the point of view of a computer scientist, they are a kind of metrics [19]. These data allow very individualized hints. We hope to be able to exploit these resources in the future.

We will evaluate in the E-BRAiN project which kind of patients accepts the collaboration with Pepper using our apps.

References

1. Ahn, H.S., Choi, J., Moon, H., Lim, Y.: Social human-robot interaction of human-care service robots. In: Companion of the 2018 ACM/IEEE International Conference on Human-Robot Interaction (HRI 2018), ACM, New York, NY, USA, 385–386 (2018). https://doi.org/10.1145/3173386.3173565
2. Buchholz, G., Forbrig, P.: Extended features of task models for specifying cooperative activities. PACMHCI 1(EICS), 7:1–7:21 (2017)
3. E-BRAiN: https://wwwswt.informatik.uni-rostock.de/webebrain/. Accessed 30 Sept 2020
4. Forbrig, P., Dittmar, A., Kühn, M.: A textual domain specific language for task models: generating code for CoTaL, CTTE, and HAMSTERS. In: EICS 2018 Conferences, Paris, France, pp. 5:1–5:6 (2018)
5. Forbrig, P., Bundea, A.: Using the social humanoid robot pepper for training tasks. In: 1st Workshop on Adapted intEraction with SociAl Robots (cAESAR), IUI 2020, 17 March 2020, Cagliari, Italy (2020)
6. Forbrig, P., Platz, T.: Supporting the arm-ability training of stroke patients by a social-humanoid robot. In: Accepted for IHIET-AI 2020 conference, 24–26 April Lausanne, Switzerland (2020)
7. Forbrig, P., Bundea, A.: Modelling the collaboration of a patient and an assisting humanoid robot during training tasks. In: Accepted for HCI 2020, Copenhagen, Denmark, 19–24 July (2020)
8. GBD 2015 Disease and Injury Incidence and Prevalence Collaborators. Global, regional, and national incidence, prevalence, and years lived with disability for 310 diseases and injuries, 1990–2015: a systematic analysis for the Global Burden of Disease Study 2015. Lancet. 388:1545–602 (2016)
9. Harte, R., et al.: A human-centered design methodology to enhance the usability, human factors, and user experience of connected health systems: a three-phase methodology. JMIR Hum. Factors 4(1), e8 (2017)
10. Manca, M., et al.: The impact of serious games with humanoid robots on mild cognitive impairment older adults. Int. J. Hum.-Comput. Stud. (2020). https://doi.org/10.1016/j.ijhcs.2020.102509
11. Palanque, P., Martinie, C.: Designing and Assessing Interactive Systems Using Task Models. In Proceedings of the CHI EA 2016, ACM, New York, NY, USA, pp. 976–979 (2016). https://doi.org/10.1145/2851581.2856686

12. Paternò, F.: ConcurTaskTrees: an engineered approach to model-based design of interactive systems. In: The Handbook of Analysis for Human Computer Interaction, pp. 1–18 (1999)

13. Petersen, S., Houston, S., Qin, H., Tague, C., Studley, J.: The utilization of robotic pets in dementia care. J. Alzheimer's Dis. JAD **55**(2), 569–574 (2017). https://doi.org/10.3233/JAD-160703

14. Platz, T., Pinkowski, C., van Wijck, F., Kim, I.H., di Bella, P., Johnson, G.: Reliability and validity of arm function assessment with standardized guidelines for the Fugl-Meyer Test, Action Research Arm Test and Box and Block Test: a multicentre study. Clin. Rehabil. **19**(4), 404–411 (2005). https://doi.org/10.1191/0269215505cr832oa

15. Platz, T., van Kaick, S., Mehrholz, J., Leidner, O., Eickhof, C., Pohl, M.: Best conventional therapy versus modular Impairment-oriented training (IOT) for arm paresis after stroke: a single blind, multi-centre randomized controlled trial. Neurorehabil. Neural Repair **23**, 706–716 (2009)

16. Platz, T., Lotze, M.: Arm Ability Training (AAT) promotes dexterity recovery after a stroke-a review of its design, clinical effectiveness, and the neurobiology of the actions. Front. Neurol. **9**, 1082 (2018). https://doi.org/10.3389/fneur.2018.01082

17. Platz, T., Roschka, S., Doppl, K., Roth, C., Lotze, M., Sack, A.T., et al.: Prolonged motor skill learning - a combined behavioural training and theta burst TMS study. Restor Neurol Neurosci. **30**, 213–224 (2012). https://doi.org/10.3233/RNN-2012-110205

18. Pulver, T.: Hands-On Internet of Things with MQTT: Build Connected IoT Devices with Arduino and MQ Telemetry Transport (MQTT). Packt Publishing Ltd., Birmingham (2019)

19. Singer, B., Garcia-Vega, J.: The fugl-meyer upper extremity scale. J. Physiotherapy **63**(1), 53 (2017). https://doi.org/10.1016/j.jphys.2016.08.010

20. SoftBank Robotics. https://www.softbankrobotics.com/corp/robots/. Accessed 11 Nov 2019

Model-Based and Model-Driven
Approaches

A Generic Multimodels-Based Approach for the Analysis of Usability and Security of Authentication Mechanisms

Nicolas Broders[1]([⊠]), Célia Martinie[1]([⊠]) [iD], Philippe Palanque[1] [iD], Marco Winckler[3] [iD], and Kimmo Halunen[2] [iD]

[1] ICS-IRIT, Université Toulouse III-Paul Sabatier, Toulouse, France
{nicolas.broders,celia.martinie,philippe.palanque}@irit.fr
[2] VTT Technical Research Centre of Finland Ltd., Espoo, Finland
Kimmo.Halunen@vtt.fi
[3] Université Côte D'Azur, Nice, France

Abstract. Authentication is a security function, added on top of an interactive system, whose role is to reduce organizations and users' risks to grant access to sensitive data or critical resources to unauthorized users. Such a security function interfere with users' goals and tasks by adding articulatory activities, which affect each dimension of usability. In order to mitigate their negative effect on usability, security functions must be designed following a User Centered Approach. In order to ensure their efficiency in terms of security, security processes have to be followed. With this respect, this paper focuses on the representation of user tasks (using task modelling techniques) to be performed during authentication. For security aspects, we propose the use of an approach called "attack trees" which represents threats and their effect. To integrate both aspects in a single framework, we propose an extended task modelling technique that is able to represent explicitly security threats and their potential effect together with users' tasks performed during authentication. We show how such models can be used to compare the usability and the security of different authentication mechanisms and to make explicit conflicts between these properties. We exemplify the use of the approach on two sophisticated authentication mechanisms demonstrating its applicability and its usefulness for representing and assessing in a single framework, usability and security of these security mechanism.

Keywords: Usability · Security · Tasks descriptions · Authentication

1 Introduction

Authentication is one of the most common and repetitive activity users have to carry out every day when accessing information technologies. Security mechanism are designed to protect users' assets by preventing a straightforward access to them, thus adding complexity to the user interaction with the system and ultimately degrading the system usability and, in particular the users' performance [48]. For example, early studies have

© IFIP International Federation for Information Processing 2020
Published by Springer Nature Switzerland AG 2020
R. Bernhaupt et al. (Eds.): HCSE 2020, LNCS 12481, pp. 61–83, 2020.
https://doi.org/10.1007/978-3-030-64266-2_4

demonstrated [21] that users have an average of 25 accounts requiring identification while user's capability of recalling multiple passwords is still questioned [7]. In their early work, Adams and Sasse [1] advocated that "Security Needs User-Centered Design". The User Centered Design (UCD) process, as defined in ISO 9241 part 210 [30], determines that the identification of the users' goals and needs is one of the key elements to produce usable interactive system. The same ISO 9241 standard in the part 11 [29], defines usability by three dimensions: efficiency, satisfaction, and effectiveness. Efficiency is assessable via user testing for instance counting the time needed to complete tasks and the number of user errors occurring during the performance of these tasks. User satisfaction can be assessed by direct observation of users (ex. positive/negative comments and analysis of facial expression) and/or using specialized questionnaires such as the System Usability Scale (SUS) [11]. For the effectiveness, the best way to assess it according to [19] is to identify exhaustively the tasks the users have to perform in order to reach their goals and to check that each task is supported by the system [34]. Assessing the cost of user errors and the cost of recovering from them is also an important aspect that can be addressed using dedicated structuring [44] or adding specific extensions to task models [17].

Even though a lot of work has been carried out on evaluating the usability of authentication mechanisms two by two [12] or more globally [8], the current state of the art demonstrates that the design and development of security mechanisms does not systematically takes into account the three before mentioned dimensions of usability, and in particular the effectiveness. Indeed, one of most cited analysis from Bonneau et al. [8], which compares the usability of 35 different authentication mechanisms, does not recognize effectiveness among the 8 different aspects covering by the so-called « Usability Benefits». It is also the case in more recent work that classifies properties that have to be supported by user authentication methods and which does not contain effectiveness [26].

This paper demonstrates how tasks models can be used to systematically represent the quantity and the complexity of work that users have to perform to complete an authentication on a given system. Moreover, we propose to extend a task-modelling notation to represent explicitly the security threats and their effect. The proposed use of this integrated representation of security and usability aspects consists in modelling users' activity for authentication on different authentication mechanisms. These models can then be used to compare the usability and security of the mechanisms under consideration both in terms of security and usability. As the design of these systems usually consists in a trade-off between these two properties, the proposed approach provides means to make these trade-off explicit. This combined representation makes it also possible to identify potential countermeasure to mitigate the effect of threats but also to identify ways to improve the usability of the mechanisms without degrading their security. This aspect related to design of usable and secure authentication mechanisms is beyond the scope of this paper that focusses on the analysis part of extant systems.

The paper is structured as follows: Sect. 2 presents the related work on methods for the analysis of usability and security as well as their main limitations in terms of identifying exhaustively user tasks and potential threats. Section 3 presents an extension to the task modelling notation called HAMSTERS-XL which was specifically designed to represent the possible threats and their effects for each relevant task in the task model. Then, using a simple case study of password authentication, we illustrate how the combined description of tasks and threats enable to identify which threats are covered or not covered by the authentication mechanism. Section 4 presents the applications of theses notations to the case study of comparing the usability and security of two authentication mechanisms. Section 5 concludes on the main benefits of the proposed approach.

2 Existing Approaches for the Analysis of Usability and Security of Interactive Systems

Research and industry have been producing, at a very high pace, diverse authentication mechanisms with increasing complexity for the users. The current practice in authentication is promoting multi-factor authentication methods (i.e. the access to the system is granted after the user provides two or more pieces of evidence, the so-called factors, to the authentication system). Even though the adoption and acceptance by users is questioned [45], other user studies (based on Mechanical Turk users) suggest that two factors authentication mechanisms are, overall, perceived as usable [16]. Most of the work concerning the usability of security mechanisms lies in one of the following categories:

- analysis of user behavior when confronted to security mechanisms (e.g. user behavior when password expires [25]),
- recommendations to enhance usability of a specific existing security mechanism (e.g. authentication in a smart home [28]),
- comparative studies of the usability of security mechanisms (e.g. which authentication mechanism would better replace CAPTCHAs [23]),
- techniques that might improve users' performances (e.g. improving users' memorability of authentication mechanisms [39]).

As we shall see, most of the existing work focuses on specific security mechanisms (such as authentication) on a case-by-case basis and they mainly address user performance and/or user satisfaction. Nonetheless, the analysis of effectiveness requires the identification of all possible user tasks [19]. Hereafter, we discuss a few generic methods that can be used to analyze the tradeoffs between usability and security of interactive systems. Then, we highlight the methods explicitly addressing the effectiveness.

2.1 Generic Methods for the Systematic Analysis of Usability and Security

Despite of a large literature, very few work propose generic methods that can be used to compare diverse types of security mechanisms and systematically assess the trade-offs between security and usability. Alshamari [3] highlights the recurrent conflicts between usability and security. That author proposes a generic process to identify these conflicts between usability and security at design time, and to select a strategy to handle them using a decision support system for eliciting requirements. Other works employ inspection methods to analyze the effect of security mechanisms on the usability of interactive system. Braz et al. [10] propose a set of heuristics and an inspection method for the analytical evaluation of the effects of security mechanisms on the system's usability. Alarifi et al. [2] propose a structured inspection model dedicated to the analysis of usability and security of e-banking platforms. Bonneau et al. [8] propose a set of heuristics for comparing usability and security benefits between several authentication techniques. Such inspection methods and heuristics provide support to compare security mechanisms and to make tradeoffs during design. However, these approaches cannot ensure an exhaustive coverage of all possible user actions with the system and they might fail in detecting problems related to specific scenarios. Ben-Asher et al. [6] propose an experimental environment to collect systematically any possible user behavior facing security mechanisms. They propose to use the output of user tests run in the experimental environment to explore possible tradeoffs between security and usability for the system under design. That approach can help to identify usability problems and/issues with security mechanism with tasks performed by users during the experimental phase. As such, the logistic required to run the user test limits the coverage of the study to a small subset of tasks that are possible with the system.

2.2 Generic Methods that Take into Account Effectiveness

All the existing approaches for systematically assessing usability and security rely on scenarios. A "scenario describes a sequence of actions and events that lead to an outcome. These actions and events are related in a usage context" [47]. Kainda et al. [32] propose a security-usability analysis process. They first present a so called "security-usability threat model" which is a set of important factors for the analysis of usability and security. Then, they produce both threat and usage scenarios that are used to assess whether (or not) the set of elicited factors are met by the security mechanisms. Faily and Fléchais [18] propose a scenario-based approach for assessing the effect of security policies on usability. The specificity of this approach is that it is based on "misusability" cases which are produced using systematic questioning of system development and deployment documentation (e.g. architecture specification, user manual…). This approach aims to inform re-design of security mechanisms.

Like other inspection methods, scenario-based methods allow to identify security threats and support the analysis of the range of user behaviors when facing threats. Scenarios bring the attention to specific tasks, thus promoting systematic inspections and reducing the risk of finding problems only by change. However, because scenarios are focused on specific tasks they do not cover all possible temporally ordered sets of user tasks and, as a consequence, the analysis of the effect of potential target threat on user tasks may be incomplete.

3   Describing Security Threats and Their Effects with Task Models

This section introduces an illustrative authentication mechanism and its corresponding description using a task model notation called HAMSTERS-XL. As we shall see, the task model is enriched to represent threats and the effects of these threats.

3.1 Illustrative Example: Text-Based Login with Short Display of User Input

Figure 1 presents a storyboard of some of the users actions required for logging in an online bank to check the accounts' balance. The middle figure shows that user input is shown for 2 s, thus providing feedback and potentially preventing user mistakes. After the 2 s, a dot visually conceals the manual entry to ensure security (right-hand side Figure of Fig. 1).

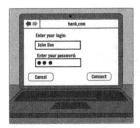  

Fig. 1. Storyboard of a text-based authentication featuring short display (2s) of user entries.

3.2 Modeling Tasks

The systematic identification of potential security threats on user actions and the effects of authentication mechanisms on user tasks requires the description of:

- user actions: a threat can arise from a type of user action, e.g. drawing a gesture password on a tactile screen is subject to smudge attacks whereas typing a password on a keyboard is subject to keylogging attack,
- their temporal ordering and/or temporal constraints: a threat can arise from the specific ordering of user actions, e.g. the user takes too long to input a password,
- the information, knowledge and objects being manipulated during these actions: a threat can arise from an information, knowledge or object that the user has lost, forgotten or misused, e.g. a credit card lost in a public space.

Hereafter, we describe how these elements are taken into account using the task model notation named HAMSTERS.

Description of the Task Modelling Notation
HAMSTERS (Human – centered Assessment and Modelling to Support Task Engineering for Resilient Systems) is a tool-supported task modelling notation for representing human activities in a hierarchical and temporally ordered way [37]. The HAMSTERS notation provides support for representing a task model, which is a tree of nodes that can be tasks or temporal operators (Fig. 3 presents a HAMSTERS task models describing the users actions to login). The top node represents the main goal of the user, and lower levels represent sub-goals, tasks and actions. Task types are elements of notation that enable to refine and represent the nature of the task as well as whether it is the user or

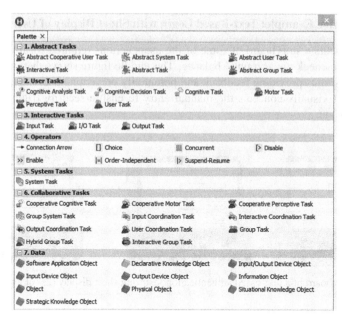

Fig. 2. Palette of the elements of notation of HAMSTERS

the system who performs the task. The main task types are abstract, user, interactive and system tasks (parts numbered 1, 2, 3, 5 in Fig. 2).

Abstract tasks (part numbered 1 in Fig. 2) provide support to describe sub-goals in the task model. They also provide support to describe tasks for which the refinement is not yet identified, at the beginning of the analysis process. User tasks (part numbered 2 in Fig. 2) provide support to describe the detailed human aspects of the user activities. User task types can be refined into perceptive, motor, cognitive analysis, and cognitive decision tasks. For example, the user may perform a motor task (such as grabbing a card) or cognitive task (such as remembering a PIN code). Such refinement enables the analysis of several aspects of the tasks performed by the user such as cognitive load, motor load, required perceptive capabilities. Such refinement also enables to identify possible threats that can be associated to specific types of user actions. Temporal operators are used to represent temporal relationships between sub-goals and between activities. Interactive tasks (part numbered 5 in Fig. 2) provide support to describe tasks that are action performed by the user to input information to the system (interactive input task) or action perform by the system to provide information to the user and that are meant to be perceived by the user (interactive output task). Interactive input/output tasks provide supports to describe both cases. System tasks (part numbered 5 in Fig. 2) provide support to describe the tasks that the system executes. The system may execute an input task, i.e. the production and processing of an event produced by an action performed by the user on an input device. It may also execute and output task, i.e. a rendering on an output device (such as displaying a new frame on a screen). The system may execute a processing task (such as checking the user login and password).

In addition to elements of notation for representing user activities and their temporal ordering, HAMSTERS provides support to represent data (e.g. information such as perceived amount of money on an account, knowledge such as a known password), objects (e.g. physical objects such as a credit card, software objects such as an entered password) and devices (e.g. input devices such as keyboard, output device such as a screen) that are required to accomplish these activities (part numbered 7 in Fig. 2).

HAMSTERS and its eponym interactive modelling environment is the only environment providing structuring mechanisms as real-life models are usually large and reuse is useful [36]. HAMSTERS also provides elements of notation to identify and describe human errors [17], which is useful to detect possible user errors and then re-design the system or estimate the costs of recovering the error. Furthermore, HAMSTERS provides functions to extend tasks types and data types if required for the analysis [37]. For all of these reasons, expressiveness of the notation and modelling support, we chose HAMSTERS to be used with our approach.

The Task Model of the Illustrative Example

Figure 3 shows the task model featuring temporally ordered user actions required for logging in as set in Sect. 3.1. First, the computer perform the task "Display the login page" (an output system task) so that the user can "See the login page" (a perceptual user task). In the sequence the user must "Fill in the username" (an abstract task, not detailed here) and "Fill in the password (an abstract task). To reach this sub-goal, the user must "Recall password" (a cognitive user task connected to a declarative knowledge object "known password"). This task is linked to the information "recalled password" (an information object) to indicate that the user was able to remembered the password.

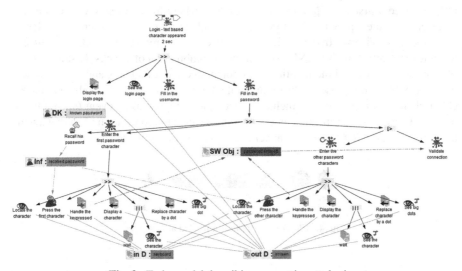

Fig. 3. Tasks model describing user actions to login

With the password in the mind, the user can "Locate the character" (a perceptive task) and "Press the first character" of the password (a motor task). This user action on the keyboard is transmitted to a computer that will "Handle the keypressed" (an input system task), "Display a character" on the screen (an output system task) and "wait" (a system task). The waiting time of 2 s prompts the user to "See the character" (an optional perceptual user task) and detect any possible mistakes while typing. After 2 s the system will "Replace character by a dot" (an output system task) and from there the user will "See big dot" (an optional perceptual user task) instead of characters. The next task "Press the other password characters" (an iterative task) repeats as many times as characters left to complete the password. To complete the login, users must "Validate connection" (an abstract task, not detailed).

For the following figures, we will not describe again the details of the task types. You can find these task types in Sect. 3.2 describing the task modeling notation.

3.3 Modelling Threats and Effects

The systematic identification and representation of threats and effects of threats require a description of user actions and all possible threats that are not directly related to the user actions (e.g. network, electronic components…). Such information is essential to design and implement mechanisms to avoid or to mitigate the threats [41].

The Attack Tree Notation
We selected Attack Tree to address security aspects as they are major tools in analyzing security of a system [41]. They can be decorated with expert knowledge, historical data and estimation of critical parameters as demonstrated in [22] even though early versions of them were lacking formal semantics [41]. Attack tree notation is a formal method to describe the possible threats or combination of threats to a system. B. Schneier [49] provided a first description of an attack tree, where the main goal of the attack is represented by the top root node and where the combinations of leaves represent different way to achieve that goal. In the original notation, OR nodes refer to alternatives of attacks to achieve the attack whilst AND nodes refer to combination of attacks. Nishihara et al. [41] proposed to extend the notation with potential effect of attacks and with a logical operator, SAND to represent constraints in the temporal ordering of combined attacks. Other elements of the notation include a rectangle to represent an event (such a threat or attack), an ellipse to represent an effect and a triangle to represent the fact that a node is not refined. All elements of the attack tree notation are shown at Fig. 4.

Fig. 4. Elements of notation for the attack trees

The Attack Tree of the Illustrative Example
The Fig. 5 shows an example of attack tree that has been produced using taxonomies of cyber security threats [33] and by grouping relevant threats into categories. For example, one category of possible threats to login is eavesdropping which gathers:

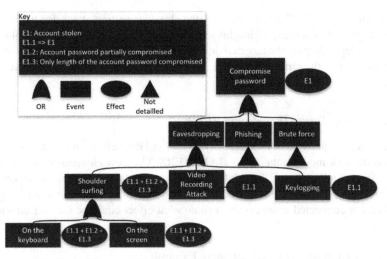

Fig. 5. Attack tree of the keyboard login authentication mechanism

- keylogging: "The key logger makes the log file of the keys pressed by the user and then sends to that log file to the attacker's email address" [46],
- video recording attack: "The attacker uses a camera (ex. mobile phones or miniature camera) to record and analyze users typing password" [46],
- shoulder surfing: "Alternative name of spying in which the attacker spies the user's movements to obtain the password…, how the user enters the password i.e. what keys of keyboard the user has pressed [46].

In Fig. 5, we read that an "Eavesdropping" (an event depicted as a rectangle) can be trigger by an attacker using one of the following attacks (connected by an OR node): "Shoulder surfing", "Video recording attack", or "Keylogging" the machine. The attacker can also "Brute force" the password or use some "Phishing" techniques but these threats are not refined in this extract (see nodes depicted by triangles).

Depending on the attacker's effectiveness and on the user device on which the attacker will be shoulder surfing, the outcome of the attack may generate different combinations of effects (represented in Fig. 5 by the ellipse containing the effect "E1.1 + E1.2 + E1.3" respectively designing "Account stolen", "Account password partially compromised" and "Only length of the account password compromised").

Fig. 6. Representation of a threat (a), and effect (b), with extended HAMSTERS notation

Video recording attack and keylogging attack may generate one effect each, which are more critical (represented in Fig. 5 by the ellipse containing the effect "E1.1" designing that "Account stolen"). The refinement of the shoulder surfing attack for two types of devices (keyboard or screen) highlights more precisely how attacks may take place and their effects depending on the targeted device. In our example, the attacks on both types of devices generate the same effects ("E1.1 + E1.2 + E1.3" possible effects on keyboard and screen).

3.4 Integrating Tasks, Threats and Effects

In order to represent explicitly the security threats and their effect on user tasks, we have extended the task model notation of HAMSTERS-XL. New elements of notation are: **threat, effect of a threat**, and the **relationships between tasks, threats and effects**. The icon representing a threat is show by Fig. 6.a, and the effect is represented by Fig. 6.b. Each threat is connected to an effect to show what effect could be the consequence of this threat.

The Integrated Model of the Illustrative Example

Figure 7 presents a HAMSTERS task model that embeds the representation of three eavesdropping potential threats (namely keylogging, shoulder surfing, and video recording attack) and their effects.

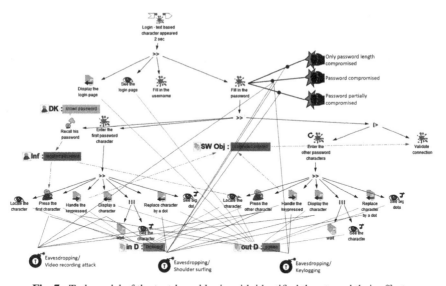

Fig. 7. Task model of the text-based login with identified threats and their effects

Each threat can be connected to one or more tasks to show that which tasks may be targets for or more threats. These relationships are depicted as strokes as we shall see in Fig. 7. Video recording attack is connected to the two user motor tasks respectively labelled "Press the first character" and "Press the other character" and the corresponding effect "password compromised". Shoulder surfing is connected to the two motor tasks respectively labelled "Press the first character" and "Press the other character" and the corresponding effects "Password compromised" or "Password partially compromised", depending on the effectiveness of the hacker. Shoulder surfing is also connected to two system output tasks "Display big dot" and "Display big dots" and the effect is to have "Only password length compromised"). The keylogging attack is connected to the two input system tasks labelled "Handle the key pressed" and the effect of this threat is to have "Password compromised".

4 Comparing Two Authentication Mechanisms: "Google 2 Step" and "Firefox Password Manager"

In order to demonstrate how our modelling approach can be used to compare authentication mechanisms we have designed a small case study focused on two authentication mechanisms ("Google 2 step login" and "Firefox password manager") that are applied to an online bank application.

We first present the main user tasks (which refer to checking account balance and wire transfer) and then we present the task models including the representation of security threats for each of the two authentication mechanisms. The models are then used to support a comparative analysis to find out which mechanism has the best trade-off between usability and security. Authentication mechanisms presented in this case study (for logging in an online bank application) aim at demonstrating the approach and do not precisely reflect precisely security mechanisms deployed.

4.1 Presentation of the Main Tasks

Figure 8 presents a task model that describes the main users' tasks with our online bank application: "Check accounts' balance and make a wire transfer".

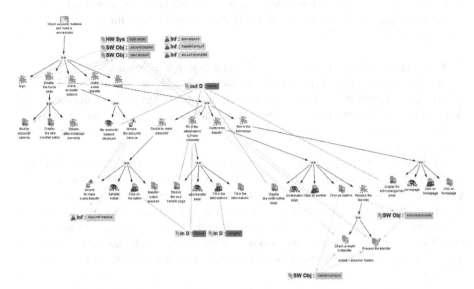

Fig. 8. Check accounts' balance and make a wire transfer task model

- First, the user visits the web page of the bank website to perform the "login".
- The consecutive task shows that the browser "Display the home page". This abstract system task is decomposed into three concurrent sub-tasks: "display accounts' balance", "Display the wire transfer button", and "Display other homepage element".
- The user can then perform the abstract task "Check accounts' balance abstract task", which is refined in: "See the accounts' balance displayed" and "Analyse the accounts' balance".
- After that, the user can perform the abstract task "Make a wire transfer", which encompasses a sequence of four abstract tasks: "Decide to make a transfer", "Fill in the information to make a transfer", "Confirm the transfer" and "Go back to the home page". The abstract task "Make a wire transfer" is refined in the four following sub-tasks: "Decide to make a wire transfer", "See the transfer button", "Click on the button", and "transfer button pressed". The abstract task "Fill in the information to make a transfer" is refined in four sub-tasks: "Fill in the information", "Fill in the information", and "Display the confirmation page". The abstract task "Confirm the transfer" is refined in the following sub-tasks: "See the confirmation page", "Click on confirm", and "Process the transfer" which is made up of a sequence of system tasks "Check amount to transfer" and "Process" the transfer". The abstract task "Go back to the home page" is refined in: "Display the acknowledgement", "See the homepage perceptive task, "Click on homepage".

4.2   Authentication Mechanism: Google 2-Step Verification

"Google 2-step Verification" is a multifactor authentication mechanism adding an extra layer of security on simple password-based authentication mechanisms [24]. After setting up of the mechanism, the user can connect to the account by entering a password, then Google sends a verification code to the user's smartphone (the user needs a smartphone to complete to login), the authentication is complete when the user confirms by pressing "yes".

Task Model of the User Tasks with the Google 2-Step Verification
Figure 10 presents the task model for the Google 2-step verification mechanism; it contains the description of the threats and effects on user tasks that are detailed latter. The first task is to perform the text-based login. The precondition "device is not recognized" on the software object "recognized device" be true to enable users to perform the abstract task "Validate the second step".

At the end of this step, the user receives a notification "Display the second authentication factor". Due to space constraints, we cannot present here the refinement of the abstract task "Validate the second step" but the refinement of this sub-goal is also used to perform the analysis presented in Sect. 4.4. The main tasks of this second step are: "Make the second step necessary" for future logging, "Display the second authentication" factor, "Grab the phone" (we assume that the phone is unlocked and close to the user), "See the second authentication notification", and finally "Press 'yes'" to confirm the login.

Attack Tree of the Google 2-step Verification
Figure 9 presents the attack tree of the Google 2-steps Verification mechanism. The goal of the attack is to get access to the bank account bypassing this mechanism. Three conditions are necessary (under the top level goal node, all the branches are linked by a SAND operator) to compromise the account of the user. First, the attacker needs to compromise the text-based password mechanism (left branch in Fig. 9). As in Sect. 3.3, the attacker has several possibilities to do it using eavesdropping techniques, phishing or brute force. Secondly, the attacker needs to get access to the smartphone of the user (second branch), at least temporarily, to confirm the login. There are two possibilities to achieve this sub-goal: the attacker uses eavesdropping techniques such as shoulder surfing or video recording attack and then unlocks the phone, or the attacker unlocks the phone by brute force or using a smudge attack. Finally, the attacker needs to press "yes" to confirm the login.

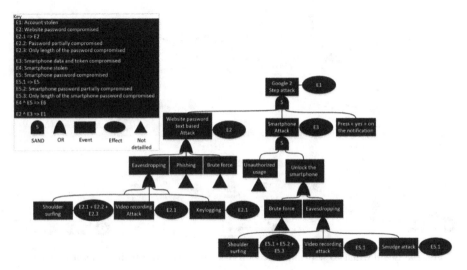

Fig. 9. Attack tree of Google 2 step mechanism

Integrated Model of Tasks, Threats and Effects for the Google 2-Step Verification
Figure 10 describes user tasks and the possible threats and their associated effects. In this example, we show the threats and effects only on the text-based login. Those threats are of the same types than the one we presented in the illustrative example section (keylogging attack, shoulder surfing or video recording attack that may cause the length of the password compromised, password totally or partially compromised).

4.3 Authentication Mechanism: Firefox Password Manager

The password manager authentication mechanism is used by several internet browsers such as Firefox [20]. This mechanism allows the user to remember only one master password and the password manager securely archives and provides the relevant username and password according to the target website for which the user has entered a username and password one time.

Task Model of the User Tasks with the Password Manager
Figure 12 presents the task model of the user tasks, the threats and effects on user tasks with the Password Manager mechanism that are discussed latter. This mechanism involves two types of passwords: password the user needs to log in websites, and a master password to access to all passwords in the password manager. We assume that the configuration of the master password of the password manager is complete.

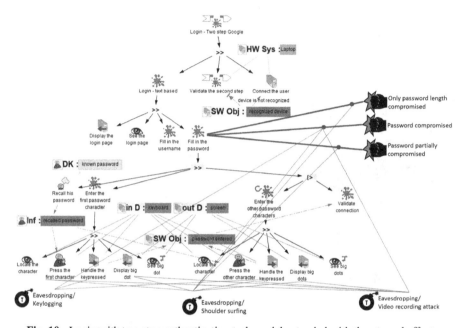

Fig. 10. Login with two step authentication task model extended with threats and effects

To login with this mechanism, there are two options (modeled using the choice operator"[]") but the activation of the options depends on the value of the software object "saved password" (shown as a pre-condition on the "saved passwords" software object), as follows: for activating the first option, we assume that the password manager "does not contain website password" (a pre-condition on the software object "saved password"), so that the user must to filling in the password using the abstract task "Login – text based". From this point, the user might "Save password" in the password manager for activating the second option, we assume that the password manager "contains website password", so instead of filling in the website password the user perform the abstract task "Login - master password" as follows: if the user is currently logged in and in a session for less than 30 min (a pre-condition on the time duration object), the password manager detects it and the users can go to the next step; otherwise, the user has to "Enter master password". After these login steps, the user is connected and can accomplish the tasks to complete the main goal "making a wire transfer".

The refinement of the optional abstract tasks "save password" is presented in Fig. 13. First, the system performs the output system task "Display save password into password manager" that prompts the user to record the password; then the user can perform the tasks "See the save popup" and "Click on save", thus enabling the system to handles the task "Click on save". The user might perform the task "Enter master password" by following the tasks: "Display master password edit box" and "See the password master edit box". Assuming the user recalls the password (see an incoming arrow from the "master password" declarative knowledge and "Recall master password" cognitive task), an information containing the password is produced to connecting to the system as if the user had filled in the password. After the confirmation, the system performs the task "Create session for 30 min". The session ends up if the user closes the web browser. After that, the password manager performs the task "Crypt password in database".

Attack Tree of the Password Manager
Figure 11 presents the attack tree where the goal is to get access to the bank account by bypassing the Password Manager mechanism. To reach that goal, two conditions are necessary: the attacker needs to compromise the website password as well as the master password. The possible attack techniques are eavesdropping, brute force or phishing.

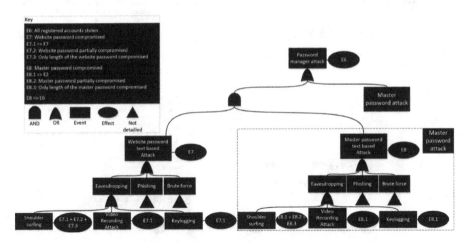

Fig. 11. Attack Tree of the Firefox Password Manager Mechanism

Integrated Model of Tasks, Threats and Effects for the Password Manager
In addition to the description of user tasks, the task models in Fig. 12 and Fig. 13 present the possible threats and their associated effects. In Fig. 12, "Login - text based", "Save password" and "Enter master password" are abstract tasks concerned by the same threats (keylogging, shoulder surfing, and video recording attacks). The effects of these threats can be that only length password compromised, or that password partially/entirely compromised. Figure 13 concerns the shoulder surfing threat.

In Fig. 13 the representation of objects, knowledge and information has been filtered out so that the reader can focus on threats and effects. The shoulder surfing threat may occur when an attacker looks at characters are entered ("Press the first character" or "Press the other character"). The effects can be that the password is partially or entirely compromised, depending on the attacker's efficiency. An attacker may look how many big dots are displayed ("Display big dot") and may know the password length. As the abstract tasks "Login text based" and "Enter master password" are concerned by the same threat and effects, they are connected with those threats and effects.

4.4 Analysis of Usability and Security of the Two Authentication Mechanisms

This section presents the principles of the analysis of usability and security of authentication mechanisms, as well as the results of this analysis for the Google 2 Step Verification and the Firefox Password Manager mechanisms.

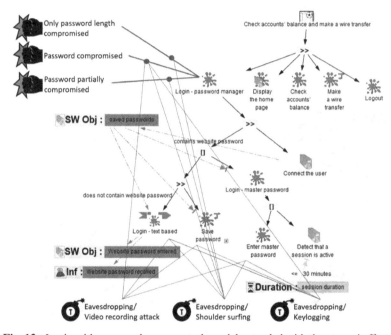

Fig. 12. Login with password manager task model extended with threats and effects

The proposed comparative analysis of usability and security of authentication mechanisms is based on the following steps:

1. Predictive assessment (from task models) of user effectiveness, user workload and temporal efficiency when using the authentication mechanism;
2. Calculation (from task models) of the amount and type of data, objects and devices required to use the mechanism from task models;
3. Calculation (from the attack tree) of the coverage of the security threats by the authentication mechanism;

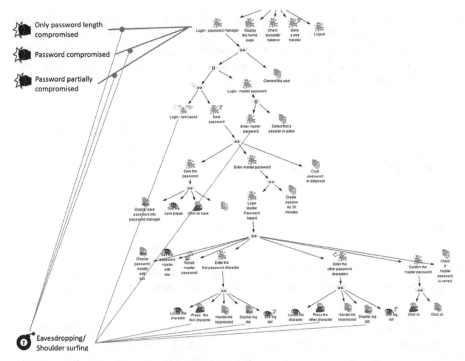

Fig. 13. Login with password manager task model (refinement of "Save password" task)

4. Calculation (from the attack tree) of the minimum and maximum number of attacks required to compromise user password, as well as interdependencies between these attacks (represented by AND and SAND operators).

These steps must be performed for each authentication mechanisms that have to be analyzed. The output of these steps is the predicted cost of the authentication mechanism in terms of effectiveness and efficiency, as well as the expected benefits of the authentication mechanisms in terms of security. The last step of the analysis is to compare the costs and benefits of the two authentication mechanisms.

From the task models of the usage of the two authentication mechanisms, we see that the planned user tasks with both mechanisms lead to reach the login sub-goal. Both authentication mechanisms are thus effective. The task models enable to identify systematically all the possible sequences of actions. From these possible sequences of actions, we calculate the minimum and maximum amount of perceptive, cognitive and motor tasks. The results are presented in Fig. 14 a. For the calculation of the minimum amount of tasks, we take as a basis the fact that the minimum password length required is 8 characters. And for the maximum amount of tasks, we chose to take a password length of 9 for the calculation. In Fig. 14 a), we can see that the minimum amount of actions is similar between the two authentication mechanisms. However, we can also see that the situation is completely different when the whole set of actions has to be performed for the Firefox Password Manager authentication mechanism, in case where the password has to be saved using the master password. In this case the number of perceptive and motor actions is more than 3 times higher. This conclusion also arises when calculating the minimum and maximum amount of time taken to login with the two authentication mechanisms, as presented in Fig. 14 b. The calculation of the time costs has been done using the Keystroke Level Model [13].

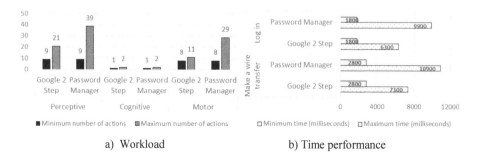

a) Workload   b) Time performance

Fig. 14. Results of the predictive assessments of user workload and user time performance with Google 2 Step and Password Manager Mechanisms for reaching the sub-goal of "Login"

Figure 15 presents the minimum and maximum number of data, objects and devices required to use the authentication mechanisms. For the Google 2 Step mechanism, two I/O devices are at least always required, whereas only one device is always required to use the Firefox Password Manager. It is also highlighted that more knowledge is required to use the Firefox Password Manager. The amount of software object and information required is similar for both authentication mechanisms. The two authentication mechanisms cover the same types of attacks: Eavesdropping (key logging, video recording, shoulder surfing), brute force, phishing. There are thus no differences between the two authentication mechanisms in terms of types of attacks covered. However, there are differences in terms of complexity to achieve an attack.

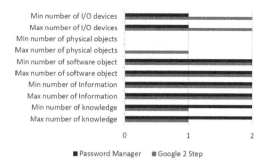

Fig. 15. Comparison of the required data, objects and devices

Figure 16 presents the minimum and maximum number of attacks that have to be performed to compromise the user password, as well as the minimum number of operators AND and SAND in the attack tree. These values provide support to analyze the complexity of the authentication mechanisms. For both authentication mechanisms, several attacks are required to compromise user password (at least one AND or SAND element in the attack trees), which makes the hacking process not easy. However, the Google 2 Step is more complicated as at a specific temporal ordering is required for performing the attacks (at least two SAND elements in the attack tree).

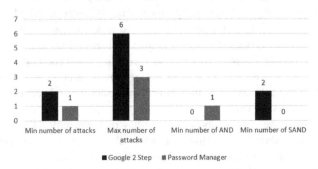

Fig. 16. Comparison of the attack trees

To conclude this analysis, the Google 2 Step seems to be more usable for entering one password than the Firefox Password Manager. It also appears to be and more secure as to compromise the password, the attack has to be more complex than for the Firefox Password Manager.

We have shown the comparison of the two authentication mechanisms for a user that logs in one time. But, users are everyday login several times with different passwords they have to remember and recall. Users have an average of 25 accounts requiring identification [21], and as capability of users to remember and recall multiple passwords is questioned [7], the usage of password manager brings a usability benefit as the user needs to remember and recall a single password once the password manager has been configured. From a security point of view, the impact of an attack on the Firefox Password Manager is more important because the attacker may compromise all the user passwords.

5 Conclusion

The goal of this paper was to present two complementary modelling techniques used to analyze jointly usability and security. We presented how the modelling techniques were used to compare usability and security of two authentication mechanism: Google 2 Step and Firefox Password Manager. From a security perspective, the approach supports the explicit and systematic analysis of threat coverage and of authentication mechanism complexity. From a usability perspective, the presented modelling approach supports the explicit and systematic analysis of the effectiveness and efficiency contributing factors. Compared to user testing techniques, a task modelling based approach enables to analyze the possible tasks for several activities to be performed on authentication mechanisms (e.g. to learn to use, to configure, to reset the password…) and to compare authentication mechanisms without performing empirical evaluations and involving users. However, the proposed approach is compatible with empirical user testing and the measures of users' satisfaction are also relevant for the analysis [50]. In the area of security measurement of user's subjective perception is critical as it is the main mean to assess trust in the security mechanisms as demonstrated in [38].

The presented work is currently extended to assess more sophisticated authentication mechanisms such as EEVEHAC that ensure secure authentication on potentially compromised devices. Beyond, as it was performed in [35] with "standard" task models, we are working on the connection of the integrated task models to the actual authentication mechanism to do predictive performance evaluation [43] and to support automatic assessment of effectiveness. Beyond, such coupling (as it encompasses visual and behavioral aspects [5]) would allow precise description of interaction techniques (such as multi-touch ones [27]) and their impact on both usability and security, beyond the authentication mechanism itself.

Lastly, due to space constraints, the paper has only presented the verification of identity sub task of authentication. However, other sub tasks such as enrolment (creation of account), modification of credential and revocation can be captured in a similar way (including both tasks and threats) using the notation presented in the paper.

References

1. Adams, A., Sasse, M.A.: Users are not the enemy. Commun. ACM **42**(12), 40–46 (1999)
2. Alarifi, A., Alsaleh, M., Alomar, N.: A model for evaluating the security and usability of e-banking platforms. Computing **99**(5), 519–535 (2017). https://doi.org/10.1007/s00607-017-0546-9
3. Alshamari, M.: A review of gaps between usability and security/privacy. Int. J. Commun. Network Syst. Sci. **9**, 413–429 (2016)
4. Balfanz, D., Durfee, G., Smetters, D.K., Grinter, R.E.: In search of usable security: five lessons from the field. IEEE Secur. Priv. **2**(5), 19–24 (2004)
5. Bastide, R., Palanqie, P.: A visual and formal glue between application and interaction. J. Vis. Lang. Comput. **10**(5), 481–507 (1999). ISSN 1045-926X
6. Ben-Asher, N., Meyer, J., Möller, S., Englert, R.: An experimental system for studying the tradeoff between usability and security. In: International Conference on Availability, Reliability and Security, Fukuoka, 2009, pp. 882–887 (2009)
7. Bonneau, J., Schechter, S.: Towards reliable storage of 56-bit secrets in human memory. In: USENIX Security Symposium (2014)
8. Bonneau, J., Herley, C., van Oorschot, P.C. Stajano, F.: The quest to replace passwords: a framework for comparative evaluation of web authentication schemes. In: 2012 IEEE Symposium on Security and Privacy, pp. 553–567 (2012)
9. Brainard, J., Juels, A., Rivest, R.L., Szydlo, M., Yung, M.: Fourth-factor authentication: somebody you know. In: Proceedings of the 13th ACM CCS 2006, pp. 168–178. ACM (2006)
10. Braz, C., Seffah, A., M'Raihi, D.: Designing a trade-off between usability and security: a metrics based-model. In: Baranauskas, C., Palanque, P., Abascal, J., Barbosa, S.D.J. (eds.) INTERACT 2007. LNCS, vol. 4663, pp. 114–126. Springer, Heidelberg (2007). https://doi.org/10.1007/978-3-540-74800-7_9
11. Brooke, J.: SUS - A quick and dirty usability scale (2006)
12. Brostoff, S., Sasse, M.A.: Are passfaces more usable than passwords? In: A Field Trial Investigation BCS HCI Conference, People and Computers XIV—Usability or Else! (2000)

13. Card, S.K., Moran, T.P., Newell, A.: The model human processor: an engineering model of human performance. In: Handbook of Perception and Human Perf., pp. 1-35 (1986)

14. Chiasson, S., Biddle, R.: Issues in user authentication. In CHI Workshop Security User Studies Methodologies and Best Pracfices, April 2007

15. Clark, R.M., Hakim, S. (eds.): Cyber-Physical Security: Protecting Critical Infrastructure at the State and Local Level, vol. 3. Springer, Cham (2016). https://doi.org/10.1007/978-3-319-32824-9

16. De Cristofaro, E., Du, H., Freudiger, J., Norcie, G:. A comparative usability study of two-factor authentication. In: Proceedings of the Workshop on Usable Security (USEC) (2014)

17. Fahssi, R., Martinie, C., Palanque, P.: Enhanced task modelling for systematic identification and explicit representation of human errors. In: Abascal, J., Barbosa, S., Fetter, M., Gross, T., Palanque, P., Winckler, M. (eds.) INTERACT 2015. LNCS, vol. 9299, pp. 192–212. Springer, Cham (2015). https://doi.org/10.1007/978-3-319-22723-8_16

18. Faily, S., Fléchais, I.: Finding and resolving security misusability with misusability cases. Requirements Eng. 21(2), 209–223 (2016)

19. Fayollas, C., Martinie, C., Navarre, D., Palanque, P.: A generic approach for assessing compatibility between task descriptions and interactive systems: application to the effectiveness of a flight control unit. i-com, 14(3), 170–191 (2015)

20. Firefox password manager. https://support.mozilla.org/en-US/kb/password-manager-remember-delete-edit-logins

21. Florencio, D., Herley, C.: A large-scale study of web password habits. In: Proceedings of the WWW Conference 2007, pp. 657–666. ACM Press (2007)

22. Fraile, M., Ford, M., Gadyatskaya, O., Kumar, R., Stoelinga, M., Trujillo-Rasua, R.: Using attack-defense trees to analyze threats and countermeasures in an ATM: a case study. In: Horkoff, J., Jeusfeld, Manfred A., Persson, A. (eds.) PoEM 2016. LNBIP, vol. 267, pp. 326–334. Springer, Cham (2016). https://doi.org/10.1007/978-3-319-48393-1_24

23. Golla, M., Bailey, D.V., Dürmuth, M.: I want my money back!" Limiting Online Password-Guessing Financially. In: SOUPS 2017 (2017)

24. Google 2-step Verification. https://www.google.com/landing/2step/. Accessed May 2020

25. Habib, H., et al.: User behaviors and attitudes under password expiration policies. In: USENIX Security Symposium 2018, pp. 13–30 (2018)

26. Halunen, K., Häikiö, J., Vallivaara, V.A.: Evaluation of user authentication methods in the gadget-free world. Pervasive Mob. Comput. 40, 220–241 (2017)

27. Hamon, A., Palanque, P., Silva, J.-L., Deleris, Y., Barboni, E.: Formal description of multi-touch interactions. In: 5th ACM SIGCHI Symposium on Engineering Interactive Computing Systems (EICS 2013), pp. 207–216 (2013)

28. He, W., et al.: Rethinking access control and authentication for the home Internet of Things (IoT). In: USENIX Security Symposium, pp. 255–272 (2018)

29. ISO. "ISO 9241-11 :2018". ISO. International Organization for Standardization. https://www.iso.org/standard/63500.html

30. ISO. "ISO 9241-210:2019". ISO. International Organization for Standardization. Accessed 17 Feb 2020. https://www.iso.org/standard/77520.html

31. ISO/IEC 27000:2018 Information technology—Security techniques—Information security management systems (2018)

32. Kainda, R., Fléchais, I., Roscoe, A.W.: Security and usability: analysis and evaluation. In: 2010 International Conference on Availability, Reliability and Security, pp. 275–282 (2010)

33. Launius, S.M.: Evaluation of Comprehensive Taxonomies for Information Technology Threats. SysAdmin, Audit, Network and Security (SANS) (2018)

34. Martinie, C., Navarre, D., Palanque, P., Fayollas, C.: A generic tool-supported framework for coupling task models and interactive applications. In: Proceedings of the 7th ACM SIGCHI Symposium on Engineering Interactive Computing Systems (EICS 2015). ACM DL, pp. 244–253 (2015)
35. Martinie C., Navarre D., Palanque P., Fayollas, C.: A generic tool-supported framework for coupling task models and interactive applications. In: 7th ACM SIGCHI Symposium on Engineering Interactive Computing Systems (EICS 2015). ACM DL, pp. 244–253 (2015)
36. Martinie, C., Palanque, P., Winckler, M.: Structuring and Composition Mechanisms to Address Scalability Issues in Task Models. In: Campos, P., Graham, N., Jorge, J., Nunes, N., Palanque, P., Winckler, M. (eds.) INTERACT 2011. LNCS, vol. 6948, pp. 589–609. Springer, Heidelberg (2011). https://doi.org/10.1007/978-3-642-23765-2_40
37. Martinie, C., Palanque, P., Bouzekri, E., Cockburn, A., Canny, A., Barboni, E.: Analysing and demonstrating tool-supported customizable task notations. PACM Hum.-Comput. Interact. **3** (2019). EICS, Article 12, 26 pages
38. Merdenyan, B., Petrie, H.: Perceptions of risk, benefits and likelihood of undertaking password management behaviours: four components. In: Lamas, D., Loizides, F., Nacke, L., Petrie, H., Winckler, M., Zaphiris, P. (eds.) INTERACT 2019. LNCS, vol. 11746, pp. 549–563. Springer, Cham (2019). https://doi.org/10.1007/978-3-030-29381-9_34
39. Micallef, N., Gamagedara Arachchilage, N.A.: A Gamified Approach to Improve Users' Memorability of Fall-back Authentication. SOUPS 2017 (2017)
40. Mihajlov, M. Jerman-Blazič, B., Josimovski, S.: A conceptual framework for evaluating usable security in authentication mechanisms - usability perspectives. In: 2011 5th International Conference on Network and System Security, Milan, 2011, pp. 332–336 (2011)
41. Nishihara, H., Kawanishi, Y., Souma, D., Yoshida, H.: On validating attack trees with attack effects. In: Casimiro, A., Ortmeier, F., Bitsch, F., Ferreira, P. (eds.) SAFECOMP 2020. LNCS, vol. 12234, pp. 309–324. Springer, Cham (2020). https://doi.org/10.1007/978-3-030-54549-9_21
42. Ortega-Garcia, J., Bigun, J., Reynolds, D., Gonzalez-Rodriguez, J.: Authentication gets personal with biometrics. IEEE Signal Process. Mag. **21**(2), 50–62 (2004)
43. Palanque, P., Barboni, E., Martinie, C., Navarre, D., Winckler, M.: A model-based approach for supporting engineering usability evaluation of interaction techniques. In: 3rd ACM SIGCHI Symposium on Engineering interactive Computing Systems (EICS 2011), pp. 21–30 (2011)
44. Palanque, P., Basnyat, S.: Task patterns for taking into account in an efficient and systematic way both standard and erroneous user behaviors. In: IFIP 13.5 Working Conference on Human Error, Safety and Systems Development (HESSD), pp. 109–130. Kluwer Academic Publishers (2004)
45. Petsas, T., Tsirantonakis, G., Athanasopoulos, E., Ioannidis, S.: Two-factor authentication: is the world ready? quantifying 2FA adoption. In: Proceedings of the Eighth European Workshop on System Security (EuroSec 2015). ACM, Article 4, 1–7 (2015)
46. Raza, M., Iqbal, M., Sharif, M., Haider, W.: A survey of password attacks and comparative analysis on methods for secure authentication. World Appl. Sci. J. **19**(4), 439–444 (2012)
47. Rosson, M.B., Carroll, J.M.: Usability Engineering: Scenario-Based Development of Human-Computer Interaction. Elsevier (2001)
48. Sasse, A.: Computer security: anatomy of a usability disaster, and a plan for recovery. In: Proceedings of CHI 2003 Workshop on HCI and Security Systems. Fort Lauderdale, Florida (2003)
49. Schneier, B.: Attack Trees. Dr. Dobb's J., December 1999

50. Seiler-Hwang, S., Arias-Cabarcos, P., Marín, A., Almenares, F., Díaz-Sánchez, D., Becker, C.: "I don't see why I would ever want to use it": analyzing the usability of popular smartphone password managers. In: Proceedings of the ACM SIGSAC CCS 2019, pp. 1937–1953. ACM (2019)
51. Weaver, A.C.: Biometric authentication. Computer **39**(2), 96–97 (2006)

Model-Based Product Configuration in Augmented Reality Applications

Sebastian Gottschalk[1](✉), Enes Yigitbas[1], Eugen Schmidt[2],
and Gregor Engels[1]

[1] Software Innovation Lab, Paderborn University, Paderborn, Germany
{sebastian.gottschalk,enes.yigitbas,gregor.engels}@uni-paderborn.de
[2] Paderborn University, Paderborn, Germany
eschmidt@mail.uni-paderborn.de

Abstract. Augmented Reality (AR) has recently found high attention in mobile shopping apps such as in domains like furniture or decoration. Here, the developers of the apps focus on the positioning of atomic 3D objects in the physical environment. With this focus, they neglect the configuration of multi-faceted 3D object composition according to the user needs and environmental constraints. To tackle these challenges, we present a model-based approach to support AR-assisted product configuration based on the concept of Dynamic Software Product Lines. Our approach splits products (e.g. table) into parts (e.g. tabletop, table legs, funnier) with their 3D objects and additional information (e.g. name, price). The possible products, which can be configured out of these parts, are stored in a feature model. At runtime, this feature model can be used to configure 3D object compositions out of the product parts and adapt to user needs and environmental constraints. The benefits of this approach are demonstrated by a case study of configuring modular kitchens with the help of a prototypical mobile-based implementation.

Keywords: Product configuration · Augmented Ueality · Runtime adaptation · Dynamic Software Product Lines

1 Introduction

Mobile shopping has become a big trend in the last years, as it allows purchasing from anywhere and at any time [22,27]. Because of the growing performance of mobile devices, Augmented Reality (AR) is becoming one key focus of these shopping apps [9]. AR allows users to virtually try-out physical objects in their environment before purchasing them. Examples of these apps are IKEA Place[1]

---

[1] IKEA Place App: https://apps.apple.com/us/app/ikea-place/id1279244498.

This work was partially supported by the German Research Foundation (DFG) within the Collaborative Research Center "On-The-Fly Computing" (CRC 901, Project Number: 160364472SFB901).

R. Bernhaupt et al. (Eds.): HCSE 2020, LNCS 12481, pp. 84–104, 2020.
https://doi.org/10.1007/978-3-030-64266-2_5

to determine the appearance of furniture in certain rooms, the configuration of products like windows in the VEKA Configurator AR App[2], or the placement of multiple products in an environment as recently announced by Amazon[3]. With these apps, the users have the possibility to get more information about the products, be more certain about buying what they want, and have a greater product choice and variety [12]. For this, most of the existing solutions focus on the positioning of atomic 3D objects in the physical environment. With this focus, they neglect the configuration of multi-faceted 3D object composition. This 3D object composition, in turn, can support a runtime adaptation of parts of the product according to the product requirements (e.g. exclusion of different product parts to each other), the user needs (e.g. maximum price), and the environmental constraints (e.g. detection of obstacles).

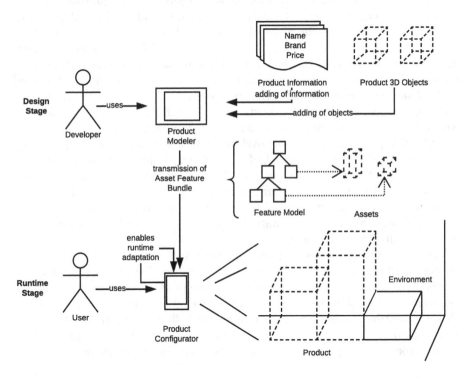

Fig. 1. Overview of the approach, where the *Developer* can model products at the *Design Stage* which can be configured by the *User* at the *Runtime Stage*

To overcome these limitations, we present a model-based AR-assisted product configuration that uses the concept of Dynamic Software Product Lines (DSPLs)

---

[2] VEKA Configurator AR App: https://apps.apple.com/us/app/vD0B5kD0B0-configurator-ar/id1450934980.

[3] Announcement of Amazon: https://techcrunch.com/2020/08/25/amazon-rolls-out-a-new-ar-shopping-feature-for-viewing-multiple-items-at-once/.

[8] to provide a runtime adaptation of product parts to the product requirements, user needs, and environmental constraints. An overview of the approach, which consists of a *Design Stage* and a *Runtime Stage*, can be seen in Fig. 1. At the *Design Stage*, we use the concept of reusable assets [3] to split the definition of products and their possible configurations from their actual representation in 3D objects. For this, the *Developer* uses the *Product Modeler* to model valid product configurations. These configurations are based on the *Product Information* (e.g. name, brand, price) which are used to create a *Feature Model* where each feature (e.g. tabletop, table leg) can be linked to a specific *Product 3D Object* (e.g. tabletop model, table leg model). This so-called *Asset Feature Bundle* is then transmitted to the *Product Configurator* at the *Runtime Stage*.

At the *Runtime Stage*, we use the MAPE-K architecture [21] to monitor the user needs in the form of user inputs, the actual product configuration, and the environment. The gathered information is validated and used to adapt to the product configuration in the physical environment. For this, the *User* uses the *Product Configurator* by defining his own needs (e.g. favorite brand, maximum price). After that, she starts the configuring process by selecting features (e.g. table) and placing them in the environment. During the placement, the need of the *User* (e.g. price too high), the configuration of the *Product* (e.g. missing fridge in the kitchen), and the constraints of the *Environment* (e.g. collisions with other objects) are checked dynamically in the background.

With this paper, we present a novel model-based approach, which provides a twofold contribution to the research of AR-assisted product configurations: First, the separation of product modeling from 3D object implementation ensures a fast and flexible extension the configurator for new products. Second, the runtime configuration provides validation of product requirements and adaptation to user needs and environmental constraints. We demonstrate both benefits with a case study of a kitchen configurator.

The rest of the paper is structured as follows: Sect. 2 is providing the background of DSPLs which is used in our approach. Section 3 defines the requirements of our solution for the three models of the product, the customer, and the environment. Based on these requirements, Sect. 4 explains a solution concept that architecture is presented in Sect. 5. Section 6 shows the benefits of our approach based on the case study of a kitchen configurator. Section 7 presents the related work of our approach. Finally, we conclude our paper in Sect. 8.

2   Background

In this section, we explain the background on which we built our approach. We divide this background into Software Product Lines (SPLs) and Dynamic Software Product Lines (DSPLs).

2.1   Software Product Lines

Software Product Lines (SPLs) can be defined as "a set of software-intensive systems sharing a common, managed set of features that satisfy the specific needs of a particular market segment or mission and that are developed from a common set of core assets in a prescribed way" [10]. Here, a feature refers to a prominent characteristic of a product which can be, depending on the stage of development, a requirement, a component in an architecture, or a piece of code [6]. To use these SPLs, a structure and an engineering process are needed.

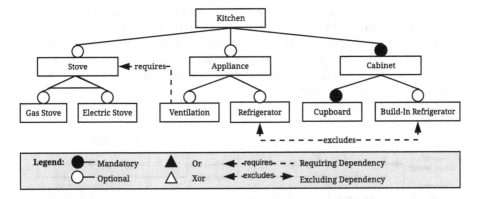

Fig. 2. Structure of feature models illustrated with a subset of a kitchen model which is used in the case study

The structure of SPLs can be represented using hierarchical feature modeling which is shown in Fig. 2. Features can be mandatory (i.e. *Cabinet*) or optional (i.e. *Ventilation*) for the model instances. Moreover, there can be Or (at least one sub-feature is selected), and Xor (exactly one sub-feature is selected) relationships between a parent and a child feature. To refine the model instance, cross-tree constraints for requiring (i.e. *Stove* requires *Ventilation*) and excluding (i.e. *Refrigerator* and *Build-In Refrigerator*) dependencies can be made. A big issue in SPL development is to find the right granularity for the features [20]. While the classical feature model does not allow modelings like the usage of multiple feature instances and additional attributes, some approaches extend the modeling approach for these cases [11]. For this, they add these additional modelings to the meta-model of the feature model. In our approach, we use feature models to structure the possible product configuration. For this, we need to extend the meta-model of feature models with meta-data in the form of attributes, positioning, and links to 3D objects.

The engineering process for SPLs is shown in Fig. 3. The process can be divided into the *Domain Engineering*, which consists of the analysis of the domain and the development of reusable artifacts, and the *Application Engineering*, which uses these artifacts for the development of a specific software product for a user group. Moreover, the *Problem Space* describes the user perspective on the requirements of the software product, while the *Solution Space* covers the developer's perspective on the design and implementation of the software product. Based on this classification the process consists of the following four steps [3]:

- **A. Domain Analysis** identifies the domain scope of the different products which can be developed with the SPL. From this analysis the reusable artifacts are identified and modeled as a feature model.
- **B. Domain Implementation** develops the different reusable artifacts (e.g. source code, test scripts) for further usage in the product derivation.
- **C. Requirement Analysis** extracts the requirements of a single user for the product. This requirements can lead to a feature selection of the SPL or the adding of new requirements to the domain analysis.
- **D. Product Derivation** is the matching of user requirements and reusable artifacts to build a product.

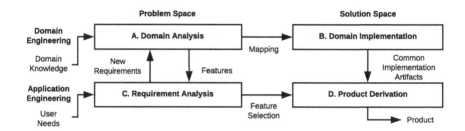

Fig. 3. Engineering process of SPLs which splits the generic *Domain Engineering* from the specific *Application Engineering*

We use the division of *Domain Engineering* and *Application Engineering* to configure different possible products from the same model. Moreover, we use the division of problem and solution space to separate the information about the product from their 3D objects.

2.2 Dynamic Software Product Lines (DSPLs)

Dynamic Software Product Lines (DSPLs) extend "the concept of conventional SPLs by enabling software-variant generation at runtime. The reason for this extension is that typical SPL approaches do not focus on dynamic aspects: the adaptation of their products is known and occurs during product line development" [7]. For this, adaptive systems can be used [19].

One of the most prominent reference architectures for autonomic computing is the MAPE-K loop [21]. MAPE-K, see Fig. 4 for the example of a socket detector consists of a *Managed Element* and an *Adaptation Manager*. The *Managed Element* provides sensors to get corresponding data (e.g. camera screens) and effectors to change its state (e.g. display view). The *Adaptation Manager* monitors the sensors (e.g. screen the environment) and analyzes the gathered data

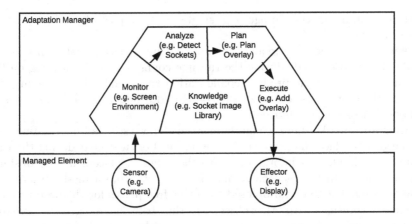

Fig. 4. Process of MAPE-K illustrated with the example of detecting and marking sockets in the environment

(e.g. detect sockets). Based on that, an adaptation is planned (e.g. plan an overlay for the sockets) and executed (e.g. add the overlay). Moreover, the knowledge base stores knowledge which can support the different steps (e.g. socket library for image recognition). Depending on the use case, the adaptation can be divided into different dimensions of goal (type, evolution), cause (type), and mechanism (autonomy, type) [4].

We use the MAPE-K loop to continuously monitor the user needs and environmental constraints for the product configuration. Moreover, the goal of the configurator will be of type self-configuring with static evolution. Moreover, the cause types are the user, product, and environment together of the manual component mechanism [4].

3 Model Requirements

In this section, we describe the requirements on the models for model-based AR product configuration. Based on the context in the *Runtime Stage*, we divide the requirements and the resulting models into the primary sources of *Product*, *User*, and *Environment*.

- **Product:** Within the product model, also referred to as the feature model in the next sections, we store all information that is needed to congure the products out of their parts. For this, we use the modeling structure of feature models [10] to model each product part as a single feature. Therefore, each valid product configuration of the feature model is also a valid AR product configuration. We extend this model with product information and asset management. In the product information, we store additional attributes (e.g. name, price, brand) for each product part. In asset management, we link the product parts to specific assets (e.g. 3D object, texture) and give additional information about their usage (e.g. single product, part of product, texture of product).

– **User:** Within the user model, we store all information that is needed to validate the user needs during the runtime configuration. Depending on the actual use case of the product configuration this could the maximum price which the user wants to pay for the configured product or the handedness to choose the side of the hinges.

– **Environment:** Within the environment model, we store all information that is needed to place the products in the physical environment during the runtime. We divide this information into the types of placement and obstacle management. In the placement management, we store a mesh structure of the environment that can be used to detect free places for the products and validates collisions with other objects. In the obstacle management, we store the positions of obstacles which can be needed by parts of the product (e.g. sockets, water supply).

Moreover, there can be dependencies between the different models. Because the product configuration is our main artifact, we consider just the combinations of *Product-User* and *Product-Environment*.

– **Product-User:** Between the product and the user, we specify dependencies that can exist between both models. Mostly these connections are between some product information and a specific user need. and For example, the product can have the dependency of a minimum height for a user or the user can prefer a specific brand of the product part.

– **Product-Environment:** Between the product and the environment, we specify dependencies that can exist between both entities. Mostly these connections are between some product information and a specific constraint in the environment. For example, the product can have the dependency of a water supply or the environment sets a maximum height for products because of a window as an obstacle.

4   Solution Concept

In this section, we present a solution concept for model-based AR product configuration. For this, we first show how the model requirements for the product, user, and environment can be modeled. Based on that we apply the engineering process of SPLs to AR product configuration. In the end, we show how the runtime adaptation to the models can be done.

4.1   Modeling of Product, User and Environment Requirements

To create a model-based AR product configuration, we have to first create models for all parts which our approach should effect. Based on the model requirements in the last section, we create models for the user (*UserModel*), the environment (*EnvironmentModel*), and the product (*FeatureModel*). The model of the user consists of simple attributes of the user (e.g. gender, maximum budget) which are characterized as important by the developer. Moreover, the modeled environment consists of a mesh structure of the physical environment together with positions of obstacles (e.g. windows, sockets) that need to be defined by the developer. Last, the model of the product consists of configuration parts that can be resolved to complete products. Because of the special interest of the product model in AR product configuration, we focus on this model within this section.

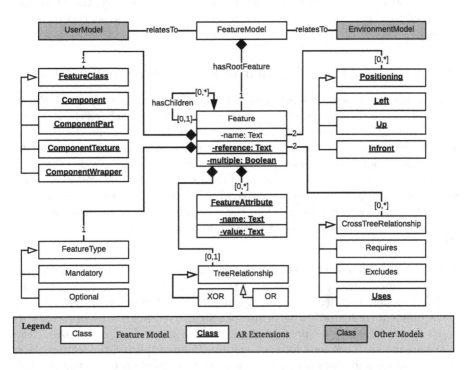

Fig. 5. Meta-Model of the *FeatureModel* with extensions for modeling the AR products and dependencies to the *UserModel* and the *EnvironmentModel*

The model of the product, see Fig. 5, is based on the concept of feature models [10]. For this, we implement all classes of feature models and extend the model with an AR specific extension. Each feature consists of a reference to a 3D object and an attribute if multiple instances (e.g. multiple cabins in one kitchen) can be created. Moreover, we added the classes of *FeatureClass*, *FeatureAttribute*, and *Positioning* together with extending *CrossTreeRelationship*. The *FeatureClass*, which is interpreted within the product configurator. Here, a *Component* relates to a 3D object which can be placed within the environment (e.g. table). A *ComponentPart* is a 3D object which can not be placed in the environment alone but as a part of another *Component* (e.g. tabletop). A *ComponentTexture* is a texture that can be applied to an existing *Component* (e.g. wood). A *ComponentWrapper* is used to structure the features within the product modeler and is not interpreted within the product configuration (e.g. electrical appliances). The *FeatureAttribute* is used to add product information (e.g. name, price) to each feature. The *Positioning* restricts the placed of features to each other. The new class of *Uses* within *CrossTreeDependencies* can be used to link *Components* to *ComponentTextures*.

Moreover, the model of the product has relationships with the models for the user and the environment. Here, the *FeatureAttributes* are linked to the requirements of the user (e.g. specific brand or color). Moreover, the *Feature[s]* are linked to obstacles that are needed to use the feature (e.g. sockets or water supply).

4.2   Engineering Process of Model-Based Product Configuration

The engineering process for AR product configuration can be seen in Fig. 6. The process can be divided into the *Design Stage*, which analyses the different product configuration parts and links them to the 3D objects, and the *Runtime Stage*, which analyses the needs of the user and environmental constraints to derive valid product configurations. Moreover, the *Problem Space* describes the user's perspective on the requirements of the product, while the *Solution Space* covers the developer's perspective on the implementation in the physical environment. Based on this classification, the process consists of the following four steps of *Product Analysis*, *Product Implementation*, *Configuration Analysis*, and *Configuration Derivation*.

- **A. Product Analysis** identifies the domain scope of the different products and develops a feature model out of them. In *A.1. Product Scoping* the possible products are identified, additional product information is collected and the different configuration parts are split up into reusable parts. In *A.2. Product Scoping* the possible product configurations are modeled as features of the feature model. Therefore, for each features the multiplicity, the feature class, the product information in the form of feature attributes and the possible positions are set (i.e. see Subect. 4.1).
- **B. Product Implementation** develops the reusable assets which are used in the configuration derivation. In *B.1. Assets Modeling* the 3D objects and textures are created and split up into the parts of possible product configurations of the feature model. In the *B.1. Assets Binding* the created assets are linked to the feature model. So that the assets are inserted as a reference in the feature model (i.e. see Subsect. 4.1).
- **C. Configuration Analysis** extracts the requirements of a single user based on user needs and possible product configurations. In *C.1. User Input Validation* the user input is validated against the current product configuration to detect violations that need to be resolved. In *C.2. Product Selection Validation* the product configuration is validated according to the underlying feature model.
- **D. Configuration Derivation** is the matching of selected features and assets to place the product configuration in the environment. In the *D.1.*

Environment Validation the configuration is validated against possible obstacles in the environment. Moreover, the *Feature Selection Change* of the *C. Configuration Analysis* can be changed. In the *D.2. Product Configuration Derivation*, the current *Product Configuration* is selected and can be exported for further usage (e.g. save for later, buy the product).

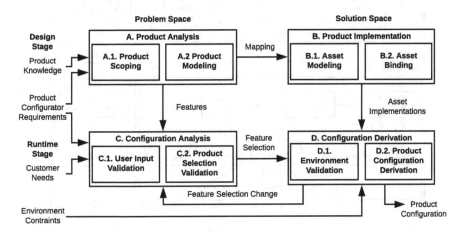

Fig. 6. Engineering process for an AR product configurator with a *Design Stage* to model the products and a *Runtime Stage* to configure the products

4.3 Runtime Adaptation According to the Modeled Requirements

The runtime adaptation for AR product configuration can be seen in Fig. 7. The concept can be divided into the *Mobile Application*, which provides the sensors and effectors for the adaptation and the *Configuration Manager*, which structures the adaptation process.

The *Mobile Application* provides sensors to provide information for the monitoring and effectors to change the display according to the execution. In the *Context Service* the inputs of the *Camera* and *User Input Management* are detected to update the *Configuration Model*, the *User Model*, and the *Environment Model*. These models can be monitored by the *Context Monitoring*. The effectors of the *Display Service* are triggered by the *Display Adaptation*. They are used to change the screen of the mobile application by *Display [the] AR Configuration* and *Display [the] Validation Issues*.

The *Configuration Manager* provides the adaptation logic to change the product configuration according to the requirements of the product, the user, and the environment. For this, the *Monitor* measures changes in the models of the configuration, the user, and the environment. While the user and configuration requirements can be directly used in the models, the environments need to be

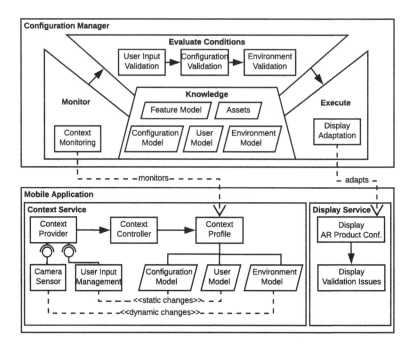

Fig. 7. Runtime adaptation based on the MAPE-K with a *Configuration Manager* (Adaptation Manager) and a *Mobile Application* (Managed Element)

interpreted to create a mesh structure and detect the obstacles which should be considered. In *Evaluate Conditions* these changes are validated if the user needs, valid product configurations, or environmental constraints are violated. While the user and the configuration can be validated with the *FeatureModel*, the for the environment the positions in the configuration need to be compared to the structure in the *EnvironmentModel*. If all conditions are fulfilled, the *Execute* process the instructions to change the screen of the application are given. During the full configuration process, *Knowledge* is stored which can be used in the different steps. This *Knowledge* consists of the *FeatureModel*, which holds all possible product configurations, and the *Assets*, which display these configurations in the form of 3D objects and textures. Moreover, the current state of the *ConfigurationModel*, the *UserModel* and the *EnvironmentModel* are stored from the *Monitor* to use them in the other steps.

5   Solution Architecture

In this section, we provide a solution architecture for model-based AR product configuration. Based on our definition of the engineering process in Subsect. 4.2, we provide a component-based architecture for the implementation. This architecture is divided into the *Design Stage*, which consists of the *Product Modeler* and the *Asset Modeler*, and the *Runtime Stage*, which consists of the *Product Configurator*.

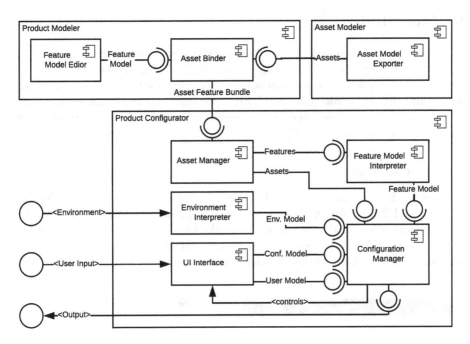

Fig. 8. Component overview of the developed *Product Modeler* and *Product Configurator* together with the external *Asset Modeler*

In the *Design Stage*, the configuration parts of the products are modeled through a *Feature Model Editor* together with the attributes for additional product information. Moreover, the assets for the configuration parts are made available with the *Asset Model Exporter*. Both, the *Feature Model* and *Assets*, are connected so that each feature can consist of an asset with the type (e.g. product, part of product, texture). Next, both are serialized through the *Asset Binder* to create a single *Asset Feature Bundle* which can be transmitted to the *Product Configurator*. By choosing the *Asset Feature Bundle* as a loose coupling between both stages, the tools of each stage can be exchanged independently (Fig. 8).

In the *Runtime Stage*, the *Asset Manager* is used to deserialize the *Asset Feature Bundle* into components. While the *Assets* can be directly used in the *Configurator Manager*, the *Features* need to be analyzed by the *Feature Modeler Interpreter* to derive the *Feature Model*. Moreover, the *Configuration Manager*, whose activities are explained in Subsect. 4.3, received the requirements of the user, the configuration, and the environment during the runtime. While the *User Input* of the *UI Interface* can be directly restricted to use the *Configuration Model* and *User Model*, the *Environment* needs to be analyzed by the Environment Interpreter to derive the *Environment Model*. This is done by analyzing the images of the camera. With all these requirements the *Configuration Manager* can control the *UI Interface* and provide the configuration to the *Output*.

6 Case Study

In this section, we show how the principles of the solution concept can be applied in a concrete usage scenario. For this, we present a use case in which a manufacturer of modular kitchens uses our approach to provide to their customers the ability to order customized kitchens. First, we show our implementation of the *Product Modeler* and the *Product Configurator*. Second, we discuss the current limitations of the implementation.

6.1 Instantiation

To show the benefits of our approach, we implemented a prototype of the *Product Modeler* and the *Product Configurator*. While the *Product Modeler* is based on a web-based implementation of a feature modeler in [17], the *Product Configurator* is based on the Unity framework[4]. Although this section gives an overview of the implementation, our demonstration paper shows more technical details [18].

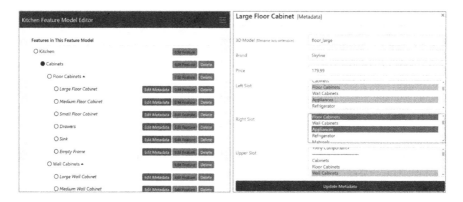

Fig. 9. *Product Modeler*: Creation of product parts and adding of meta-data inlcuding the 3D object for later AR representation

The *Product Modeler*[5], see Fig. 9 for screenshots, can be used to create the *FeatureModel* of the product that should be configurated. For this, all dependencies and constraints of feature models [3] can be used within the configuration by using the feature modeling tool in [17]. We extend this tool by adding meta-data for each feature (i.e. product part). In this meta-data, each feature can be linked

---

[4] Unity Framework: https://unity.com/.
[5] Source Code of the Product Modeler: https://github.com/sebastiangtts/feature-modeler.

to a 3D object, which is placed in a specific folder of Unity. Moreover, we add a price and a brand as feature attributes, which can be chosen to configure the product according to the customer needs. These feature attributes are also specified in our meta-model in Fig. 5. To place the product parts (e.g. cabin, stove) to each other, we allow the selection of valid other parts of the left, right, and upper slot of each product part. This, in turn, allows the flexible configuration of the kitchen in front of a single wall. After the full feature model is created, we need to bind the features to the corresponding 3D objects. For this, we export the whole model as a JSON file. After this, we use a developed importer script in Unity, which serialized the features and 3D objects in a single file. This file can be now uploaded to a web server. From this web server, the product configurator can download the *Feature Asset Bundle* and use it in the configuration process. With the *Project Modeler* it is possible to flexibly change the possible product configurations. These changes are automatically applied to all mobile clients in the form of *Product Configurators*.

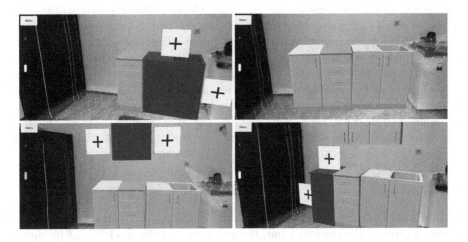

Fig. 10. *Product Configurator*: Configuring the product by selecting an existing product part and clicking on the "+"-button

The *Product Configurator*[6], see Fig. 10 and 11 for screenshots, can be used to configure a product out of the feature model. For this, the user opens the app, which downloads the *Feature Assets Bundle* from the webserver. After that, the user scans the environment to detect where the different parts of the kitchen can be placed. This information is stored inside the *EnvironmentModel* of the approach. Initially, she clicks on the screen to place the first part of the kitchen (i.e. see mesh structure on the floor). Iteratively, she now can click on an existing part of the kitchen, which makes "+"-buttons appear to extend the

---

[6] Source Code of the Product Configurator: https://github.com/sebastiangtts/ar-product-configurator.

configuration. By clicking on one of these buttons, a list of all valid product parts is shown for selection.

Fig. 11. *Product Configurator*: Validation of the product configuration during the selection process and after the configuration is finished

During the full configuration process, the app checks if product requirements, user needs, or environmental constraints are violated. As an example, the first screen of Fig. 11 shows a cabin which can not be placed because of an object collision in the environment. After the full configuration has been done, the user can go to the check out process. Here, conformance errors, which can not be modeled graphically during the configuration, are validated. As an example, the second screen of Fig. 11 shows the error message that the sink requires an empty frame. Moreover, also requirements of the *UserModel* like the maximum price are applied here. With the *Product Configurator* it is possible to detect violated requirements of the product, the user, and the environment at runtime. Based on that, the violation can be resolved or conformance errors can be shown.

6.2   Discussion

With the implementation of the modular kitchen, we show the two main benefits of our approach. On the one hand, the separation of the modeling of products from their actual configuration, and, on the other hand, the adaptation of the configuration to the requirements of the product, the user and the environment. Nevertheless, the current implementation is just a prototype and has limitations according to the *Model Management* and *Platform Compatibility*.

For the *Model Management*, we develop a feature model where the configuration parts can be enriched with meta-data like product attributes and 3D objects. In the current prototype, we have not considered the user and the environment as explicit models. While for the user we fixed the data of the user at the beginning of the implementation, the *EnvironmentModel* is based on an internal model of AR Core[7]. In the future, we want to improve the prototype so that all requirements of the product, the user, and the environment are based on distinct models and not internal models like used by AR Core. Moreover, it should be possible that changes in the models (e.g. adding new feature attributes) are also

---

[7] AR Core: https://developers.google.com/ar.

covered directly in the prototype and not need to be fixed at the beginning of the implementation.

For the *Platform Compatibility*, we develop the prototype based on the technologies of Android and Unity. While the adaptation logic is written for Angular's AR Core, the *Asset Binding* is built on a script in Unity. Here, the *Asset Feature Bundle* has also the limitation that the whole information is transmitted at the starting of the application which limits the scalability of the approach. Therefore, the current prototype has limitations in using other technology platforms. In the future, we want to modify the prototype so that different technology platforms can be used and interexchange. Moreover, we want to modify the *Asset Feature Bundle* so that assets are only transferred when they are needed at the runtime.

7   Related Work

In this section, we provide an overview of the related work of our approach. For this, we analyze relevant approaches considering the topics of Product Configuration, Augmented Reality, and Runtime Adaptation that are described and compared to our solution approach.

7.1   Product Configuration

Product configuration is a rich topic with a substantial amount of research behind it which is applied in various domains such as industrial applications, management, marketing, and computer science. In the following, we briefly focus on and describe product configuration approaches that rely on a model-based solution approach.

For model-based approaches, we use feature models to model the product features and business models of mobile applications [16]. We call our concept a Business Model Decision Line (BMDL). In this paper, we use our BMDL Feature Modeler [17] as the basis of our AR Product Modeler. Furthermore, Bashari et al. present a reference framework for dynamic software product line engineering which also serves as an inspiration for extending our feature modeler towards a DSPL approach that supports dynamic product configuration in AR [4]. For model-based approaches, one of the first things a product configuration system needs to do is validate the feature model itself. A lot of research has been conducted in the area of feature model validation [5], partially because feature models can be prone to errors (e.g. adding a new constraint might accidentally create a constraint deadlock or remove some valid products from the product line). One of the more advanced solutions in this area was proposed by Trinidad et al. who have developed a 3-step framework for automated feature model validation [26]. Their approach can detect some situations where there is a discrepancy between what the feature model describes and the actual product line it is supposed to model (e.g. feature models that produce no valid products or features that cannot appear in any valid product).

Another related area of research is optimization of product configurations (i.e. using algorithms to scan through all valid product configurations to find one that is optimal concerning some criteria). Depending on the criteria used, optimization can bring benefits to both the manufacturer and the customer. For example, an algorithm can be used by the manufacturer to find configurations that are easiest to produce or would be fastest to deliver, while the customer can use an optimization system to find a configuration with the lowest price. For example, Yeh et al. focus specifically on using advanced algorithms to optimize the price of configurable products [28]. However, using such advanced techniques is only needed in cases where the feature model is complex enough to induce a very large number of possible configurations that can only be analyzed by a highly efficient algorithm.

7.2   Augmented Reality

With the shift from mass manufacturing to mass customization, the interest in product configuration increases as more and more companies offer their customers the ability to tailor a product to their needs before manufacturing even begins. This customization step often relies on computer-based representations of the product, its variants, and sometimes the used environment. For this reason, technologies that offer computer-generated imagery, such as VR and especially AR, are being researched in this context. In the following, we discuss some of the relevant AR-based approaches for product configuration.

An early study by Gehring et al. explored the usage of a mobile AR configurator app as a means of on-the-fly customization at the point of sale [15]. The app allowed the user to customize the color of a soap dispenser on their phone, either by picking a color directly or by calculating the most fitting color from the environment. Thus, the app exhibited a form of dynamic adaptivity to both user-based and environmental constraints. However, the focus of the study was not on using adaptive techniques for product configuration. Rather, the app was envisioned to be used in concert with a smart factory.

Moreover, the usage of AR in product customization is a related topic of this work. As a result, an additional related area of study in AR-based product configuration has emerged: virtual try-on. This discipline aims to use AR's capabilities to allow the customer to not only customize a wearable product but also to immediately try their design on themselves. This research field is in certain aspects similar to the idea of mobile product configuration, as both aim to enable the end-user to test and preview a product with the help of computer-generated imagery. Here, Eisert et al. developed an AR-based try-on system that they called Virtual Mirror [13]. This system was essentially an AR-based mirror that recorded the customer's feet and displayed the video output in real-time, horizontally flipped. The customer could then use a computer to select a shoe model and make various cosmetic changes such as color, materials, and embroidery.

Overall, approaches that focus purely on the try-on aspect, as exemplified by Eisert et al., can be considered as fulfilling the user–product requirement type due to their often minimal configuration capabilities [13]. Furthermore, they can be said to display a degree of adaptivity to the user, because they adapt their video output to the user's physical properties and movement. However, despite being AR-based, virtual try-on systems do not take their environment into account, as their AR capabilities are aimed at augmenting the image of the user, rather than the environment.

7.3 Runtime Adaptation

For enabling runtime adaptation in software systems, the research area of self-adaptive software systems [24] has emerged which provides extensive approaches to support the adaptation of software systems to changing context situations. As AR-based product configuration approaches have to monitor and adapt a viable product configuration regarding various aspects such as user and environmental requirements, we discuss relevant approaches based on runtime adaptation.

Here, especially adaptive UIs have been promoted as a solution for context variability due to their ability to automatically adapt to the context-of-use at runtime [1]. RBUIS [2] and Adapt-UI [31] are two representative approaches that present methods, techniques, and tools for supporting the development of adaptive UIs. With regard to adaptive UIs, most existing approaches make use of a context model consisting of a user, platform, and environment model as described by us in [30]. Besides these approaches, there are also approaches that apply the idea of runtime adaptation for AR applications. While in [29], we apply the idea of context-awareness for VR applications, in [23] we propose a development framework for context-aware AR applications. Mostly, the before mentioned approaches are based on a runtime monitoring and adaptation loop which is characterized through the MAPE-K loop [21] which was also applied in this work. In contrast to the described approaches, our proposed solution in this paper combines the advantages of DSPLs with runtime adaptation to support model-based product configuration.

Moreover, some approaches use the concept of DSPLs to model the UI and the context of use (user, platform, environment) as feature models. Here, Gabillon et al. create a single feature model for the UI features and the contexts of use [14]. Moreover, they add logic rules to the UI features so that they can adapt to changes in the context and apply the concept of a case study of a desktop application. Sboui et al. model both as separate feature models and create a configuration model to link both feature models together [25]. They apply their approach to a case study of a mobile application. In contrast to the described approaches, our proposed solution in this paper combines the advantages of DSPLs with runtime adaptation to support model-based product configuration of AR products.

8 Conclusion

Augmented Reality (AR) has recently found high attention in mobile shopping apps such as in domains like furniture or decoration. While these apps focus on the displaying of atomic 3D objects, they neglect 3D object composition and their configuration according to the user and environmental requirements. To solve both issues, we develop a model-based AR-assisted product configuration approach based on the concept of Dynamic Software Product Lines. For this, we split the engineering process into a *Design Stage* and a *Runtime Stage*. While in the *Design Stage* we create a feature model where each product part is modeled as a feature can be linked to an asset, the *Runtime Stage* uses the feature model and assets to display a product configuration in the physical environment. Moreover, this product configuration can adapt to the requirements of the user and the environment. The benefits of this approach are demonstrated by a case study of configuring modular kitchens with the help of a prototypical mobile-based implementation.

Our future work is twofold and deals with the generalization of the introduced concepts: First, we want to improve the modeling of the user and the environment by separating them into distinct models. Second, we want to create a cross-platform solution for supporting model-based AR/VR product configuration. By combining both, our goal is to develop a model-driven framework for developing AR/VR product configurators.

References

1. Akiki, P.A., Bandara, A.K., Yu, Y.: Adaptive model-driven user interface development systems. ACM Comput. Surv. **47**(1), 9:1–9:33 (2014). https://doi.org/10.1145/2597999
2. Akiki, P.A., Bandara, A.K., Yu, Y.: Engineering adaptive model-driven user interfaces. IEEE Trans. Softw. Eng. **42**(12), 1118–1147 (2016). https://doi.org/10.1109/TSE.2016.2553035
3. Apel S., Batory D., Kästner C., Saake G.: Software Product Lines. In: Feature-Oriented Software Product Lines. Springer, Berlin (2013). https://doi.org/10.1007/978-3-642-37521-7_1
4. Bashari, M., Bagheri, E., Du, W.: Dynamic software product line engineering: a reference framework. Int. J. Software Eng. Knowl. Eng. **27**(02), 191–234 (2017). https://doi.org/10.1142/S0218194017500085
5. Benavides, D., Segura, S., Cortés, A.R.: Automated analysis of feature models 20 years later: a literature review. Inf. Syst. **35**(6), 615–636 (2010). https://doi.org/10.1016/j.is.2010.01.001
6. Benavides, D., Trinidad, P., Ruiz-Cortés, A.: Automated reasoning on feature models. In: Pastor, O., Falcão e Cunha, J. (eds.) CAiSE 2005. LNCS, vol. 3520, pp. 491–503. Springer, Heidelberg (2005). https://doi.org/10.1007/11431855_34
7. Bencomo, N., Hallsteinsen, S., de Almeida, E.S.: A view of the dynamic software product line landscape. Computer **45**(10), 36–41 (2012). https://doi.org/10.1109/MC.2012.292
8. Capilla, R., Bosch, J., Trinidad, P., Ruiz-Cortés, A., Hinchey, M.: An overview of dynamic software product line architectures and techniques: observations from research and industry. J. Syst. Softw. **91**, 3–23 (2014). https://doi.org/10.1016/j.jss.2013.12.038

9. Chatzopoulos, D., Bermejo, C., Huang, Z., Hui, P.: Mobile augmented reality survey: from where we are to where we go. IEEE **5**, 6917–6950 (2017). https://doi.org/10.1109/ACCESS.2017.2698164

10. Clements, P., Northrop, L.: Software product lines: Practices and patterns. SEI series in software engineering, Addison-Wesley, Boston, 7. print (edn.) (2009)

11. Czarnecki, K., Helsen, S., Eisenecker, U.: Staged configuration through specialization and multilevel configuration of feature models. Softw. Process. Improv. Pract. **10**(2), 143–169 (2005). https://doi.org/10.1002/spip.225

12. Dacko, S.G.: Enabling smart retail settings via mobile augmented reality shopping apps. Technol. Forecast. Soc. Chang. **124**, 243–256 (2017). https://doi.org/10.1016/j.techfore.2016.09.032

13. Eisert, P., Fechteler, P., Rurainsky, J.: 3-d tracking of shoes for virtual mirror applications. In: Proceedings of the IEEE Computer Society Conference on Computer Vision and Pattern Recognition (CVPR). IEEE (2008). https://doi.org/10.1109/CVPR.2008.4587566

14. Gabillon, Y., Biri, N., Otjacques, B.: Designing an adaptive user interface according to software product line engineering. In: ACHI 2015 (2015)

15. Gehring, S., et al.: Mobile product customization. In: Proceedings of the 28th International Conference on Human Factors in Computing Systems (CHI), pp. 3463–3468. ACM (2010). https://doi.org/10.1145/1753846.1754002

16. Gottschalk, S., Rittmeier, F., Engels, G.: Intertwined development of business model and product functions for mobile applications: a twin peak feature modeling approach. In: Hyrynsalmi, S., Suoranta, M., Nguyen-Duc, A., Tyrväinen, P., Abrahamsson, P. (eds.) ICSOB 2019. LNBIP, vol. 370, pp. 192–207. Springer, Cham (2019). https://doi.org/10.1007/978-3-030-33742-1_16

17. Gottschalk, S., Rittmeier, F., Engels, G.: Hypothesis-driven adaptation of business models based on product line engineering. In: Proceedings of the 22nd Conference on Business Informatics (CBI). IEEE (2020). https://doi.org/10.1109/CBI49978.2020.00022

18. Gottschalk, S., Yigitbas, E., Schmidt, E., Engels, G.: ProConAR: a tool support for model-based AR product configuration. In: Human-Centered Software Engineering. Springer (2020). https://doi.org/10.1007/978-3-030-64266-2_14

19. Hallsteinsen, S., Stav, E., Solberg, A., Floch, J.: Using product line techniques to build adaptive systems. In: Proceedings of the 10th International Software Product Line Conference (SPLC), pp. 141–150. IEEE (2006). https://doi.org/10.1109/SPLINE.2006.1691586

20. Kästner, C., Apel, S., Kuhlemann, M.: Granularity in software product lines. In: Schäfer, W., Dwyer, M.B., Gruhn, V. (eds.) Proceedings of the 13th international conference on Software engineering (ICSE), p. 311. ACM (2008). https://doi.org/10.1145/1368088.1368131

21. Kephart, J.O., Chess, D.M.: The vision of autonomic computing. Computer **36**(1), 41–50 (2003). https://doi.org/10.1109/MC.2003.1160055

22. Ko, E., Kim, E.Y., Lee, E.K.: Modeling consumer adoption of mobile shopping for fashion products in Korea. Psychol. Mark. **26**(7), 669–687 (2009). https://doi.org/10.1002/mar.20294

23. Krings, S., Yigitbas, E., Jovanovikj, I., Sauer, S., Engels, G.: Development framework for context-aware augmented reality applications. In: Proceedings of the Symposium on Engineering Interactive Computing Systems (EICS), pp. 9:1–9:6. ACM (2020). https://doi.org/10.1145/3393672.3398640

24. Salehie, M., Tahvildari, L.: Self-adaptive software: landscape and research challenges. ACM Trans. Auton. Adapt. Syst. **4**(2), 14:1–14:42 (2009). https://doi.org/10.1145/1516533.1516538

25. Sboui, T., Ayed, M.B., Alimi, A.: A UI-DSPL approach for the development of context-adaptable user interfaces. IEEE Access **6**, 7066–7081 (2018). https://doi.org/10.1109/ACCESS.2017.2782880

26. Trinidad, P., Benavides, D., Durán, A., Cortés, A.R., Toro, M.: Automated error analysis for the agilization of feature modeling. J. Syst. Softw. **81**(6), 883–896 (2008). https://doi.org/10.1016/j.jss.2007.10.030

27. Yang, K.: Determinants of US consumer mobile shopping services adoption: implications for designing mobile shopping services. J. Consum. Mark. **27**(3), 262–270 (2010). https://doi.org/10.1108/07363761011038338

28. Yeh, J.Y., Wu, T.H., Chang, J.M.: Parallel genetic algorithms for product configuration management on pc cluster systems. Int. J. Adv. Manuf. Technol. **31**(11/12), 1233–1242 (2007). https://doi.org/10.1007/s00170-005-0283-7

29. Yigitbas, E., Heindörfer, J., Engels, G.: A context-aware virtual reality first aid training application. In: Alt, F., Bulling, A., Döring, T. (eds.) Proceedings of Mensch und Computer 2019, pp. 885–888. GI/ACM (2019). https://doi.org/10.1145/3340764.3349525

30. Yigitbas, E., Jovanovikj, I., Biermeier, K., Sauer, S., Engels, G.: Integrated model-driven development of self-adaptive user interfaces. Softw. Syst. Model. **19**(5), 1057–1081 (2020). https://doi.org/10.1007/s10270-020-00777-7

31. Yigitbas, E., Sauer, S., Engels, G.: Adapt-UI: an IDE supporting model-driven development of self-adaptive UIs. In: Proceedings of the Symposium on Engineering Interactive Computing Systems (EICS), pp. 99–104. ACM (2017). https://doi.org/10.1145/3102113.3102144

A Scrum-Based Development Process to Support Co-creation with Elders in the eHealth Domain

Jose Barambones[1](✉)(iD), Cristian Moral[1](✉)(iD), Xavier Ferre[1](✉)(iD),
and Elena Villalba-Mora[1,2](✉)(iD)

[1] Centre for Biomedical Technology, Universidad Politécnica de Madrid,
Madrid, Spain
{j.barambones,cristian.moral,xavier.ferre,elena.villalba}@upm.es
[2] Biomedical Research Networking Centre in Bioengineering Biomaterials
and Nanomedicine (CIBER-BBN), Madrid, Spain

Abstract. Since the publication of agile manifesto in 2001, agile methodologies has been gaining significant interest in both software industry and research community. Agile User-Centered Design (AUCD) assesses the challenge of integrating agile development with user experience and usability techniques. Although both methodologies have similarities, their scope and perspective are different and difficult to integrate. The eHealth domain implies additional challenges in terms of usability, due to the differences between healthcare professionals, and lack of knowledge of the day-to-day work carried out in different care tiers. Therefore, the challenge is twofold: to achieve an adequate symbiosis of work between teams, and design a solution adapted to the needs of diverse stakeholders with vast differences in their context of use. We designed a lightweight AUCD process adapted to such situation, and we present our experience in the design and implementation of such development process for the development of a system to monitor frailty in elder patients with support for both community and specialized care. As a result, our UCD process has achieved both iterative and incremental value generation, maintaining a good coordination between developers and UX designers, and resulting on a usable solution with regard to target users.

Keywords: Agile User-Centered Design · Experience report · eHealth · Elder users

1 Introduction

Scrum is an agile process framework for software development aimed to address complex adaptive problems, while productively and creatively delivering products with the highest possible value. Scrum teams are subject to a series of roles,

© IFIP International Federation for Information Processing 2020
Published by Springer Nature Switzerland AG 2020
R. Bernhaupt et al. (Eds.): HCSE 2020, LNCS 12481, pp. 105–117, 2020.
https://doi.org/10.1007/978-3-030-64266-2_6

rules, events and artifacts; and orchestrated through a set of well-defined relationships and interactions between them [16]. In an agile process, development is organized into a series of short and fixed-length iterations or sprints. The outcome of each sprint is a tested, integrated, and executable partial system, including its own requirements analysis, design, implementation, and testing activities. The system grows incrementally with subsequent iterations, becoming an incremental development [13].

User-Centered Design (UCD) includes activities such as the specification of the context of use and the user requirements, producing design solutions, and evaluating them against such requirements [1]. UCD is inherently iterative to cope with the uncertainty of the human part in the human-computer interaction. Each iteration includes some kind of usability evaluation of the produced solution that determines if it is required to perform a new iteration, but repeating only the UCD activities that require some refinement.

Integration of UCD into agile approaches has traditionally found obstacles related to the lack of usability awareness and the different focus of Human-Computer Interaction (HCI) techniques compared to other development activities. The Agile User-Centered Design (AUCD) approach emerged to address these problems [4,8,9,17]; however, although scrum is considered a lightweight process easy to adopt, the integration of UCD with agile methods remains challenging. The agile Manifesto[1] focuses directly on providing value as functioning software for the customer, whereas UCD aims for a proper understanding of users and their context to take design decisions according to their goals and expectations. Extensive user research activities, necessary for proper UCD, can be identified as big design up-front from an agile perspective, that defends having running software built from the very beginning. Both methodologies coincide in the need for and iterative approach and handle requirements and uncertainty in development from different approaches, either by integrating the client needs as the product owner or the objective user. However, there is a need to fit UCD activities into the overall agile process and to define how UCD findings drive redesign efforts in the software product.

Participatory design methods from UCD need to take into account technical and resource constraints. In our case we need to add the difficulties of applying UCD in the eHealth domain. User experience research with healthcare professionals show that they prioritize the medical error reduction to avoid unforeseen or harmful decisions to patients [2,12]. Accordingly, special effort is required for understanding and designing for all stakeholders. Healthcare professionals are a scarce resource, and it is difficult to have them continuously as part of the development team, as agile approaches suggest. From the patient perspective, user satisfaction is critical to preserve his/her engagement and ensure proper adherence to treatment. Designing any software product for elders requires considering their possible limitations in technology background and physical and cognitive abilities. These limitations linked to elder users require the consideration of specific usability guidelines.

---

[1] See http://agilemanifesto.org/.

We present in this paper the instantiation of an AUCD software development process for the development of a telemedicine system to monitor elder patients with risk of frailty, merging a scrum-based approach with co-creation UCD activities. We extract measures from both scrum and usability metrics to discuss how the process fulfills the project objectives.

2   Related Work

With regard to AUCD adoption, Brhel et al. conducted a literature review on agile and UCD integration techniques, resulting on a foundation based on a set of principles, such as to merge effectively iterative and incremental development, and continuous stakeholder involvement, among others [4]. Fox and Ferreira defined different approaches to integrate agile methods with UCD and compare them in respective study cases with experienced software teams from industry [5,6]. Garcia et al. identify through an ethnographic study the artifacts used to facilitate the communication between designers and developers in an AUCD approach [7].

Apropos of development and design for ageing, Ruzic et al. designed a set of guidelines to ensure usability of mobile eHealth devices by elder based on design principles from literature: universal design, design for aging, universal usability, and guidelines for handheld mobile interface design [15]. Lerouge et al. investigate how User Profiles and Personas techniques improve the design and development of consumer health technologies and devices for an aging population [14]. The study provides guidelines to tap into the conceptual models of elder population to reflecting their preferences and capabilities, but user motivation and adherence is considered superficially.

3   Context

Elder-associated conditions, e.g. frailty, and other health-related conditions are becoming a huge challenge to the sustainability of healthcare systems. Concretely, frailty condition is an intermediate state in the ageing trajectory, preceding the onset of disability.

POSITIVE project (maintaining and imPrOving the intrinSIc capaciTy Involving primary care and caregiVErs), funded by EIT Health, proposes a new organizational ecosystem to manage frailty, based on the basic model centered into the Geriatric Comprehensive Assessment (CGA) detailed in [18], but extending it to primary care professionals to allow for a closer contact with patients and their caregivers. This project implies the participation of health professionals at different levels (nurses, general practitioners, geriatricians, physiotherapists, occupational therapists, etc.), patients and their informal caregivers. The system allows professionals to carry out CGA in clinical settings and to remotely monitor patient's intrinsic capacity and prevent frailty through tailored intervention in community dwellings. Figure 1 shows the POSITIVE services offered through the developed platform. In a nutshell, POSITIVE system is composed by three main components: the professional app, the patient app, and the support ruled-based engines. Through the professional app healthcare professionals manage their activities such as patient monitorization, messaging and gathering patient data during clinical visits. The patient app includes the functionality to assist and assess in a remote manner the patient intervention at dwelling. The rule-based engines are a sever-side service that receives patient data from clinical visits and home activities. Later, the engine analyzes the data to support care professional decision process for referring to specialized care professionals. Co-creation activities defined and refined the screens of the Patients Dashboard (Fig. 4), New Visit, and Home activities (Fig. 5), and served for defining the rules of the side support components (alerts and referral engines).

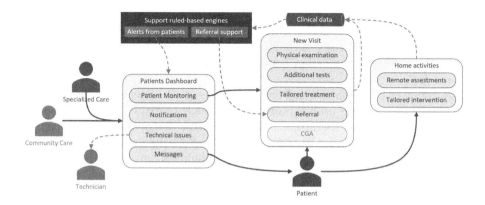

Fig. 1. POSITIVE platform schema.

4   AUCD Process Proposal

The project team is composed by two sections: Development (Dev team) and User eXperience (UX team). The UX team deals with user research and is responsible for the high-level design of the solution, through co-creation activities, while the Dev team is responsible for the implementation and software testing activities. A set of healthcare professionals participate in co-creation activities as a relaxed case of product owners. These participating stakeholders are exempt of backlog/project management, though the UX team acts as spokesperson for the users in the generation of the backlog, collaborating with the Dev team in such purpose.

Figure 2 shows the deployed AUCD process for the POSITIVE project. Subteams possess their own work pipeline, where each team processes the data from the other team at the previous iteration. Accordingly, the Dev team performs a scrum sprint given the backlog generated, whilst the UX team works in the design of the following iteration in co-creation activities. Prototype validation, design, and refinement are performed over subsequent releases, thus both iterative pipelines converge onto an incremental development. The following subsections describe the iteration process and its activities.

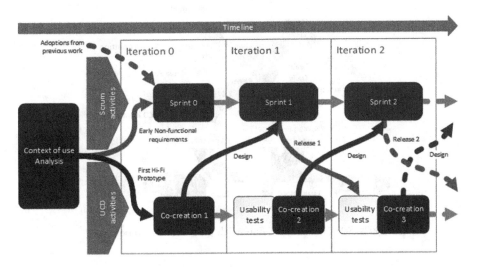

Fig. 2. Integration of UCD and base scrum sprints in our applied process.

4.1 Sprint Iteration

Figure 3 describes the activity flow over a single iteration from Fig. 2. As mentioned above, the sprint receives the design requirements and works over the last deployed release. In other words, the backlog from current iteration is generated and updated from design results obtained on the previous UCD iteration. As output, a new release is deployed and a new set of design requirements from co-creation and usability tests are delivered. In this way, development activities can be parallelized with the next design iteration. Indeed, this flow enables both teams to be coordinated through different meetings, appointments and common activities in such a way that ongoing decisions are made with up to date information. Team dailies are held with the entire team allowing for the status of both teams to be effectively shared and coordinated.

Kick-Off: Previous work consisted on extensive user research activities, including observation at the Geriatrics Unit of the University Hospital of Getafe and semi-structured interviews with key stakeholders [18], followed by several iterations of prototypes for the UI of the system to support the CGA carried out by geriatricians. The overall POSITIVE ecosystem, including primary care professionals, was designed at time of project proposal, so when the actual development started there was a clear product concept defined, even if the prototypes were

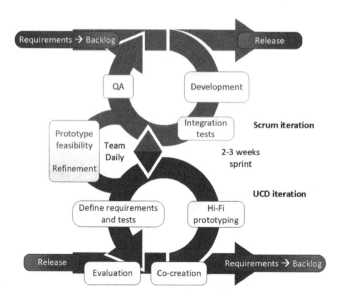

Fig. 3. AUCD iteration flow with activities per pipeline.

outdated and needed to be considered from scratch due to the new organizational model implied in the project.

4.2   UX Activities

Co-Creation: Co-creation activities can effectively involve different stakeholders on design decisions, revealing hidden requirements and restrictions which may be difficult to identify otherwise. Based on participatory design principles, they are aimed to understand properly the potential users of a product, to identify the real context of use, and to ensure that the proposed design actually fits both users and context [10].

Co-creation requires users to be actively involved in the design process. The aim of the scheduled co-creation sessions was to define the context of use through activities where stakeholders are actively implied. In our case, we have used two methods: focus groups and pluralistic walkthroughs. A Focus Group is a qualitative research technique that is specified as a meeting of potential users where participants give their opinion about one or more topics [11]. The most interesting output of this technique is the debate created between the participants, as this forces them to defend, argue and justify their ideas, and then to externalize their real mental model. Having a total of 15 primary professionals and 5 geriatricians participating in the co-creation activities allowed us to uncover different viewpoints and lack of knowledge about how other care tiers work. A single product owner would have not been able to provide enough information for such a complex care ecosystem. A pluralistic Walkthrough is a usability inspection method where stakeholders, including users of any role, designers and developers revise the design. This helps specifying in detail the tasks that must be developed from different role-perspectives and brought together [3].

Hi-Fi Prototyping: The early design output is generated from co-creation decisions. The Hi-Fi prototype is extended with that output, in such a way that design becomes incremental along the iterations. Subsequent usability testing the generated prototypes allows for the required design refinement. Fig. 4 and 5 show some prototypes used later in UX activities.

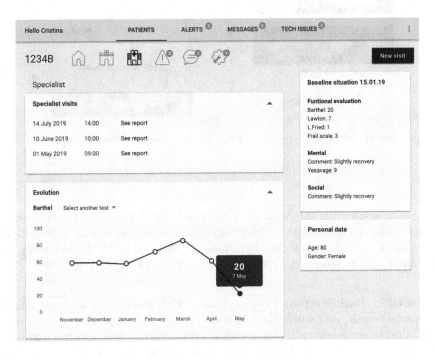

Fig. 4. Hi-Fi prototype for the professional view.

Requirements and Tests: From co-creation activities, requirements are collected according to the professional knowledge and their mental model. This data is formatted into documentation for the dev team in different assets. The Hi-Fi prototype validated by stakeholders through co-creation activities embodies the system requirements. Such source of requirements include the set of acceptance tests for the subsequent evaluation. Requirements and tests are translated to simple input/output tasks or user stories with pre/post conditions and attached test cases. Such tasks are classified by story points from scrum estimation. In our case, the difficulty emerges given a backlog that is increased with new features or epics in further iterations. This implies that the estimation and priority can

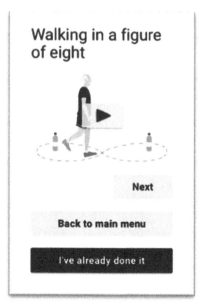

Fig. 5. Hi-Fi prototype for the patient view.

only be done with the information of the current iteration plus the remaining undone tasks. To overcome this, co-creation activities were scoped in initiatives or big epics, in such a way that iterations are differentiated, dependencies are minimized, and to ensure the critical tasks from each epic are prioritized.

Evaluation: Usability tests were performed with community and specialized care professionals, and with elders in their homes. During testing, participants were asked to complete typical tasks while observers watched, listened and took field notes with the aim of identifying usability problems, collecting qualitative/quantitative data and determining the user satisfaction. Quantitative results were collected using System Usability Scale (SUS) questionnaires, while qualitative findings were gathered through deep contextual interviews. The Think Aloud protocol was used for the usability tests to collect qualitative data allowing to explain when and why errors were made, and to identify the reasons for the user problems.

4.3 Dev Activities

Development Environment: The Dev team follows the Dev-QA-Prod pipeline. The Dev environment is used to code new features, to perform functional tests, and to fix bugs. The process is iterated until the code is ready for the next stage of testing. The quality assessment environment (QA) is used for testing by the UX team and domain experts carry out heuristic usability evaluation, with redesign decisions reported back to the Dev team if necessary. The end-user release is deployed in the production environment once the QA environment has been thoroughly tested and its stability and performance has been checked. The pipeline is managed by a control version software with a continuous integration framework that allows to automatically deploy and test the releases in their respective environment.

Integration and Quality Assessment: Integration assets have been grouped in different test sets according to their purpose. Integration tests are non-functional tests related to networking and infrastructure assets, and incremental tests ensuring the correct integration of the new release onto the current deployment. QA consists on passing a set of test cases designed by the Dev team that ensure a proper system response according to the elicited requirements and acceptance tests.

4.4 Team Daily

Dailies are the most important activity of our AUCD process. Both teams participate in team dailies to ensure coordination between them. On the one side, the UX team provides information about the subsequent design decisions, shows the current prototype and provides feedback about the integration in terms of interaction with regard to the current release. On the other side, the Dev team provides the current status of the development, including dev planning, functionality priority and tests. From the output given by both teams, daily agreements are achieved. At this point, team objectives are well-defined: the UX team aims to control and support refinement tasks for developers to fix possible deviations or slips during development, while the Dev team evaluates and agrees design decisions based on their technical viability. Thus, the whole team information is up to date, and priorities, deviations and issues are properly managed.

5 Application Results

The proposed process was applied during 6 iterations until the first release was completed. The team was composed by 4 software engineers and 1 dev lead senior, 2 UX researchers, and 1 scrum master. Figure 6 summarizes both usability and scrum results: bars represent the different SUS values obtained at the end of each iteration. It is important to note that SUS questionnaires were conducted with the involved stakeholders on the sprint, either professionals, patients, or both. Lines represent the story points progression, where the yellow line determines the estimated story points at the beginning of the iteration, and the green one the completed at the end of it.

The UX team conducted during this period a set of five consecutive walkthrough sessions to progress iteratively and incrementally co-design with the potential users. Those workshops ensure that all the required functionalities

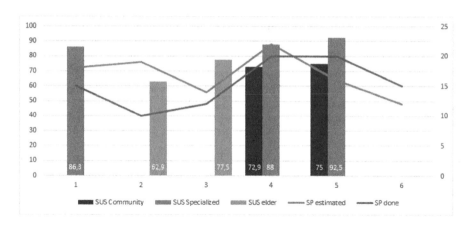

Fig. 6. Quantitative results by iteration. On the left axis, SUS values are broken down by user profile according to the different focus groups during co-creation activities and evaluation. On the left axis, story points estimated vs. done in each sprint.

have been considered and that they are implemented based in the users' needs and preferences. Usability tests were always conducted by one UX researcher, and at least a second UX researcher observed, took notes and collected the data during the test. Usability testing results were used as the main criterion to iterate. Regarding the development pipeline, submitted releases are related to the different components briefly described in Fig. 1. The first iteration was focused on the first release of the CGA for specialized care professionals (geriatricians). Second and third iterations were focused on patients' tasks, monitoring, and intervention at dwelling. Iteration 4 was focused on tasks were primary and specialized care professionals converge (referral, communication, alerts, and sharing data, among others). In this iteration the Dev team participated in the walkthrough session due to the complexity of several tasks to be designed. Thus, issues, solutions and decisions related with viability, alternatives, and technical requirements were held from the beginning. Iteration 5 consisted on the incremental inclusion of the remaining stakeholders (technical, staff, caregivers, other professionals, etc.). The last iteration performed tackled the different pending tasks carried over from previous iterations, refinement of certain user stories, and low priority tasks.

In iteration 2, the first one with elder patients, users expressed they would like to interact with the system frequently, but at the same time, they thought there was too much inconsistency in the system, resulting on an overall SUS value of 62.92, which is below the average (68). The subsequent iterations were mainly focused on solving and mitigating the detected issues on priority tasks. Finally, patients stated that they would like to use the system regularly, in case they would need to monitor their health status, but still expressed that there were some problems about lack of well-described instructions for some complex tasks. Regarding healthcare users, they perceived that the system is easy to use, well-adapted to their needs, and that they would not require help or further assistance by the UX facilitator to perform the tasks. On the other hand, we detect on later iterations the different work constraints between profiles. For example, primary care professionals have very short medical visits to attend their patients, so they are more reluctant to add a new system to their work routine. Due to these results, task refinements were critical in sprints 3 and 5, so the expected new story points to complete were significantly reduced. Later iterations reflect how once the main user stories were successfully finished and refined, the Dev team could focus on low priority and pending stories from the backlog. Indeed, this situation allowed to turnaround the trend where more stories were performed than estimated.

6   Discussion

Overall, the design and adoption of this AUCD process was successful in different perspectives. From an organizational point of view, to allocate team members to UX or Dev pipelines allowed to focus the best effort according to their skills. Activities where the UX and Dev team worked together, such as daily meetings and a pluralistic walkthroughs, allowed both teams to stay up to date and react to problems from different perspectives. Regarding the artifacts delivered by the UX team, such as prototypes, task descriptions and acceptance tests, they were easily adopted by the Dev team due to their similarity with common agile artifacts. From a product/value-perspective, incremental design and development has been usually accompanied by good acceptance by target users; where the different stakeholders found the app easy to use and well-adapted to their needs.

There were relevant deviations in the estimation of effort for different parts of the system, due the complexity of dealing with multiple stakeholders and the specificities of the health domain. In particular, some tasks were downplayed in the system after identifying that the initial overall approach for such section was not possible, and effort estimations had to be modified accordingly. In addition, from the UCD part, it is worth mentioning that, although patient acceptance was achieved, several difficulties during UX activities were found. Additional iterations were required to better accommodate the designed user interfaces to the elders and their caregivers, due to the specific interaction limitations of this user base.

In a project involving different care tiers, like primary and specialized care, it is more difficult to identify a single customer. Lack of availability of healthcare professionals for development activities may cause that eHealth projects cannot carry out a traditional scrum inception. In our case, this led to some prioritisation mismatches, that both teams had to deal with. Our experience is an example of the inherent difficulties of integration of UCD and agile approaches in the eHealth domain.

7 Conclusions and Future Work

We have designed and deployed an AUCD process based on co-creation and scrum activities for a frailty monitoring eHealth platform. The process was aimed to apply a scrum-based methodology in a context with strong requirements on usability that includes quite differentiated contexts of use. Such contexts include different roles/profiles: community and specialized care professionals, elder patients and other stakeholders like caregivers, occupational therapists and nurses, among others. The process consists of two interlaced pipelines focused on agile and UCD activities and their specialized teams. Requirements and prototypes from co-creation are used as input for Dev team as user stories and tests, whilst releases are submitted to UX team and users for validation and further design. The Dev-QA-Prod pipeline was used to properly parallelize development and tests with design, the validation and the staging. As a result, both iterative processes properly converge to contribute to incremental development and create value. Usability evaluation results state that users found the platform easy-to-use and learn, and adapted to their needs.

Providing tools and activities to improve the big picture of the backlog and help users to compare the value between different epics are proposals for future adoption. In our further steps, the platform will be deployed in a clinical pilot involving 75 elders and 25 professionals from Spain, Poland and Sweden.

References

1. 210:2010, I.: Ergonomics of human-system interaction - part 210: Human-centred design for interactive systems (2010)
2. Ash, J., Berg, M., Coiera, E.: Some unintended consequences of information technology in health care: the nature of patient care information system-related errors. J. Am. Med. Inform. Assoc. JAMIA **11**, 104–12 (2004)
3. Bias, R.G.: The Pluralistic Usability Walkthrough: Coordinated Empathies, p. 63–76. Wiley, USA (1994)
4. Brhel, M., Meth, H., Maedche, A., Werder, K.: Exploring principles of user-centered agile software development: a literature review. Inf. Softw. Technol. **61**, 163–181 (2015)
5. Ferreira, J., Sharp, H., Robinson, H.: Values and assumptions shaping agile development and user experience design in practice. In: Sillitti, A., Martin, A., Wang, X., Whitworth, E. (eds.) XP 2010. LNBIP, vol. 48, pp. 178–183. Springer, Heidelberg (2010). https://doi.org/10.1007/978-3-642-13054-0_15
6. Fox, D., Sillito, J., Maurer, F.: Agile methods and user-centered design: how these two methodologies are being successfully integrated in industry. In: Agile 2008 Conference, pp. 63–72 (2008)
7. Garcia, A., da Silva, T.S., Silveira, M.S.: Artifact-facilitated communication in agile user-centered design. In: Kruchten, P., Fraser, S., Coallier, F. (eds.) XP 2019. LNBIP, vol. 355, pp. 102–118. Springer, Cham (2019). https://doi.org/10.1007/978-3-030-19034-7_7

8. Hussain, Z., Slany, W., Holzinger, A.: Current state of agile user-centered design: a survey. In: Holzinger, A., Miesenberger, K. (eds.) USAB 2009. LNCS, vol. 5889, pp. 416–427. Springer, Heidelberg (2009). https://doi.org/10.1007/978-3-642-10308-7_30

9. Hussain, Z., Slany, W., Holzinger, A.: Investigating agile user-centered design in practice: a grounded theory perspective. In: Holzinger, A., Miesenberger, K. (eds.) USAB 2009. LNCS, vol. 5889, pp. 279–289. Springer, Heidelberg (2009). https://doi.org/10.1007/978-3-642-10308-7_19

10. Jansen, S., Pieters, M.: The 7 Principles of Complete Co-Creation. Laurence King Publishing, Amsterdam (2018)

11. Krueger, R.: Focus Groups: A Practical Guide for Applied Research. SAGE Publications, Thousand Oaks (2014)

12. Kushniruk, A.W., Triola, M.M., Borycki, E.M., Stein, B., Kannry, J.L.: Technology induced error and usability: the relationship between usability problems and prescription errors when using a handheld application. Int. J. Med. Informatics **74**, 519–526 (2005)

13. Larman, C.: Applying UML and Patterns: An Introduction to Object-Oriented Analysis and Design and Iterative Development, 3rd edn. Prentice Hall PTR, Upper Saddle River (2004)

14. Lerouge, C., Ma, J., Sneha, S., Tolle, K.: User profiles and personas in the design and development of consumer health technologies. Int. J. Med. Informatics **82**, e251–e268 (2011)

15. Ruzic, L., Lee, S.T., Liu, Y.E., Sanford, J.A.: Development of universal design mobile interface guidelines (UDMIG) for aging population. In: Antona, M., Stephanidis, C. (eds.) UAHCI 2016. LNCS, vol. 9737, pp. 98–108. Springer, Cham (2016). https://doi.org/10.1007/978-3-319-40250-5_10

16. Schwaber, K., Sutherland, J.: The scrum guide (2017). www.scrumguides.org

17. Silva da Silva, T., Martin, A., Maurer, F., Silveira, M.: User-centered design and agile methods: A systematic review. In: Proceedings of the 2011 Agile Conference, AGILE 2011, pp. 77–86. IEEE Computer Society, Salt Lake City (2011)

18. Sánchez Sánchez, A., Villalba Mora, E., Peinado, I., Rodríguez-Mañas, L.: Integrated care program for older adults: analysis and improvement. J. Nutr. Health Aging **21**, 867–873 (2017)

BPMN Extensions and Semantic Annotation in Public Administration Service Design

Carmelo Ardito[1]([⊠]) [ID], Danilo Caivano[2] [ID], Lucio Colizzi[2] [ID],
and Loredana Verardi[2] [ID]

[1] Dipartimento di Ingegneria Elettrica e dell'Informazione, Politecnico di Bari, Via Orabona, 4, 70125 Bari, Italy
carmelo.ardito@poliba.it
[2] Dipartimento di Informatica, Università degli Studi di Bari Aldo Moro, Via Orabona, 4, 70125 Bari, Italy
{danilo.caivano,lucio.colizzi,loredana.verardi}@uniba.it

Abstract. Internet of Things (IoT), and in general the Internet of Everything (IoE), are deeply influencing the business processes Digital Transformation, also in the Public Administration context, introducing new actors and interactions among People, Process, Data and Things. Therefore, a re-design of the processes or the creation of new ones is necessary, in a way that the design of a public service meets needs and skills of different end users (citizens, business managers, experts, etc.). This paper presents a framework for the design of public service user interfaces that, on the basis of domain ontologies and BPMn extensions, support the modeling of new interactions with IoT and bot services, in particular Telegram Bots, in the context of public administration processes. A service semantic annotation model can be shared with and reused by other organizations, thus reducing the user interface design and implementation time, and consequently the overall service development time.

Keywords: Business processes · Internet of Things · Bot · BPMN · Ontology · UI design

1 Introduction and Motivation

In the Smart Cities context, the revolution triggered by Internet of Things (IoT) and, more generally, by Internet of Everything (IoE), enables new processes and modifies the existing ones, such as signaling of inefficiencies via APP, geolocalized tourist information service provided via OpenData, thus creating new value and new business opportunities for the involved communities. People and new types of information are increasingly connected, autonomous and semi-autonomous things are now active participants in digital processes. The four pillars of the IoE (People, Things, Process and Data) are being increasingly crucial factors in the Digital Transformation of Public Administration (PA) processes, which move from traditional document workflows to processes that involve both human and non-human actors.

© IFIP International Federation for Information Processing 2020
Published by Springer Nature Switzerland AG 2020
R. Bernhaupt et al. (Eds.): HCSE 2020, LNCS 12481, pp. 118–129, 2020.
https://doi.org/10.1007/978-3-030-64266-2_7

Effective Business Process (BP) digitalization is essential to provide efficient services, and to quickly respond to the citizens' needs. Smart City actions aim to enhance city performance by using data, information and information technologies, such as IoT, in order to provide a more efficient service to citizens, monitoring and optimizing existing infrastructure, increasing collaboration among various stakeholders and encouraging innovative business models in the public and private sectors.

The potential value of a Smart City is fully exploited when data from multiple IoT networks are combined to enable new knowledge in a process, and even in a different application domain. In addition, social media, instant messaging platforms, chatbots, Artificial Intelligence, and OpenData have transformed the communication between PAs and citizens in an increasingly "smart" way, enabling new processes, also through citizens' involvement. We can identify three different communication types between PAs and citizens:

- broadcast (1:N): via different institutional communication channels (web site, Facebook page, etc.) to inform the citizenship;
- direct (1:1): via email, Instant Messaging, user identification;
- participative (N:M): via social platforms, active citizenship platforms, etc.

However, there are several gaps introduced by the implementation of IoT/IoE in business processes, and generally by the BP Digital Transformation in Smart Communities contexts:

- the Business Process Management notation (BPMn) 2.0 [1], used for modeling processes, does not provide classes and artifacts able to model the interactions with IoT/IoE elements;
- in IoT-based processes and in Public Administration contexts the same data (possibly provided by a smart device, such as a sensor) may be of interest in multiple processes and application domains. This introduces semantic issues about assigning the most appropriate meaning to data and information;
- technical interoperability issues due to IoT devices heterogeneity, which affect the of device description;
- different types of end users interacting with the processes, who are characterized by different skills and have to be provided with graphic layouts and semantics representations suitable to their skills.

To address these issues we refer to the KSM - Knowledge Stratification Model framework [2], which guides technical experts in designing IoT and IoE based public service interfaces with a user centered perspective and semantic approach. This paper introduces a PA service interface design framework, based on ontologies to describe the three KMS layers and an extended BPMn process modeler able to manage the specificities of IoT and IoE. The framework aims to contextualize data in PA processes and public service user interfaces (UIs) from a semantic point of view, through ontologies and controlled dictionaries, in a multi-stakeholder - user-centered - development process. In fact the interaction and knowledge sharing among all stakeholders (technicians, process analysist, domain experts, end users) is necessary both in the process modeling and in service design phases, in order to ensure usability and user experience of the final PA service UI.

This paper is organized as follows. Section 2 provides a brief overview of the existing studies on BPMn extensions and on semantic approaches in IoT and IoE contexts. Section 3 illustrates the proposed BPMn extension for IoT and bot-based processes. Section 4 introduces the proposed framework to support PA service UI design by means of a semantic approach. Section 5 reports conclusions and future work.

2 Related Work

Traditionally, IoT-based information and events are represented via web services in BPM systems (BPMs) [3], because BPMn 2.0 supports modeling URI-based service tasks. This approach simplifies the systems for business process management and is compatible with existing BPM tools. Unfortunately, many IoT devices do not work as regular web service entities. For example, there is often the need of intermediary services to enable systems to access the devices; or tasks such as sensor data streaming are continuous tasks that cannot be explicitly represented by standard BPM notation [4]. A common solution is to extend the notation introducing specific IoT elements, thus differentiating the tasks in which they are involved from those with standard BPM services [5].

In the literature, there are several proposal of introducing IoT elements in existing modelling standards as BPMn, according to different perspective: as Events [6], Resources [7], Services [5], Participants [8]. They define new notations in order to represent IoT elements in the models, i.e., an IoT process is described as a Pool and IoT device activities are modelled in Lane [7], real world Physical Entity are modelled through Participant notation [8], etc.

Some research projects [7, 9] propose frameworks for theoretical IoT-driven business process modelling, others for practical system integration in order to involve IoT elements in the intra-organisational or in the inter-organisational level [5]. The IoT-A project [10] focuses on designing IoT-driven BP models, proposes a meta-model of BPMn extensions, and provides a guidance for the (re)design of processes.

To the best of our knowledge IoE elements have not been much investigated. Only *social media* have been deeply explored and BPMn extensions and design patterns have been defined to represent their behavior [11].

Finally, semantic technologies are applied both to IoT domain [12] and BP modeling in order to re-use and include semantic models, as IoT-BPO or IoT-Lite. In Italy, several ongoing initiatives are coordinated on digital and technological transformation of PAs, promoted by AGID[1] (Agency for Digital Italy) and the Department For Digital Transformation of the Presidency of the Council of Ministers. In this frame, the OntoPia project[2] defines a common language for data exchange among Italian PAs. By means of shared ontologies and controlled vocabularies, the project aims to the standardization and semantic interoperability of Italian PAs' knowledge, data integration, sharing and reusing of public data. The *Designers Italia*[3] project is developing guidelines for Italian PA service design.

---

[1] http://www.agid.gov.it.

[2] https://github.com/italia/daf-ontologie-vocabolari-controllati.

[3] https://designers.italia.it.

3 Extending BPM Notation to IoT and Bot-Based Processes

Integrated tools and approaches, such as BPM, are needed to support the Digital Transformation of public process. BPM is a structured approach to process modeling and management, which can be extended in order to include other constructs, for modelling and managing new relationships and interactions enabled by technology.

We have defined BPM extensions for IoT and Telegram Bot according to Stroppi's approach [13], which defines a procedure to transform a conceptual domain model to a BPMn compliant extension model through mapping and transformation rules. The approach is based on the following steps: 1) definition of a conceptual domain model of the extension as UML class diagram; 2) transformation of the conceptual domain model into a validable BPMn extension model (BPMN+X); 3) transformation of BPMN+X into an XML Schema Extension Definition Model; 4) transformation of XMLSchema Extension Definition Model into an XML Schema Extension Definition Document (XSD).

3.1 BPMn Extension for IoT

We consider IoT elements as process Participant, and we start from the domain model defined by the IoT-A project [10]. This model was modified and extended according to ISO/OGC Observation and Measurement (O&M)[4] and to the IoT Ontology defined in OntoPIA project[5]. In the UML conceptual model we propose for the IoT-domain (see Fig. 1), *IoTService* is a generalization of the *Performer* class that defines the resource performing an *Activity* (SendTask, ActuationTask, etc.); *IoTDevice* is a pool, its features are assigned using the *IoTSpecifications* relationship, and is referred to a DeviceType (sensor, actuator, gateway, etc.). In this way future extensions are possible. Moreover, the *Observation* class describes observations, results and sampling features; the *Measurement Quality* class represents the observation quality or measurement parameters defined by the IoT ontology, such as Latency, Accuracy, Replicability, etc.

Then, according to Stroppi's methodology [13], an XML-schema extension model was defined and finally an XSD with the BPMN+X model transformation was generated. The XML schema is used into a process modeler tool in order to design processes with new extensions that are visually represented by new graphic constructs (Fig. 2).

3.2 BPMn Extension for Bot

To the best of our knowledge, there are no BPMn extensions modeling bot interaction, although these bot services are widely spreading in Open Government context.

Bots are programs that can perform autonomous actions or execute commands when receiving inputs; their applications are various (marketing, customer care, search engines, etc.), good or bad (fraudulent), but all share the same capability to imitate human behavior. For example, chat-bots mimic human conversations; bots programmed for search engines or for fraudulent purposes copy the way human browse the Web. Telegram Bots, in particular, have spread, also in Public sectors, because they exploit the potential of

---

[4] OGC 10-004r3 and ISO 19156:2011

[5] https://github.com/italia/daf-ontologie-vocabolari-controllati.

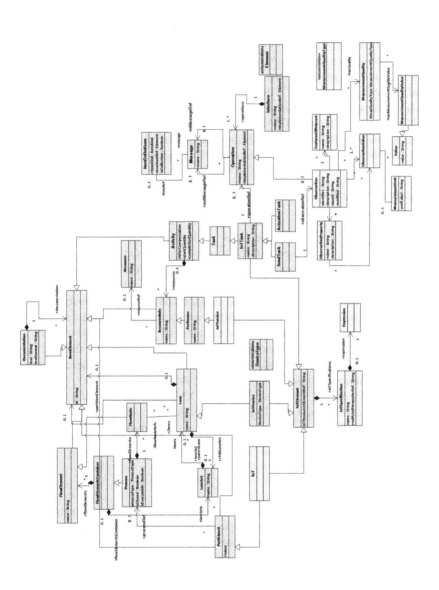

Fig. 1. UML representation of the BPM conceptual model of the IoT-domain; classes in blue are a subset of those proposed by the IoT-A initiative [10], classes in pink are the proposed extensions. High-resolution image available at http://tiny.cc/HCSE2020_material (Color figure online)

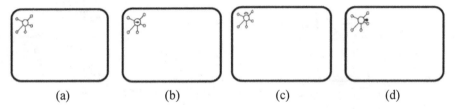

Fig. 2. IoT-extension graphic constructs: (a) sensing task; (b) actuation task, (c) gateway task, (d) stream task.

the Telegram instant messaging platform, thus improving user's requests response and taking advantage of mobile device popularity. In the PA context, bot usage scenarios are various: personalized news, virtual desks, Open data browsing, alerts from citizens, etc. These services allow targeted communication from the PA to the citizen or to a community. From the other side, they enable citizen's interaction with the internal processes of the PA: for example, the bot can start specific PA processes for managing a problem reported or a claim submitted by citizens.

The Telegram Bot is configured as an active participant in the PA process, able to interact with other actors, to automate some steps of a traditional process, to call up external services or other bots, to activate social services, custom tools, payments and games[6]. The UML domain conceptual model provided in Fig. 3 shows an excerpt of BPMn meta-model classes, highlighted in blue, extended with bot classes.

The *BOT* class is a generalization of *Participant* class, because BOT has a role in the process, i.e., it is responsible for performing tasks. Its graphical representation is a Pool. The *BOT Lane* is a generalization of the *Lane* class, because bots can interact with other bots. The *BOT Task* class represents a program that resides in the Telegram server; it is specialized in other classes: *BOT Commands* is the communication task to execute activities scheduled for the command; *BOT answer* is the activity for posting a response via chat, group or channel, represented by the corresponding classes; *BOT Game* allows users to play with another user or in a group by receiving a game message; *BOT Payment* allows to accept payments from Telegram users; *BOT Service Integration* combines responses from external services, third-party REST services or other bots (*BOT Inline*[7]). The *BOT Message* is a generalization of the *Message* class that represents different bot message types: voice, text, audio, video, document, game.

Figure 4 shows our proposal of graphic constructs to be embedded in process modelling tools in order to model bot behaviour.

---

[6] https://core.telegram.org/bots.

[7] Inline bots are embedded in other bots that cite them through the "@ <inlineBotName" call.

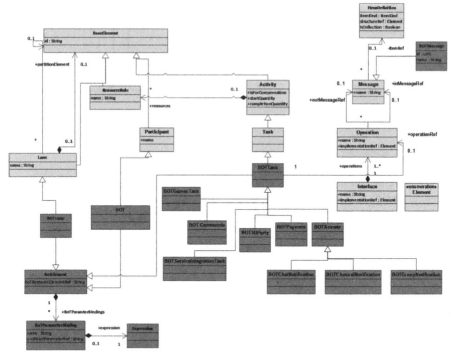

Fig. 3. UML representation of the BPM standard meta-model (classes in blue) extended with Telegram Bot classes (in pink). High-resolution image available at http://tiny.cc/HCSE2020_mat erial (Color figure online)

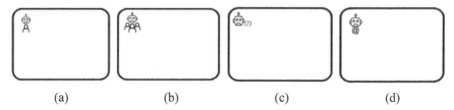

| (a) | (b) | (c) | (d) |

Fig. 4. Graphic constructs to model bot behaviour: (a) chat notification, (b) group or channel notification, (c) commands, (d) inline.

3.3 IoT and Bot BPMn Extensions: A Case Study

The proposed IoT and bot extensions have been used for modelling already existing PA processes and to define new ones. The Municipality of Lecce (Italy), for example, has implemented a process, managed by the municipal police via a Telegram channel (*@polizialocalelecce*[8]), to deliver communications to citizens. The channel has 6378 subscribers (data referred to March 2020), who, through messages, photos, links,

---

[8] https://t.me/polizialocalelecce.

receive weather alerts, traffic and road incidents information, and any other relevant communication for the community (Fig. 5a).

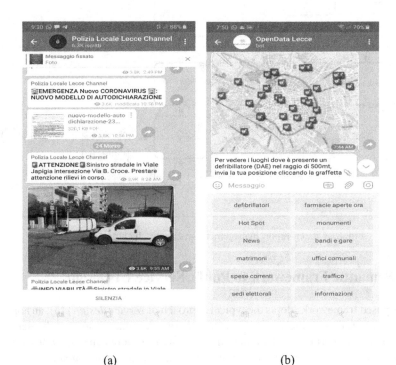

(a)   (b)

Fig. 5. (a) Telegram channel of the municipal police of Lecce. (b) Telegram Bot to explore OpenData of municipality of Lecce.

When the municipal police receives a report of an event from a citizen, it is verified and inserted it in the internal information system; then, after complementing the event with further details, the alert is possibly broadcasted to citizens via the Telegram channel. These data are organized in datasets, published on the OpenData website[9] that, as shown in (Fig. 5b), can be explored by means of a bot telegram (*@opendataleccebot*[10]) [14].

The alerting and management process of the municipal police, as outlined in Fig. 6, has been designed with the Bpmn.io[11] open source process modeler, extended with the IoT and IoE graphic constructs we have presented in the previous subsection.

---

[9] http://dati.comune.lecce.it/.

[10] https://telegram.me/opendataleccebot (https://www.piersoft.it/i-miei-bots-telegram/).

[11] http://www.bpmn.io.

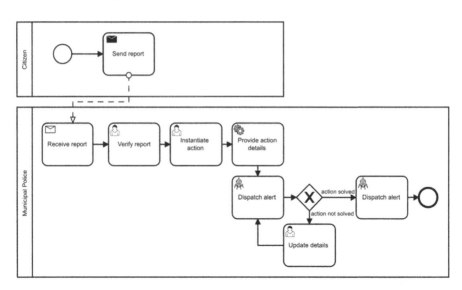

Fig. 6. Citizen-report management process by the municipal police.

4   A Semantic Framework to Public Service UI Design

The proposed framework adopts the typical approach of *service design* [15], an approach to design according to the needs of customers or participants, so that the service is user-friendly (for participants), competitive (for organizations) and generates a quality experience for both parties involved allowing to achieve the desired goal.

In the PA context it is important to focus on the citizens' needs: it means to investigate, through user research activities (such as web analytics or interviews and focus groups), how the user uses the system, and to ensure that all features are designed around her needs and mind models, allowing her to get easily and quickly what she requires, also by means of new technologies, without unnecessary steps and with understandable instructions. Through a multidisciplinary approach, services must be designed around the citizens' needs and not on the basis of the requirements of the organization that provide them. This affects the semantic constructs to be used, the graphic design and the implementation on the different devices.

We are creating a tool that supports the design of the public user interfaces of a service through a semantic annotation of the service management processes, the graphical constructs adopted and the intended users. By involving domain experts, technicians, PA employees and end users, the semantic annotation is performed according to the three layers of the KMS [2], i.e. real world data provided by IoT/IoE resources, domain knowledge embedded in the business processes and user needs to be satisfied by the final application.

The framework is composed of three main elements (see the top layer of Fig. 7):

1) the *Semantic Annotator tool*. It provides a BPM modeler, extended to visualize the IoT or IoE based process that manages the resulting service; an *Annotator* that

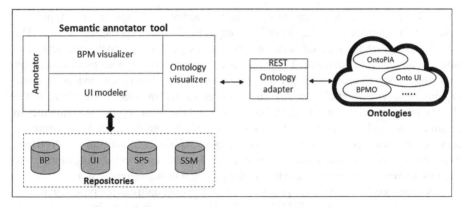

Fig. 7. High level overview of the semantic framework.

enables the annotation of the process by means of the concepts available through
the *Ontology Visualizer*; a *UI modeler*, based on open source Rdf forms library[12],
that creates RDF descriptions of public service user interface.

2) the shared *Ontologies* (e.g., Ontopia, BPM, domain), which contain the concepts
to be used into the service annotation activity performed by means of the Semantic
Annotator tool.

3) the *Ontology Adapter*, which allows the Semantic Annotator tool to access via REST
services the Ontologies.

The data layer consists of four *Repositories*. The *Business Process (BP)* repository
stores metadata and references to BP models that manage services; the *UI template
(UI)* repository includes the specifications of UI patterns; the *Semantic Public Service
(SPS)* repository stores service metadata descriptions, the included BP and UI components references and semantic annotation model references; the *Semantic Service Model
(SSM)* repository stores service semantic annotation models defined with the Semantic
annotator tool.

The framework enables the semantic annotation of a UI-Process-IoE triad and the
definition of public service metadata, which will be used for software development by
programmers. The Onto adapter facilitates the introduction of new ontologies, thus to
guarantee extensibility over time.

The framework generates a semantic annotation model and a RDF description of
Public service UI, that can be browsed, shared, or reused by other PAs, in order to reduce
UI-design time, and consequently development time, according to the code sharing and
reusing objective of the Open Government approach.

5 Future Work

In this paper, we presented a framework to support the design of user interfaces of a public
administration service. Such services use increasingly pervasive technologies such as

---

[12] http://www.rdforms.org.

IoT and IoE and are characterized by a multi-stakeholder design process, typical of Smart City initiatives, involving technical experts, PA domain experts, and citizens. The processes that manage such services are new or redesigned to include the interactions of non-human elements such as IoT or bots; for this reason, an extended process modeler tool with BPMn extensions for IoT and Telegram bots has been presented. A semantic tagging of service interfaces and business processes that manage it will allow, in the development phase, to identify the UI constructs and the most appropriate semantics in relation to the end user, to use a semantics shared throughout the entire PA community, and a correlation between interfaces and processes within the organization. Moreover, semantically annotated interface models can facilitate the reuse and sharing of the same models within the community, exploiting the potential of the semantic web.

As future work, we are in the process of assessing the quality of the proposed framework. We are working with an ENAC accredited European laboratory for software product certification based on ISO 25010 standards. A qualitative and quantitative analysis has been defined, which can respond to two hypotheses: do the notation and process patterns introduced improve the usability in use, i.e. the user's understanding of the model both in terms of aesthetic layout and model interpretation time? Do the introduced patterns improve the quality of the model, in terms of comprehensibility, modularity? A study will be defined to investigate the understanding of the process model and the patterns by the end users, i.e. the technical experts who model the processes. For this reason, participants will be recruited among the employees of an IT company, who are the final recipients of what has been achieved with this research work.

Acknowledgments. This work is funded by Italian Ministry of Education, University and Research (MIUR) through **PON Ricerca e Innovazione 2014–2020** - Asse I "Investimenti in capitale umano" - Azione I.1 "Dottorati Innovativi con caratterizzazione industriale" (CUP H92H18000210006 and H92H18000200006 approved with D.R.n.991 on 29/03/2018 of University of Bari Aldo Moro).

References

1. Object Management Group: Business process model and notation (BPMN) version 2.0 (January 2011)
2. Ardito, C., Caivano, D., Colizzi, L., Verardi, L.: Towards a model to address the interplay between IoT applications and users in complex heterogeneous contexts. In: Bogdan, C., Kuusinen, K., Lárusdóttir, M.K., Palanque, P., Winckler, M. (eds.) HCSE 2018. LNCS, vol. 11262, pp. 283–293. Springer, Cham (2019). https://doi.org/10.1007/978-3-030-05909-5_17
3. Zeng, D., Guo, S., Cheng, Z.: The web of things: a survey. J. Commun. **6**, 424–438 (2011)
4. Appel, S., Kleber, P., Frischbier, S., Freudenreich, T., Buchmann, A.: Modeling and execution of event stream processing in business processes. Inf. Syst. **46**, 140–156 (2014)
5. Chang, C., Srirama, S., Buyya, R.: Mobile cloud business process management system for the Internet of Things: a survey. ACM Comput. Surv. **49**, 1–42 (2016). https://doi.org/10.1145/3012000
6. Chiu, H.-H., Wang, M.-S.: A study of IoT-aware business process modeling. Int. J. Model. Optim. **3**, 238–244 (2013). https://doi.org/10.7763/IJMO.2013.V3.274

7. Meyer, S., Ruppen, A., Magerkurth, C.: Internet of Things-aware process modeling: integrating IoT devices as business process resources. In: Salinesi, C., Norrie, M.C., Pastor, Ó. (eds.) CAiSE 2013. LNCS, vol. 7908, pp. 84–98. Springer, Heidelberg (2013). https://doi.org/10.1007/978-3-642-38709-8_6

8. Meyer, S., Ruppen, A., Hilty, L.: The things of the Internet of Things in BPMN. In: Persson, A., Stirna, J. (eds.) CAiSE 2015. LNBIP, vol. 215, pp. 285–297. Springer, Cham (2015). https://doi.org/10.1007/978-3-319-19243-7_27

9. Yous, A., de Freitas, A., Dey, A.K., Saidi, R.: The use of ubiquitous computing for business process improvement. IEEE Trans. Serv. Comput. **9**(4), 621–632 (2015)

10. Bauer, M., et al.: Internet of Things – architecture IoT-A deliverable D1.5 – final architectural reference model for the IoT v3.0 (2013)

11. Brambilla, M., Fraternali, P., Vaca, C.: BPMN and design patterns for engineering social BPM solutions. In: Daniel, F., Barkaoui, K., Dustdar, S. (eds.) BPM 2011. LNBIP, vol. 99, pp. 219–230. Springer, Heidelberg (2012). https://doi.org/10.1007/978-3-642-28108-2_22

12. Szilagyi, I., Wira, P.: Ontologies and semantic web for the Internet of Things - a survey. In: Conference of the IEEE Industrial Electronics Society (IECON 2016), pp. 6949–6954 (2016)

13. Stroppi, L.J.R., Chiotti, O., Villarreal, P.D.: Extending BPMN 2.0: method and tool support. In: Dijkman, R., Hofstetter, J., Koehler, J. (eds.) BPMN 2011. LNBIP, vol. 95, pp. 59–73. Springer, Heidelberg (2011). https://doi.org/10.1007/978-3-642-25160-3_5

14. https://github.com/piersoft

15. Stickdorn, M., Schneider, J.: This is Service Design Thinking: Basics, Tools, Cases. Wiley, Hoboken (2011). ISBN:9781118156308

Software Development Strategies

Identifying the Mood of a Software Development Team by Analyzing Text-Based Communication in Chats with Machine Learning

Jil Klünder$^{(\boxtimes)}$ (ID), Julian Horstmann, and Oliver Karras (ID)

Software Engineering Group, Leibniz University Hannover, Hannover, Germany
{jil.kluender,oliver.karras}@inf.uni-hannover.de
julian.horstmann@se.uni-hannover.de

Abstract. Software development encompasses many collaborative tasks in which usually several persons are involved. Close collaboration and the synchronization of different members of the development team require effective communication. One established communication channel are meetings which are, however, often not as effective as expected. Several approaches already focused on the analysis of meetings to determine the reasons for inefficiency and dissatisfying meeting outcomes. In addition to meetings, text-based communication channels such as chats and e-mails are frequently used in development teams. Communication via these channels requires a similar appropriate behavior as in meetings to achieve a satisfying and expedient collaboration. However, these channels have not yet been extensively examined in research.

In this paper, we present an approach for analyzing interpersonal behavior in text-based communication concerning the conversational tone, the familiarity of sender and receiver, the sender's emotionality, and the appropriateness of the used language. We evaluate our approach in an industrial case study based on 1947 messages sent in a group chat in Zulip over 5.5 months. Using our approach, it was possible to automatically classify written sentences as positive, neutral, or negative with an average accuracy of 62.97% compared to human ratings. Despite this coarse-grained classification, it is possible to gain an overall picture of the adequacy of the textual communication and tendencies in the group mood.

Keywords: Communication · Development teams · Software projects · Human aspects · Interpersonal behavior

1 Introduction

Due to the increasing complexity of software, most software projects require some kind of teamwork [17]. Having a team working on a project requires coordination

© IFIP International Federation for Information Processing 2020
Published by Springer Nature Switzerland AG 2020
R. Bernhaupt et al. (Eds.): HCSE 2020, LNCS 12481, pp. 133–151, 2020.
https://doi.org/10.1007/978-3-030-64266-2_8

and an adequate collaboration [6,17], for example, appropriate requirements communication between the development team and the customer. To succeed with the project, the team and the customer must share the same vision [4]. Otherwise, the team cannot develop a software satisfying the customer [2].

An adequate collaboration requires knowledge and information sharing to have a successful project closure [21,24]. Lost or insufficiently shared information can cause – in the worst case – project failure, e.g., due to missing functionality of the final software product. Mitigating this risk requires a sufficient amount of communication during the whole development process [21]. This communication can take place, e.g., in meetings, via e-mail, or during phone calls [16].

As meetings enable team members to share a lot of information with many team members in a short time, they are an established medium in the development process [23,26]. However, inappropriate behavior and interactions in meetings decrease the success of a meeting and the participants' satisfaction afterwards [24,26]. This, in turn, has an influence on the project and the collaboration. To avoid inappropriate behavior in meetings, interaction analyses are an established medium in psychology [13,19] and gain increasing attention in software engineering [15,24,26].

In addition to the increasing complexity of software projects, the share of globally distributed projects is high [18] and complicates a close collaboration [27,31]. In case of regionally or globally distributed projects, it is difficult to have meetings regularly [23]. Virtual meetings are a possibility, which is, however, influenced by the requirements for technical equipment (including bandwidth) and difficulties caused by different time zones. Therefore, indirect communication using digital communication channels such as e-mails or instant messenger is widely used in software projects [16].

Problem Statement. According to Schneider et al. [26] and Kauffeld et al. [14], a single person participating in a meeting can influence the mood of all other participants – both positively or negatively. This, in turn, influences the developers' productivity [8] and has several other consequences for the project [7]. Therefore, interaction analyses in meetings take into account the amount of positive, i.e., good and appropriate, as well as negative, i.e., bad and inappropriate, behavior during the meetings [13,15]. Since the frequency and duration of meetings tend to decrease with project progress, whereas the use of other communication channels increases [16], likely, the communication behavior in text messages can also influence team satisfaction and, thus, motivation and project progress.

Objective. In this paper, *we want to analyze text-based communication, for example in e-mails or chats, in development teams with respect to its emotionality to detect development phases where the group mood is rather negative.* The emotionality of text-based communication is for example affected by the language used, the frequency, the length of the messages, the formality of the communication, the use of emoticons, and the time until the receiver replies to the message. In particular, we want to answer the following research question:

Research Question 1

How can text-based communication in development teams be holistically analyzed to derive information on the mood in the team?

Contribution. We present the current state of our approach classifying written messages as *positive*, *negative*, or *neutral* based on the sensitivity and the formality of the used words. We evaluate the approach in a case study in industry based on 1947 messages in a group chat. The results show that our tool classifies single sentences as *positive*, *negative*, or *neutral* with an average accuracy of 62.97%. When refining the analysis techniques it is possible to increase this number of correctly identified sentences either to shed light on the overall mood transported in messages or to analyze the mood in the development team based on the messages to allow interventions in case of a very dissatisfied team.

Outline. The rest of the paper is structured as follows: In Sect. 2, we present related work. Section 3 summarizes the concept and the approach followed in this paper. We evaluate the approach in Sect. 4 and present the results of the application in industry in Sect. 5 which we discuss in Sect. 6. We conclude the paper in Sect. 7.

2   Related Work

Analyzing communication behavior is not new in the area of Software Engineering. McChesney and Gallagher [22] analyze both communication and coordination in software projects. Herbsleb and Mockus [9] analyze differences in communication behavior of distributed and co-located teams. Klünder et al. [16] analyze team meetings, their frequency and duration over time in software projects. On a more fine-grained level, Schneider et al. [26] analyze interactions in team meetings of development teams. All these analyses require manual effort.

However, there are some approaches to support the analysis of communication of development teams by tools. Most existing approaches focus on meetings. Gall and Berenbach [5] present a framework to record elicitation meetings and automatically save information given by stakeholders. Shakeri et al. [1] also support the analysis of elicitation meetings. Their tool automatically collects knowledge that is important to understand the requirements. This approach is mainly based on written documentation and allows a content-related analysis. However, it has not yet been applied to written communication in text messages of development teams.

Sentiment analysis, i.e., the analysis of textual language aiming at identifying the author's mood, is also not new. Jongeling et al. [11] compare different tools for sentiment analysis in the Software Engineering domain and compare the tools' results to human evaluators. According to their results, different tools can produce contradictory results. Islam and Zibran [10] also analyze and compare the results of different tools used for sentiment analysis to understand their low accuracy. They present an improved version of one of the tools adjusted to development teams. The inaccuracy of tools can be partially explained by training the used classifiers on data sets which are not related to the Software Engineering domain and hence do not consider domain-typical language and knowledge. Lin et al. [20] trained an already existing tool for sentiment analysis using 40000 manually labeled sentences or words from Stack Overflow. Calefato et al. [3] present Senti4SD which is a classifier adjusted to development teams. The classifier was trained using communication of developers on Stack Overflow. Jurado and Rodriguez [12] analyze text in issues and tickets with sentiment analysis to extend the possibilities to investigate the development process.

In this paper, we use sentiment analysis to analyze text-based communication of developers on team level, which has, to the best of our knowledge, not been done before.

3   General Research Approach

To achieve our research goal, we combine sentiment analysis with natural language processing and machine learning to classify text-based communication. We developed an approach to classify text-based communication as *positive, neutral* or *negative* considering the emotion transported in the message. In the following, we give an overview of the process presented in Fig. 1. An exemplary application of our approach is presented in Sect. 4.

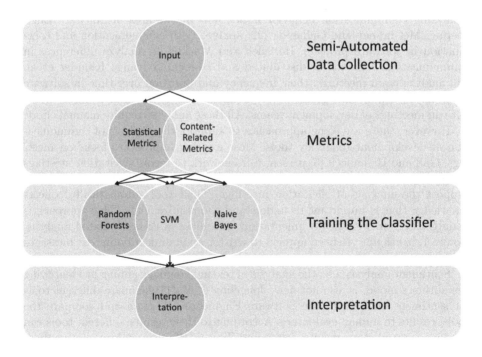

Fig. 1. Overview of the process to classify messages

Our approach consists of the four steps summarized in Fig. 1. It starts with a semi-automated data collection by crawling the respective communication channel. Afterwards, different metrics are calculated for the text messages to extract relevant characteristics of the messages to allow conclusions regarding the emotionality of the communication. These metrics are used by a trained classifier to assign one of the classes *positive, neutral,* or *negative* to each of the sentences. This classification allows an evaluation and interpretation of the whole communication, e.g., on a daily basis.

3.1   Step 1: Data Collection

Text-based communication can be found in different sources, including mailing lists, instant messengers such as Slack[1], Skype[2], or Zulip[3], and in e-mails. To analyze the communication on group level, it is most suitable to use some kind of group chat or mailing lists several team members have access to and use it to discuss team-internal project-related issues. However, the process is applicable to any kind of text-based communication, including bi-directional information exchange[4].

The semi-automated data collection strongly depends on the communication channel under consideration. Exporting text messages in Skype differs from a data export in e-mails. At the moment, our approach supports the semi-automated data collection for Zulip, which will be described in more detail in Sect. 4 as part of the application in industry.

3.2   Step 2: Metrics

Metrics are required to extract relevant characteristics of text-based communication. The identification of relevant metrics is difficult as natural language is not unique and can be interpreted in completely different ways [30]. Depending on the actual goal of the communication analysis, one may choose different metrics. In the following, we present some exemplary metrics and the rationale of why we consider them useful for emotional analysis of text-based communication.

Statistical metrics analyze the text messages from a quantitative viewpoint, for example by calculating the *length of each message* or the *average length of the used words*. The length of the words and the message allow conclusions for the formality of the communication. Consider the following situation:

---

[1] https://slack.com/.

[2] https://www.skype.com/.

[3] https://zulipchat.com/.

[4] Note that the analysis of bi-directional communication is questionable due to privacy concerns and personal messages in private chats.

> **Example**
>
> Paul has a problem and writes a message with 100 words in the group chat. In his text, he explains the problem in detail so that everybody who reads the message has a clear idea of what information he needs to solve the problem. In the end, he proposes a very time-consuming alternative if he does not get the required information. And the only answer he receives comes from Anton: "sounds good".

This huge difference in the length of the messages allows several conclusions. First, it raises the impression that nobody but Anton cares about Paul's problem. Second, as Anton's reaction is short, he may not even have read the whole text, or is at least not interested in supporting Paul. Of course, one can also interpret the short message differently. But this is one scenario, where a short message can lead to demotivation and team-internal problems. And it is not clear how Paul interprets this answer.

Besides the lengths of messages and words, counting adjectives, emoticons and the number of punctuation characters is also useful. The use of emoticons indicates familiarity in the team. In formal communication, emoticons will only be partially used, if at all. The number of punctuation characters is difficult to interpret. On the one hand, the use of commas and the like imply a formal message, but it can also indicate a huge amount of emoticons such as ":-)". Nonetheless, in conjunction with a detection of smileys using punctuation characters can help to analyze the formality of the message.

Content-Related Metrics. The statistical metrics do not allow conclusions on the emotionality of the messages which is the main topic of this paper. Therefore, the content of text-based communication has also to be taken into account. To analyze the communication on content-level, profound knowledge on a typical structure of the language, the so-called *part of speech*, is necessary. Using natural language processing, it is possible to analyze words in relation to their position in the sentence. This allows considering not only the word A itself but also other words that may influence the interpretation of the word A.

Emoticons also raise feelings, which may differ among the receiver of a message [29]. Wang and Castanon [29] investigated the use of emoticons and the intention of the use. According to their results, it is not always possible to assign exactly one of the classes *positive, neutral*, or *negative* to the emoticon [29]. Therefore, they present a list of emoticons together with a probability that the emoticon belongs to the respective class. For example, the emoticon ":D" is interpreted positively with a probability of 90%. In the approach presented in this paper, we assign the class with the highest probability to the respective emoticon. However, at the moment, we do not consider neutral emoticons. This will be part of future research.

Comparable to the feelings raised when seeing emoticons, words also have some kind of emotional shade. To identify the emotional shade of the words, we used two databases[5] summarizing words and their emotionality [25,28]. The database provided by Waltinger [28] assigns each word to one of the classes *positive (+1)*, *neutral (0)*, or *negative (−1)*, whereas Remus et al.'s [25] database assigns a value ranging from *−1 (negative)* to *1 (positive)* to each word. We use both databases to increase the number of words and to aggregate the results. Examples from the first database can be found in Table 1. If possible (i.e., if the word is also contained in the second database), we present the concrete value in brackets.

Table 1. Examples for the emotional shades [28]. The number in brackets, if available, represent the score [25].

Positive	Neutral	Negative
Agree (0.0040)	Objectively	Arbitrary (−0.3481)
Convinced (0.2381)	Fully	Confused
Innovation (0.0040)	Thought	Deficient (−0.4535)
Non-violence	Argumentation	Autocrat

In addition, we use the *CountVectorizer* and the *TF-IDF Vectorizer* to analyze the relevance of words. For example, the *TF-IDF Vectorizer* calculates the term frequency of the word in the message (TF) and the inverse document frequency (IDF) considering all messages. This helps to detect relevant words which only appear a few times in the text.

We also take the *formality* of the language into account. However, the detection of formality is language-specific (e.g., in Spanish and German (and other languages) there are specific forms to address someone formally).

3.3   Step 3: Training the Classifier

In the next step, we train the classifier to achieve good classification results. We use machine learning techniques to train the classifier, including *Random Forests*, a *Support Vector Machine*, and *Naive Bayes*. To increase the accuracy of our model, we combine the results of the three methods using a *Voting Classifier* choosing the class for a sentence that was forecasted by the majority of the three approaches.

A *Random Forest* starts with randomly creating decision trees. Each of the trees classifies the sentence. In the end, the algorithm chooses the class that is most often chosen by the trees. An schematic visualization is presented in Fig. 2.

A *Support Vector Machine* separates the multi-dimensional feature space. Consider the 2-dimensional example in Fig. 3. The gray dots represent data points, i.e., messages, labeled as *neutral*, and the black dots represent data

---

[5] Note that both databases are based on the German language as we performed our application in industry (see Sect. 4) in a German-speaking company.

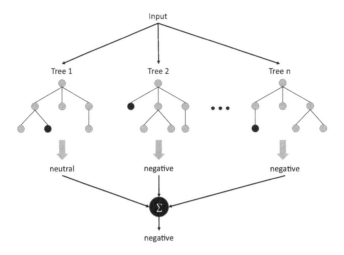

Fig. 2. Schematic Visualization of the Random Forest

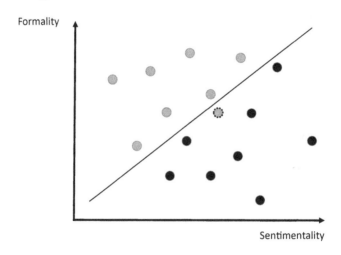

Fig. 3. Example for a two-dimensional classification by a Support Vector Machine

points classified as *negative*. The Support Vector Machine separates this two-dimensional space using a linear function. Therefore, the gray dot circled with black dots would be classified as negative even if the sentence is neutral.

The *Naive Bayes Classifier* uses probability functions indicating whether a data point in the feature space belongs to a specific class or not. As the density functions of the probability are unknown, this procedure allows only for an approximation.

As all of the three approaches have their strengths and weaknesses, we decide to combine their results using a *voting classifier*. This classifier identifies the class which was chosen by the majority of the approaches. This way, the approach is more robust against outliers and we can reduce the influence of noise in the data.

The training of the classifier can be done by dividing the data set into training and test data. The training data is then used to derive heuristics indicating that a specific type of sentence belongs to a specific class (i.e., to train the classifier) and the test data is used to check the accuracy of the classifier.

To optimize the forecast, we use an evolutionary algorithm. This algorithm uses a fitness function representing the goodness of the current solution, i.e., the classifier. In our case, the goodness is defined via the average accuracy of the classification. We repeat the learning process 20 times with different test and training sets (in a ratio of 10:90). This allows cross-validation of the classifier.

3.4 Step 4: Interpretation of the Results

The interpretation of the results is mainly part of future work. However, to summarize and visualize the emotionality of messages over time, we map the three classes *positive, neutral,* and *negative* to the integer values *+1, 0,* and *−1*. This allows to calculate mean values, for example of all messages sent on a specific day, and analyses over time.

4 Application in Industry

To show the applicability of our approach, we apply it to an industrial software project. Figure 4 shows the four steps of our general research process with its concrete instantiation in the case study which required a step for the data preprocessing. In the following, we present our proceeding when applying the approach in detail.

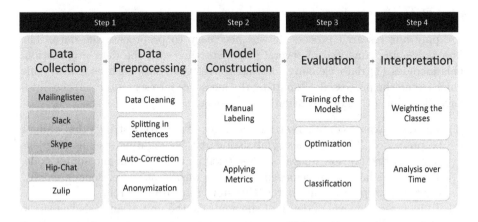

Fig. 4. Overview of the application in industry

4.1 Data Collection

We evaluated our approach in industry. However, due to privacy concerns, we cannot provide profound information on the company. We call the company *ZETA*. *ZETA* is specialized on software and consulting. There is one in-house software development team called *Team MY*. Before running the case study in the company, each team member of *Team MY* received a transparency letter describing the overall concept of our approach as well as a detailed description of the data analysis of communication data of the whole team. After a reflection period of two weeks to communicate concerns, ideas, or disagreement, we were allowed to start the case study since none of the team members disagreed.

In total, about 80 developers worked on the software project we use to prove the applicability of our approach in industry. These developers work distributed in one country. The main communication tool in the software project is *Zulip* which is a chat tool for teams[6]. The users subscribe to so-called *streams*. Each stream has a *topic* that organizes conversations in the stream. This helps to cluster messages also after hours of silence on a respective topic. The user can decide on his access to the streams. This reduces the risk of information overload with irrelevant information. Besides Zulip, the team also uses (if possible) face-to-face communication and meetings, as well as phone calls, e-mails, and a chat tool. However, Zulip is the official tool that should be used for communication.

The company granted us access to five streams of *Team MY* which were exported using the REST-API for further processing. We exported all messages that have been written between Feb 11, 2019 and Jul, 24 2019, resulting in 1947 messages consisting of 7070 sentences. In total, 65 developers actively participated in the communication in at least one of the five streams. Note that we consider a person to actively participate if and only if she wrote at least one message.

4.2 Data Processing

To apply our research process, it was necessary to preprocess the data. The data processing consisted of several steps, starting with the data preparation. This includes (1) data cleaning to remove irrelevant data such as source code which cannot be processed, (2) cutting the messages into sentences, (3) the auto-correction, and (4) anonymization of the messages.

(1) The data export contains several messages respectively strings that cannot be processed. This includes symbols for text highlighting such as asterisks (for bold text) or low lines (for italic text) as well as links and source code. These parts have to be removed. This step was, in our case, done manually. However, we plan to automatize this step in future research.

(2) To increase the level of detail of the analysis, the unit of analysis is a single sentence. Therefore, messages which consist of more than one sentence have to be split into single sentences. As start and end of a sentence cannot

---

[6] More information on Zulip can be found at https://zulipchat.com/.

always be derived by the punctuation, we use the Python package *spacy*. This package identifies sentences based on the structure of the language (and not solely on the punctuation). However, as *spacy* does not have an accuracy of 100%, we manually checked the results.

(3) Most metrics require the correct spelling of words. Otherwise, words may be identified as a different word mitigating the correctness of the classification. Therefore, we used the Python package *pyspellchecker* providing corrections for misspelled words.

(4) During the anonymization phase, we manually replaced all names and addresses (including links) by pseudonyms. This step was done by one author of this paper. Due to privacy concerns, only one researcher was allowed to process the raw data. Limitations caused by this fact will be discussed in Sect. 6.

4.3   Training the Model

In the next step, we trained the model to evaluate the accuracy of the classifier. The training consisted of two steps: (1) Labeling of existing sentences, and (2) training the classifier.

(1) We manually labeled the data by assigning one of the three classes *positive, neutral,* and *negative* to each of the sentences. Examples for words belonging to the respective class are presented in Table 2. The division in three classes is rather coarse-grained. Future research will focus on increasing the granularity of the results. Due to the privacy concerns of the company, this step was done by one researcher. Limitations caused by this fact will be discussed in Sect. 6.

(2) In the training phase, the metrics presented in Sect. 3.2 are calculated for each of the sentences. We calculated in total 5378 different metrics, mostly considering language-specific characteristics[7]. We chose this huge number of metrics as each metric which is not correlated to other metrics can increase the accuracy of the classifier. To analyze the correlation between the metrics, we calculated the correlation matrix (based on Pearson's r) for this specific data set.

4.4   Evaluating the Model

We evaluate the model by applying the classifier to some exemplary sentences of our data set. We chose a ratio of 10% for the test data set and use the remaining 90% of the data set to train the model. The selection of the concrete test data was random. The learning process of the model is based on an evolutionary algorithm which identifies the best fitting model. In our case, we achieved the best model after 80 steps. The accuracy of the model is defined by the confusion matrix summarizing the results of the classification (comparison between forecast and as-is) as well as different key indicators such as precision, recall, and F1-score.

---

[7] As the number of metrics is quite high, future research should focus on the selection of appropriate metrics.

Table 2. Exemplary emotions or types of words for each class

Positive	Neutral	Negative
Love	Facts	Fear
Happiness	Ambivalence	Hate
Euphoria	Interest	Anger
Surprise	Indifference	Trouble
Sympathy	Apathy	Regret

4.5   Interpretation of the Results

To visualize the results, we present the development of the average emotional score of the messages over time. We assign values to each of the classes, namely *positive = +1*, *neutral = 0*, and *negative = −1*. This way, it is possible to calculate the average score per day, which we call the *emotionality score*. Observing this score over time can help to detect stressful phases. However, the interpretation of the emotionality score remains future work.

5   Results

We performed the steps described in Sect. 4. The manual data labeling resulted in 845 sentences classified as *positive*, 1856 sentences classified as *neutral*, and 1077 sentences classified as *negative*. This imbalance of data points can influence the classifier's accuracy as there are more negative sentences to train the classifier than positive. However, it is unlikely to find completely balanced data in industry. Future research should, hence, focus on training the model with huge data sets containing balanced data.

In a next step, we calculated the correlation matrix of the metrics presented in Fig. 5. Most of the metrics are only partially or not at all correlated. However, the metrics for the emotions (emoji_mean, emoji_min, and emoji_max) are highly correlated. In addition, we find a weak correlation between the need for corrections (AutoCorrectionRatio) and the formality of the communication (formality).

Table 3. Confusion matrix of the classifier for the test set

	positive	neutral	negative
positive	36	46	7
neutral	10	173	11
negative	2	64	29

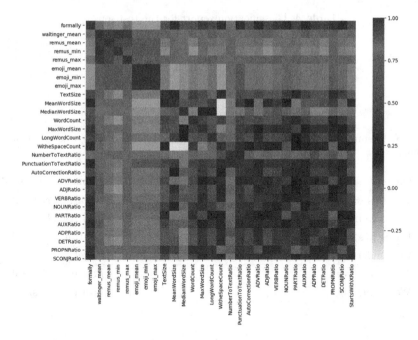

Fig. 5. Correlation matrix including 28 metrics

As described above, we trained the model using the labeled data set. The classifier assigned one of the classes *positive, neutral,* and *negative* to the sentence under consideration. The evolutionary algorithm used to train the model achieved, in his best generation, an average accuracy of 58.5%. We chose the best model from this generation which achieved an average accuracy of 62.97%. To calculate the accuracy of our model, we applied an amount of randomly chosen 10% of the data set as test data to the model trained by the remaining 90% of the data set as training data. The results of the classification are presented in Table 3 as a confusion matrix. We see only 9 out of 378 confused classifications of positive and negative, i.e., it was most difficult to distinguish between positive and neutral (56 out of 378 confusions) respectively between negative and neutral (75 out of 378). Based on these numbers, it is possible to calculate other key indicators summarized in Table 4. In total, the class *positive* has the highest precision, whereas the F1-Score is best for the neutral class. Examples for a few classifications are presented in Table 5 presenting the manual classification by a person and the predicted classification by the model.

At this point, we have evaluated the classifier leading to an accuracy of 62.97%. In the last step, we want to outline how the classification (either from a person or from the classifier) can be used to analyze emotions in the team. Presenting the shade of the emotions on a scale from −1 to 1 as described in Sect. 3.4 leads to the curve presented in Fig. 6. Note that we use the manually labeled data. However, this step can also be done using the results of the classifier

Table 4. Classification report for the test set

Class	Precision	Recall	F1-Score	Frequency
Positive	0.75	0.40	0.53	89
Neutral	0.61	0.89	0.73	194
Negative	0.62	0.31	0.41	95

Table 5. Exemplary sentences and predictions from a human rater and the trained classifier

Id	Content	Human	Classifier
1	Yes, this was my mistake	Negative	Neutral
2	Welcome in [[countryname]] :-) good decision	Positive	Positive
3	If this was not your mistake, it has to be fixed as follows:	Neutral	Neutral
4	Had understood you differently this morning	Negative	Neutral
5	Then we agree	Positive	Neutral
6	Well done!	Positive	Positive

(see Fig. 7). To derive the results in Fig. 6, we first calculate the average emotional score of the labeled data on a daily level. As evident from Fig. 6, the mood is on average rather neutral. However, it ranges from positive to negative and vice versa. When presenting the results to the company, we figured out that the negative phases coincide with stressful phases in the project, e.g., due to deadlines. Comparing the trendline in Fig. 6 with the trendline in Fig. 7 based on the forecasted data shows very similar tendencies.

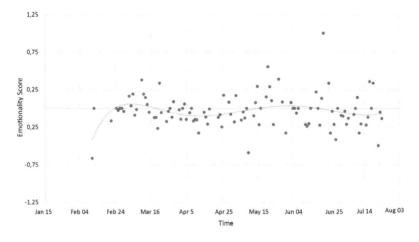

Fig. 6. Emotional niveau using the manually labeled data. The dotted curve presents the trendline.

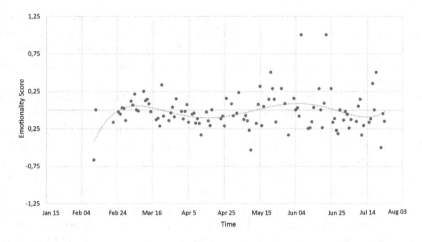

Fig. 7. Emotional niveau using the forecasted data. The dotted curve presents the trendline.

6   Discussion

In the application in industry, we analyzed text-based communication consisting of 1947 messages in a chat tool used by a development team in industry. We used several metrics ranging from the emotional shade of single words over the length of a sentence to the formality of the language. We combined three machine learning algorithms to classify each of the messages as *positive, neutral,* or *negative.*

Our approach achieved an accuracy of 62.97% which allows for improvement. However, the trained classifier was almost as good as a human rater who achieved an accuracy of 66% when coding 200 sentences twice with a temporal distance of one month.

We used the classification to aggregate the team mood on a daily level by calculating the average emotionality of all messages sent on a specific day. When interpreting the course of emotionality over time, we see an average neutral mood, with some tendencies towards positive as well as negative mood. However, one would expect to find such a rather balanced course in a professional work environment. Further possibilities to interpret the results will be subject to future research.

6.1   Threats to Validity

Our application in industry is subject to some threats to validity which we discuss now.

The *conclusion validity* is threatened by the choice of the data source. For example, communication in e-mails will differ from communication in group chats. We are aware that adjustments to the procedure are required, as the data collection and extraction strongly depends on the data source. To provide a holistic picture of the emotionality of the text-based communication in the team, we consider a huge set of metrics. To allow good learning of the model, we ensure that these metrics are only partially correlated and do not measure all the same characteristics of the communication.

Due to privacy concerns and legal restrictions from the company, only one author was allowed to handle the data. This threatens the *internal validity* since the data processing strongly depends on the subjective perception of one person. By following a structured proceeding, for example for the anonymization of the data, we tried to mitigate this threat. However, there was no possibility to review the labeling process. Therefore, the person who labeled the data labeled a randomly chosen set of 200 sentences a second time with a distance of one month. In 2 of 3 cases, the labels coincided, leading to an accuracy of 66%. This raises several questions and possibilities for future research which will be discussed in Sect. 6.3. However, the manual reference classification of the data influences the results as this defines whether the classification by the tool is correct or not.

The *construct validity* may be threatened due to the mono-operation and the mono-method bias. As we are aware of this fact, we do not draw any conclusions based on our results. We only see them as promising support to continue the development of the approach. Further studies in different settings are required to mitigate this threat.

The *external validity* of our results is very limited. The concrete results of our analysis are correct for the team under consideration, and only reflect the time frame of our analysis. However, we do not want to draw conclusions or to generalize our results for other teams. The main objective of the application to an industrial project is to prove the applicability of our approach. If this is the case, we only conclude that our approach is applicable, but the results obtained from the study cannot be transferred to any other team. How to draw conclusions based on the results will be subject to future work (see Sect. 6.3).

6.2 Answering the Research Question

With the approach presented in this paper and its application in industry, we were able to show that the analysis of text-based communication is possible using a combination of natural language processing, sentiment analysis, and machine learning. By aggregating the emotionality of the sentences, e.g., daily, it is possible to derive information on the general mood in the team as well as the development over time. However, there are some open questions and there is potential for improvement to be addressed in future work.

6.3 Future Research

Even if the results of our approach underline its potential, it might (and should) be improved to address some issues that could not have been considered in the paper at hand. These issues will be addressed in future research.

(1) One problem is the rather low accuracy of the algorithm. However, given the interrater agreement of a human rater of 66% when labeling the data twice with a temporal distance of one month, the classifier is almost as good as the human rater. This result is near to perfect as a trained model cannot perform better than the labeling allows. Consequently, to improve the accuracy of our algorithm, we first have to find possibilities to identify clear characteristics of the messages in the respective class. This finding goes along with the findings of other authors [11].

(2) The context of the single sentence is currently not considered. This should be improved in future research. Depending on the context of previous messages, an answer can be differently interpreted. Therefore, the emotionality of the sentences before also needs to be considered for the forecast and probably can also improve the classification.

(3) At the moment, we do not provide any guidance for the interpretation of the results. To gain insights based on the results, we calculate average emotionality scores and present them on a daily level. This can help to detect stressful phases or phases where the team needs support, for example by an external coach due to unsolved team-internal conflicts. However, as part of future research, it is required to apply our approach to huge data sets and investigate correlations to other factors (e.g., deadlines, conflicts, high workloads, and context factors).

(4) The usefulness of the tool for development teams is not yet proven. This is mainly because we do not provide guidance to interpret the results. As soon as we finished the research described in (3), we can evaluate the usefulness of the insights by presenting them to the team.

7   Conclusion

As text-based communication is widely distributed in software development, but often not adequate, we strive towards an automated analysis of text-based communication in different channels. Our approach analyzes interpersonal behavior in text-based communication concerning the emotional shade of the communication, considering the conversational tone, the familiarity of sender and receiver, and the appropriateness of the used language. We prove the applicability of our approach in an industrial case study, where we got access to 1947 messages in Zulip, consisting of 7070 sentences. The results of our application in industry show that it is possible to correctly classify statements with an average accuracy of 62.97% which is as good as the rating of a human classifier. In this paper, we only classified the statements as *positive*, *neutral*, or *negative*. In future work, we want to make the results more fine-grained and also consider other information contained in the data, such as emoticons. In addition, we want to support the interpretation of the results, which is not yet part of the approach.

References

1. Abad, Z.S.H., Gervasi, V., Zowghi, D., Barker, K.: Elica: an automated tool for dynamic extraction of requirements relevant information. In: Proceedings of the 5th International Workshop on Artificial Intelligence for Requirements Engineering. IEEE (2018)
2. Bjarnason, E., Wnuk, K., Regnell, B.: Requirements are slipping through the gaps– a case study on causes & effects of communication gaps in large-scale software development. In: 2011 IEEE 19th International Requirements Engineering Conference, pp. 37–46. IEEE (2011)
3. Calefato, F., Lanubile, F., Maiorano, F., Novielli, N.: Sentiment polarity detection for software development. Empirical Software Eng. 23(3), 1352–1382 (2018)
4. Fricker, Samuel A., Grau, Rainer, Zwingli, Adrian: Requirements engineering: best practice. In: Fricker, Samuel A., Thümmler, Christoph, Gavras, Anastasius (eds.) Requirements Engineering for Digital Health, pp. 25–46. Springer, Cham (2015). https://doi.org/10.1007/978-3-319-09798-5_2
5. Gall, M., Berenbach, B.: Towards a framework for real time requirements elicitation. In: Proceedings of the 1st International Workshop on Multimedia Requirements Engineering, p. 4. IEEE (2006)
6. Ghosh, T., Yates, J., Orlikowski, W.: Using communication norms for coordination: evidence from a distributed team. In: Proceedings of the 25th International Conference on Information Systems, p. 10 (2004)
7. Graziotin, D., Fagerholm, F., Wang, X., Abrahamsson, P.: Consequences of unhappiness while developing software. In: Proceedings of the 2nd International Workshop on Emotion Awareness in Software Engineering, pp. 42–47. IEEE Press (2017)
8. Graziotin, D., Wang, X., Abrahamsson, P.: Are happy developers more productive? In: Heidrich, J., Oivo, M., Jedlitschka, A., Baldassarre, M.T. (eds.) PROFES 2013. LNCS, vol. 7983, pp. 50–64. Springer, Heidelberg (2013). https://doi.org/10.1007/978-3-642-39259-7_7
9. Herbsleb, J.D., Mockus, A.: An empirical study of speed and communication in globally distributed software development. IEEE Trans. Software Eng. 29(6), 481–494 (2003)
10. Islam, M.R., Zibran, M.F.: Leveraging automated sentiment analysis in software engineering. In: 2017 IEEE/ACM 14th International Conference on Mining Software Repositories (MSR), pp. 203–214. IEEE (2017)
11. Jongeling, R., Datta, S., Serebrenik, A.: Choosing your weapons: on sentiment analysis tools for software engineering research. In: 2015 IEEE International Conference on Software Maintenance and Evolution (ICSME), pp. 531–535. IEEE (2015)
12. Jurado, F., Rodriguez, P.: Sentiment analysis in monitoring software development processes: an exploratory case study on github's project issues. J. Syst. Softw. 104, 82–89 (2015)
13. Kauffeld, S., Lehmann-Willenbrock, N.: Meetings matter: effects of team meetings on team and organizational success. Small Group Res. 43(2), 130–158 (2012)
14. Kauffeld, S., Meyers, R.A.: Complaint and solution-oriented circles: interaction patterns in work group discussions. Euro. J. Work Organizational Psychol. 18(3), 267–294 (2009)
15. Klünder, J., et al.: Do you just discuss or do you solve? meeting analysis in a software project at early stages. In: Proceedings of the 5th International Workshop on Emotion Awareness in Software Engineering. ACM (2020)

16. Klünder, J., Unger-Windeler, C., Kortum, F., Schneider, K.: Team meetings and their relevance for the software development process over time. In: Proceedings of the 43rd Euromicro Conference on Software Engineering and Advanced Applications, pp. 313–320. IEEE (2017)

17. Kraut, R.E., Streeter, L.A.: Coordination in software development. Commun. ACM **38**(3), 69–82 (1995)

18. Kuhrmann, M., Tell, P., Klünder, J., Hebig, R., Licorish, S.A., MacDonell, S.G.: Complementing materials for the helena study (stage 2). November 2018 https://doi.org/10.13140/RG.2.2.11032.65288

19. Lehmann-Willenbrock, N., Meyers, R.A., Kauffeld, S., Neininger, A., Henschel, A.: Verbal interaction sequences and group mood: exploring the role of team planning communication. Small Group Res. **42**(6), 639–668 (2011)

20. Lin, B., Zampetti, F., Bavota, G., Di Penta, M., Lanza, M., Oliveto, R.: Sentiment analysis for software engineering: How far can we go? In: Proceedings of the 40th International Conference on Software Engineering, pp. 94–104 (2018)

21. Marjaie, S., Rathod, U.: Communication in agile software projects: qualitative analysis using grounded theory in system dynamics. In: Proceedings of the International Conference of the System Dynamics Society (2011)

22. McChesney, I.R., Gallagher, S.: Communication and co-ordination practices in software engineering projects. Inf. Softw. Technol. **46**(7), 473–489 (2004)

23. Oshri, I., Kotlarsky, J., Willcocks, L.P.: Global software development: exploring socialization and face-to-face meetings in distributed strategic projects. J. Strategic Inf. Syst. **16**(1), 25–49 (2007)

24. Prenner, N., Klünder, J., Schneider, K.: Making meeting success measurable by participants' feedback. In: Proceedings of the 3rd International Workshop on Emotion Awareness in Software Engineering. ACM (2018)

25. Remus, R., Quasthoff, U., Heyer, G.: Sentiws-a publicly available german-language resource for sentiment analysis. In: LREC, Citeseer (2010)

26. Schneider, K., Klünder, J., Kortum, F., Handke, L., Straube, J., Kauffeld, S.: Positive affect through interactions in meetings: the role of proactive and supportive statements. J. Syst. Softw. **143**, 59–70 (2018)

27. Teasley, S., Covi, L., Krishnan, M.S., Olson, J.S.: How does radical collocation help a team succeed? In: Proceedings of the 2000 ACM Conference on Computer Supported Cooperative Work, pp. 339–346 (2000)

28. Waltinger, U.: Sentiment analysis reloaded-a comparative study on sentiment polarity identification combining machine learning and subjectivity features. In: WEBIST (1), pp. 203–210 (2010)

29. Wang, H., Castanon, J.A.: Sentiment expression via emoticons on social media. In: 2015 IEEE International Conference on Big Data (big data), pp. 2404–2408. IEEE (2015)

30. Watzlawick, P., Bavelas, J.B., Jackson, D.D.: Pragmatics of human communication: a study of interactional patterns, pathologies and paradoxes. WW Norton & Company (2011)

31. Zheng, J., Veinott, E., Bos, N., Olson, J.S., Olson, G.M.: Trust without touch: jumpstarting long-distance trust with initial social activities. In: Proceedings of the SIGCHI Conference on Human Factors in Computing Systems, pp. 141–146 (2002)

Towards Super User-Centred Continuous Delivery: A Case Study

Joakim Klemets[1,2(✉)] and Tore Christian Bjørsvik Storholmen[1]

[1] Department of Health Research, SINTEF Digital, Trondheim/Oslo, Norway
`tore.christian.storholmen@sintef.no`
[2] Department of Computer Science, Norwegian University of Science Technology (NTNU), Trondheim, Norway
`joakim.klemets@ntnu.no`

Abstract. To develop well designed socio-technical systems for a particular context user involvement is essential. Emerging software development approaches that enable continuous delivery of software functionalities provide new opportunities as to how users can be involved in shaping the design. We present a case study of a software project at a Norwegian engineering and construction company in their effort to move towards a user-centred development approach that leverages on continuous delivery principles. We investigate how user representatives in form of super users have been involved in the process and their role in forming and implementing new digital technology in practice. We conclude that utilising super users have been instrumental to design a system that meet users' needs. Providing opportunities to test the system in a production environment gave rise to new ideas on how to further refine the design. Involving super users also facilitated system adoption among workers.

Keywords: User-centred design · Continuous software engineering · Agile development · Super users · Qualitative research

1 Introduction

To remain competitive in a challenging market many companies seek to make work processes and procedures more effective through developing and introducing new digital tools. However, to utilise the new technology it needs to be adopted and be taken into use. From a socio-technical standpoint, developing and introducing new digital solutions is as much about forming new work practices and routines as designing the tool itself meant to support work [1]. Hence, in enhancing the possibility of the tool to be accepted into practice one should ensure that it aligns with organisational goals and values.

Scandinavia has a rich history of politically empowering workers to 'have a say' in shaping their own working environment [2]. The Scandinavian approach to participatory design has therefore emphasized principles that are today central in user-centred design approaches [3]. User involvement enhance user acceptance and ease system adoption

R. Bernhaupt et al. (Eds.): HCSE 2020, LNCS 12481, pp. 152–165, 2020.
https://doi.org/10.1007/978-3-030-64266-2_9

through generating more usable solutions [4, 5]. It has also been singled out as an important factor for project success [6–8]. Although user involvement has received limited attention in software engineering [9], there is a growing interest in looking to combine user-centred approaches with existing system development methodologies [6]. In Particularly agile approaches been singled out as a good fit with user-centred design.

While agile approaches are commonplace today, more and more companies are also moving towards continuous delivery, where new functionality is delivered to actual users frequently. To be able to release new functionality into production more rapidly, the development and operations (DevOps) teams collaborate tightly to automate parts of the delivery process. Whereas there are little empirical studies on DevOps implementations [10], there are even fewer looking at combining a continuous delivery with user-centred principles [11].

We report on a case study carried out at a large Norwegian engineering and construction services company that through a digitalisation strategy seek to transform its IT-development towards a DevOps and user-centred approach. The research objective is to investigate the transformation from a traditional and linear software engineering model towards an iterative and user-centric approach. Particularly, we zoom in on the end-user involvement and ask the following research questions: how are end-users involved in different phases of the process and what are the challenges? How do the end-users representant, or the super-user, role facilitate system improvement and implementation?

2 Background

2.1 User-Centred Design in Agile and Continuous Software Development

A number of scholars have discussed different perspectives on how to integrate agile and user-centred practices as a mean to produce more usable software [12–15]. From a process perspective [12], many scholars advocate having up-front design activities that seek to explore the problem space and possible design solutions before conducting any actual software development. To better adhere to the lean principles of agile practices, little design upfront is advocated [15], where whereas this phase often is more extensive in traditional user-centred design.

One approach to implement design up-front is through carrying out usability studies one iteration ahead of the development [12]. Kuusinen [16] argues that the approach, which usually separates developers and usability-experts into separate teams, prolongs the time to feedback, as well as risk wasting development resources on unusable functionality. Instead, she proposes a framework where cross-functional teams collaborate. First, through a short up-front exploration phase and later within the same iteration. And that feedback is collected continuously from end-users (Fig. 1).

Continuous involvement of stakeholders is another central user-centred agile software development principle that has received less attention in form of empirical studies [12]. Particularly, finding good ways to involve the end-user in the process is important [17]. However, user involvement in the development is complex, and whom to involve, when, and how is not straightforward [9, 18]. Whereas user involvement in the requirements phase has shown to be effective [8, 19, 20], studies also indicate positive effects

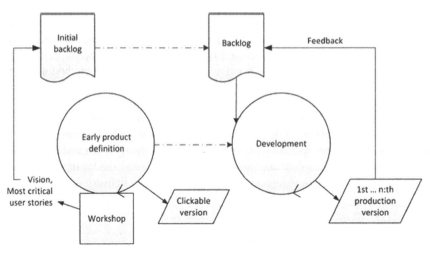

Fig. 1. The BoB framework [16].

of user involvement throughout the process [18, 21]. Doing so can, for example, enable users to feel greater ownership of the system [18] and, hence, enhance adoption.

Haake et al. [19] found that it is central that a large share of affected users are involved in the implementation phase, as failing to do so could have negative effect on project success. Bano et al. [18] reports that failing to identify motivated and positive user representatives also has negative effects. With regard to continuous software engineering (CSE), where new software functionality is realised frequently to the end-user [22, 23], data-driven approaches have been developed that automatically monitor system use and quantified user feedback [24]. However, Johanssen et al. [25] who inquired 17 companies adopting CSE, found that the companies also collected explicit (i.e. written or verbal) user feedback in addition to passively collecting user metrics. Yet, the feedback context was mostly neglected, which made it difficult to fully utilise the collected feedback [26].

2.2 Super Users and Design-in-Use

Whether it is super user, power user, or champion user, the role goes by many names.

Hansen and Anders [27] define super users as 'regular employees with in-depth knowledge of one or more of the organization's computer applications without being programmers'. Hence, skilled workers in their own field that also play a significant role as user representatives in system development, implementation, training, and support. To be successful in this role, the super user should be positive towards adopting new technology, good communicators and be patient teachers, as reported by McNeive [28].

The use of super users has also been studied within end-user development, where users are empowered to make own configurations to a system or through the close collaboration with developers and IT-professionals [27, 29, 30]. End-user development or design-in-use has been suggested as an alternative to traditional system implementation, which takes place once the design is finished. The design-in-use approach acknowledges the idea that implementation is context-dependant and tightly coupled with work practices and processes. Hence, once a minimal viable version of the system is ready to be deployed, end-users continue the design of both the system and associated practices [29, 30].

3 Methods

3.1 Research Setting

The Mill Co.[1] is a large Norwegian engineering and construction company specialised in offshore constructs that recently has initiated significant digitalisation efforts. The company operates mainly on two different sites within Norway. Whereas one of the digitalisation aims is to make existing work processes more effective through developing new information technology, it also aims to empower employees to take more control and responsibility of their work. One particular project that seek to do so is the CoConstruct project. The aim of CoConstruct is to build a mobile platform through which construction workers (welders, electricians, plumbers, etc.) and their foremen can use smartphones to access information such as work orders, plans, and documentation. It is also meant to provide a platform for team communication and allow real-time work progress reporting.

Mill Co. has an in-house IT-department that lead development projects and are responsible for operating and maintaining existing systems. However, the majority of the development workforce is hired on a project basis from another software engineering company with whom Mill Co. has a long-lasting collaboration. As part of the CoConstruct project, the development team also made the transition from using a traditional waterfall model to a more agile inspired approach, incorporating DevOps practices to release new software version to production roughly every 2 weeks. This meant that during the span of the project, the team had to acquire new skills, adopt new practices, and adopt new development tools (e.g. Azure DevOps). Further, the team also decided to incorporate user-centred design principles into their way of working by involving usability and user experience (UX) experts.

The entire CoConstruct project team consisted of a project manager, two UX researchers, a UX designer, a system architect, five front-end developers, and four back-end developers. Further, platform architects specialised in existing production systems were involved to ensure system integration. Two experts in mobile platforms (Xamarin) and cloud services were also included in the development team.

A pool of super users was established from the beginning of the project, including 15 users from each construction site (a total of 30 super users). The super users consisted of both foremen and construction workers that represented different disciplines. Particularly, super-users that were curious about new technology and positive about the project were selected. The development team tried to ensure variety by including super users that were not so experienced with digital technology, such as smartphones, and recruiting super users of different age groups.

---

[1] To preserve the anonymity of the people involved we use fictional names.

3.2 Research Design

A case study strategy [31] was adopted to investigate the development team's processes and practices, as well as experiences of the ones involved in the CoConstruct project. Particularly, we focus on how the end-user representants have been involved in the project and its implications. The case study lasted for about a year, between 2019 and 2020. The CoConstruct project was still active after the data collection ended.

Within this time period we collected qualitative data through semi-structured interviews and a focus group with a variety of people involved in the project (Table 1). An interview guide was designed that covered the different project phases: context study, requirement analysis, development, testing and implementation. A separate interview guide designed for user representatives (super users). Seven of the interviews were recorded and seven were transcribed. For the remaining we made notes during the interviews. We also got access to documents and presentations providing information about the CoConstruct project and associated work processes. All data material was thematically analysed by both authors. The study has been approved by the Norwegian Centre for Research Data (NSD) and informed consents was collected from study participants.

Table 1. Data collection occasions.

Participant(s)	Data collection method	Duration
Project manager, 1 developer, 1 UX researcher, 1 test engineer	Focus group interview	1,5 h
Developer	Interview	1 h
Test engineer	Interview	1 h
UX researcher	Interview	1 h
Project manager	3 online interviews	2,5 h in total
4 super users from 3 different construction teams	4 separate online interviews with each participant	30–45 min for each interview

4 Results

4.1 User Involvement in the Development Process

A high-level overview of the development process is illustrated in Fig. 2, which also highlights where and how in the process users were involved. An up-front context study phase initiated the process (1), which was followed by requirement analysis (2), development (3), test/deploy (4), release (5), and implementation (6).

Context Study. The first project phase was undertaken by a separate UX team, an assembly of 2 UX researchers, a UX designer, the project manager and a system architect. The aim was to gain an understanding of the context of use and user needs by

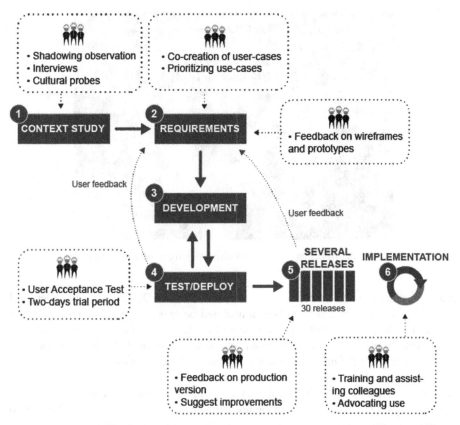

Fig. 2. User involvement in the development process

investigating current tools, processes and practices at both sites. The UX team conducted data collection that lasted for 2–3 days, for each site, and included activities such as workshops, shadowing observations, interviews, as well as utilising WhatsApp[2] and disposable cameras as cultural probes [32]. The use of WhatsApp groups made it possible to collect great amounts of photos and live data, where workers described their work situations and the work environment. This activity continued after the team had left the sites, and was, according to the team members, particularly useful to collect data from the site that was located geographically distant from the development team.

Based on the collected data, the UX team developed a timeline experience-map presenting activities and interactions between workers, as well as challenges and opportunities for new technology. The workers were invited for a co-creation session (same people that was shadowed), where they were encouraged to further refine the experience-map (Fig. 3).

Requirements. The UX team that figured in the context study phase, collaborated closely with the super users to write an prioritise initial use-cases in the subsequent

---

[2] A mobile messaging application.

Fig. 3. Workshop participants discussing the experience map.

phase. In order to make more accurate prioritisations, the UX team tried to understand how valuable a use-case is from both a user and business perspective. The team also aspired to estimate the technical complexity of implementing a certain functionality. A team member explained that 'a use-case could be very relevant, but if it would take four months to deliver the functionality it was assigned a lower priority.'

This process led to the selection of 14 use-cases. The selected use-cases were presented to super users at both sites and to a steering-committee. The super users were also asked to individually prioritize the use-cases in an Excel-spreadsheet, which led to 6 more use cases being added.

Based on these use-cases, the UX team initially developed wireframes[3] for the first planned features. Later the UX team created clickable prototypes as well. To get feedback on these early designs, the prototypes were presented to super users.

Development. To hand over the initial system requirements to the development team, a 7-day kick-off workshop was held where the UX team presented the selected use cases. Initially a total of 60 features were examined to estimate a total development time for the project.

The development was carried out using a Scrum-influenced approach with a 2-week sprint interval. Two separate teams worked in parallel iterations but delivered functionality as one unit. If one team ran out of tasks within a sprint, it assisted the other team if suitable resources were available. The teams held daily 'scrum-talks' and review meetings after each sprint. Both UX experts and the developers involved in the initial UX team was also part of the development team, which allowed the team to more fully take advantage of the experience gained from the previous phase in the development.

Test, Deploy, and Release. At the end of each sprint, the development team arranged a meeting to present the newly developed functionality to the super-users, and to run a user

---

[3] Non-interactive prototypes illustrating the applications user interface.

acceptance test (UAT). The super users participated either on site or through Skype. The number of participants varied; some participated every time while others participated less frequent. During the UAT the super users installed a test version of the CoConstruct application on their smartphones and were handed individualised test scripts to carry out during the session.

The aim was to discover potential bugs and to prioritize these in different categories according to severity. Identified defects and issues were entered into the development backlog. After this session, the super users were provided the opportunity to use the application for two days and report feedback. If still no major issues were found after the 2-day period, the application was released to production, making it available for everyone. After the release, feedback was generally collected by superusers and communicated to the development team at the following UAT meeting.

Implementation (Training, Support, and Dissemination). To support the implementation and adoption of the CoConstruct application among construction workers and foremen, the development team are establishing web-based training courses. A separate department of education at Mill Co. was also prepared to train smaller groups in how to use the application. The project manager told that they are monitoring various use statistics, which is used to more easily identify departments that possibly are in need of additional support and training.

The CoConstruct project has also developed user manuals presenting core functionality of the application to educate users. The project group have been sending out newsletters on email to keep people informed and presented teasers on information screens in the canteens, reception, etc.

4.2 Reflections on the Development Processes

Involving Super Users. The CoConstruct project ensured user involvement by establishing a pool of super users. Some were recruited from the beginning of the project; others were onboarded later. The main idea was to involve the same users throughout the project for discussing and validating needs, desires, requirements, and solutions. They were also responsible for collecting and forwarding feedback from colleagues.

Dual Roles. The super users interviewed were generally pleased with their role in the process, and some took great pride in participating. The super users admitted that the additional role sometimes caused stress due to the extra workload. The project manager suggested the possibility of rotating the super user role with others. He told: 'I believe some of them still want to continue as super users, but some are maybe getting tired. They have spent a lot of time on this.'

However, having a management that support and understand that the super user role will reduce time devoted to 'regular work' was considered important. As a super user explained: 'it has worked out nice to have the super user role in combination with regular work. The management understands that I spend time on this. This is no problem in my department. And I'm also passionate about making this work'. Further, having both a foreman and a construction worker from each construction team involved as super users was described as valuable, as it enabled them to support each other.

Super Users' Role in Dissemination and Training. According to the project manager, superusers main responsibility was to be involved in the development and to provide feedback back to the development team. In addition, the superusers were also expected to serve as 'ambassadors' for the CoConstruct application. As well as to provide some support to their work colleagues. But providing training was not part of their responsibility, the project manager explained.

However, super users from two of the construction teams involved in the study (three in total) reported that they were very engaged not only in advocating use, but also in training their colleagues in how to use the system. The superusers in these teams were very active in taking the application into use at their workplace, which was done on their own initiative. One of these teams' strategy was to hold training sessions with groups of 3–4 people at a time. They preferred smaller groups that allowed for closer interaction as the users try out the application and ask questions during the session.

For people that were not used to smartphones, or otherwise resistant to new technology, they held individual training sessions. The interviewed superuser explains: 'there has been resistance among some individuals that do not want to use digital tools, that find it difficult. We have taken these aside and gone through and thought them one and one. Walking through and repeating the tasks that the person should carry out. And at the end things have went fine.' The superuser continues, 'One-to-one walkthrough is the best way to achieve this. If you take them on one-to-one, they become a bit more comfortable with the situation, and you can explain it to them slowly, and then they understand it better. A lot of it is about lack of knowledge and insecurity. If you do this one-to-one much of the insecurity disappears.'

Feedback from Test and Production Versions. Within the span of 1,5 years, about 30 new production versions of the application were delivered to the users. Whenever a new version of the CoConstruct application had been finalised, it was made first available as a test version only for the super users. The super users said that the initial test version they got was mainly checked for major flaws regarding the applications user interface and functionalities. And most of the times, the test version was accepted by the super user without any complaints.

However, releasing the version into production meant that the application also could be tested by a larger number of users, and in a real work context. Hence, how well the new features align with work practices, and the influence of a new version on work efficiency could be scrutinised more thoroughly. The super users told that is was during this phase (after production release) that most major issues with the application emerged. And that issues became much more visible once a lot of people started complaining or simply stopped using the application.

One super user said that the feedback typically came after using the application for a while and when people had been facing the same challenges over time. He explained: 'in the beginning, there are often few people who give feedback, because they haven't been annoyed enough about it. But as time went on, people stopped using the mobile to report progress. Because it took too long compared to just ticking off the job package, like you did previously. It's mainly when many people use it that you get feedback. When you face the same problem as your colleagues'. Similarly, both the super users and the development team anticipated that the application would improve as the user base grows, which meant more feedback on how to improve it.

Another super user also suggested to speed up the feedback process when facing critical usability issues. The super users were supposed to report feedback in the following UAT meeting, which could be sometimes a month away. Considering development time, it could take a significant amount of time before the workers had an improved version available. When asked about how the process could be improved, he told: 'maybe not having to wait for another UAT meeting to address critical issues we had. It took a few extra weeks to fix the problem as well, and I noticed that the motivation to use the app was very low at that time. We should have contacted the team directly and said that this must be fixed'. The super user regretted that he had not used more effort to get the development team to resolve the issue more quickly, saying: 'I should have pushed them regardless'. A similar story is also shared by another superuser, where a software update led to that operators went back to 'doing it the old way'.

The project manager also told that they could have spent more time with the users to identify their daily challenges. But he admitted that it is challenging to know how to allocate available resources. He said: 'we should have been more visible at the construction area to follow up on daily challenges, but this is challenging. Should you spend time developing or should you focus on follow-ups and support?'

Screening of Feedback. Currently the CoConstruct application has approximately 500 unique (not necessarily active) users. This generates an amount of feedback that the developers find hard to process. The feedbacks include either bug fixes, suggestions for new functionality or suggestions on how to improve existing functionality. The team has been considering how they should screen and prioritise the feedback more effectively. A member of the development team explained the dilemma: 'the more users you get, the more feedback you get. Huge amounts of feedback. And it's only positive that you get lots of feedback, but how do you screen it? How can we ensure that what ends up on the backlog is what the company actually need, and not just what users want. We need to look at this. How can a screening be conducted?'.

The CoConstruct members are discussing if the construction department, the owner of the CoConstruct application, should establish and own a kind of 'change forum' where they discuss and screen incoming feedback. They already have existing arenas where different representatives meet and discuss topics related to work improvement, and the CoConstruct application could be a natural part of this, the project manager explains.

The Benefits of involving Super Users. The people involved in the CoConstruct project found the involvement of super users in different phases very useful. An informant from the CoConstruct project said that the user-centred approach was highly appreciated by super users as it allowed them to have genuine influence on the system design. One from the development team explained: 'some of them stated that they felt heavily involved for the first time. This led to two great benefits; firstly, we got involvement from the users, and secondly; the word started spreading about what we were doing. The users were also feeling that we are working hard to adapt the app to the way they work'. This is also reflected by the super users, as one them said: 'the development team are very eager and want to hear what we think is needed and not. We've been listened to'.

Super users reported that the CoConstruct application provided benefits to both construction workers and foremen. Particularly, in terms of increased work efficiency and empowering operators to further take control over their own work progress. As a super user said: 'I notice that many engage in reporting work progress using the app. You can see your own work progress and completion. Then it is more enjoyable to do the work. I think it makes the workers feel that they own their work'.

Both super users and developers appreciated the use of visual tools prepared by the UX teams when discussing different solutions. The visualisations made it easier for users to understand the product and share their opinions. They also explained that the experience map, for example, helped to them establish a mutual understanding of the wider socio-technical system, not just the application. The wireframes and clickable prototypes were also highly appreciated by the developers. As one developer said: 'It is a lot easier to us programmers to talk about solutions when you see a UX design, rather than just reading text. I've been in the business for 10 years, and so far, I've never seen UX been used as a basis to development. It has often been a "developer design"; a design solution that the developer feel is a good design'

5   Discussion

5.1   A Continuous Delivery Approach to User-Centred System Design

The super users had a central role as user representatives when the development team has taken its first steps towards a more agile and user-centred approach. Whereas the Mill Co. has a long tradition of utilising super users, they have not been involved in the development process to a similar extent before. Contradictory to agile principles, the CoConstruct project began with a rather extensive design up-front phase, in which super users were involved in defining the final system requirements that yielded a large initial work package.

While up-front discovery activities are recommended in the context of user-centred agile software development, there is a lack of knowledge regarding the recommended extent of this phase [12]. In the CoConstruct case study, further development and refinement of the application was needed even after a majority of the initial use cases were implemented, which led to the project contract being extended several times. Particularly, delivering production versions continuously enabled users to identify application features that was not suited to their work, which led to additional backlog entries. In this respect, continuous delivery provides mechanism that could be aligned with a design-in-use approach.

Although issues related to system implementation is often discussed within information systems research [9], it should perhaps also take a larger role in software engineering. In particular, as when moving towards continuous software engineering the boundaries of implementation and development gets blurred. While super users had an important role in influencing the system design in this project, they also were integral to the application being adopted. Some even voluntarily committed to arranging training and extended support for those struggling to take the digital leap. To ensure continues software engineering that produces useful, usable, as well as *used* software, one perhaps need to take a more holistic approach [33]. Skilled workers continuously configure the socio-technical systems they are part of through working around technical deficiencies to enhance work efficiency [34]. A continuous, user-centered system engineering approach could allow them to re-design also the technical part of the system to support such workarounds as these occur.

The approach adopted in the project somewhat reassembles the framework proposed by Kuusinen [16] in that development was carried out in multidisciplinary teams collaborating within the same iteration. However, the rather long feedback loop after a crucial deficiency was identified by the user was a significant bottleneck. This issue is interwoven with the question on how to screen a large amount of feedback to rapidly identify issues that matters the most. In addition to an enhanced dialog between users and developers implemented, for example, through a change forum, a more systemised approach to collecting feedback could be developed [26]. This could include combining descriptive contextually rich feedback with quantitative metrics of application usage. If issues related to a specific version for a specific department is detected early on, a simple version rollback could be instantiated for a limited group of people [35].

5.2 Study Limitations

Through a triangulation strategy, in which multiple data sources have been utilised and both authors being involved in the data collection and analysis we have sought to enhance research validity. Our prolonged involvement could also reduce respondent bias. A large part of the qualitative data was also recorded and transcribed to reduce researcher bias. However, due to time constrains not all interviews were transcribed verbatim. Another limitation of the study is the small number of involved super users. Further, as access to super users was managed by through a gateway inside the company, it is uncertain whether the selection was representative. While, there has been reported issues with adoption of the CoConstruct application at some departments, this was not the case at the departments of the super user that we interviewed.

Whereas the user-centred approach investigated in this study mainly focus on usability and system adoption, there are several other aspects such as, business strategies, security and privacy that need to be considered when developing and implementing IT-systems in an organisation. To this end, end-user involvement might not be sufficient, but participation of experts in other domains need to be included. However, we consider this as future work.

6 Conclusion

Through a case study we investigate how end-users representants are involved in the software development process and their influence on system design and adoption. The study shows that super-users have been central in forming the developed system according to their needs. Continuous delivery of system functionalities provides an interesting opportunity for end-users to further shape the system design along with work practices. This allows considering also aspects of work that often is overlooked in up-front design. Super users also had a central role in system adoption, taking on a role as ambassador, providing training and support to their fellow work colleagues.

References

1. Bossen, C.: Chapter 5 - Socio-technical Betwixtness: Design Rationales for Health Care IT. Designing Healthcare That Works. Academic Press, pp. 77–94 (2018)
2. van der Velden, M., Mörtberg, C.: Participatory design and design for values. In: van den Hoven, J., Vermaas, P.E., van de Poel, I. (eds.) Handbook of Ethics, Values, and Technological Design: Sources, Theory, Values and Application Domains. Dordrecht: Springer Netherlands, pp. 1–22 (2014)
3. Simonsen, J., Robertson, T.: Routledge International Handbook of Participatory Design. Taylor & Francis (2012)
4. Ritter, F.E., Baxter, G.D., Churchill, E.F.: Foundations for Designing User-Centered Systems: What System Designers Need to Know about People. Springer, London (2014)
5. Mumford, E.: The story of socio-technical design: reflections on its successes, failures and potential. Inf. Syst. J. **16**(4), 317–342 (2006). https://doi.org/10.1111/j.1365-2575.2006.002 21.x
6. Abelein, U., Paech, B.: Understanding the influence of user participation and involvement on system success – a systematic mapping study. Empirical Softw. Eng. **20**(1), 28–81 (2013). https://doi.org/10.1007/s10664-013-9278-4
7. Mohagheghi, P., Jørgensen, M.: What contributes to the success of IT projects? success factors, challenges and lessons learned from an empirical study of software projects in the norwegian public sector. In: IEEE/ACM 39th International Conference on Software Engineering Companion (ICSE-C), pp. 371–373 (2017)
8. Bano, M., Zowghi, D., da Rimini, F.: User satisfaction and system success: an empirical exploration of user involvement in software development. Empirical Software Eng. **22**(5), 2339–2372 (2016). https://doi.org/10.1007/s10664-016-9465-1
9. Iivari, J., Isomäki, H., Pekkola, S.: The user – the great unknown of systems development: reasons, forms, challenges, experiences and intellectual contributions of user involvement. Inf. Syst. J. **20**(2), 109–117 (2010). https://doi.org/10.1111/j.1365-2575.2009.00336.x
10. Lwakatare, L.E., Kilamo, T., Karvonen, T., Sauvola, T., Heikkilä, V., Itkonen, J., et al.: DevOps in practice: a multiple case study of five companies. Inf. Software Technol. **114**, 217–230 (2019). https://doi.org/10.1016/j.infsof.2019.06.010
11. Dittrich, Y., Nørbjerg, J., Tell, P., Bendix, L.: Researching cooperation and communication in continuous software engineering. In: IEEE/ACM 11th International Workshop on Cooperative and Human Aspects of Software Engineering (CHASE), pp. 87–90 (2018)
12. Brhel, M., Meth, H., Maedche, A., Werder, K.: Exploring principles of user-centered agile software development: a literature review. Inf. Software Technol. **61**, 163–181 (2015). https://doi.org/10.1016/j.infsof.2015.01.004
13. Salah, D., Paige, R.F., Cairns, P.: A systematic literature review for agile development processes and user centred design integration. In: Proceedings of the 18th International Conference on Evaluation and Assessment in Software Engineering. London, England (2014)
14. Hussain, Z., Slany, W., Holzinger, A.: Current state of agile user-centered design: a survey. In: Holzinger, A., Miesenberger, K. (eds.) USAB 2009. LNCS, vol. 5889, pp. 416–427. Springer, Heidelberg (2009). https://doi.org/10.1007/978-3-642-10308-7_30
15. Silva, T.S.D., Martin, A., Maurer, F., Silveira, M.: User-centered design and agile methods: a systematic review. Agile Conference **2011**, 77–86 (2011)
16. Kuusinen, K.: BoB: a framework for organizing within-iteration ux work in agile development. In: Cockton, G., Lárusdóttir, M., Gregory, P., Cajander, Å. (eds.) Integrating User-Centred Design in Agile Development. HIS, pp. 205–224. Springer, Cham (2016). https://doi.org/10. 1007/978-3-319-32165-3_9

17. Harris, M.A., Weistroffer, H.R.: A new look at the relationship between user involvement in systems development and system success. Commun Assoc. Inf. Syst. **24**(1), 739–756 (2009)
18. Bano, M., Zowghi, D., Rimini, F.D.: User involvement in software development: the good, the bad, and the ugly. IEEE Software, **35**(6), 8–11 (2018). https://doi.org/10.1109/ms.2018. 4321252
19. Haake, P., Kaufmann, J., Baumer, M., Burgmaier, M., Eichhorn, K., Mueller, B., et al.: Configurations of User Involvement and Participation in Relation to Information System Project Success, pp. 87–102. Springer International Publishing, Cham (2018)
20. Kujala, S.: User involvement: a review of the benefits and challenges. Behav. Inf. Technol. **22**(1), 1–16 (2003). https://doi.org/10.1080/01449290301782
21. Bano, M., Zowghi, D.: Users' involvement in requirements engineering and system success. In: 2013 3rd International Workshop on Empirical Requirements Engineering (EmpiRE), p. 24–31 (2013)
22. Bosch, J.: Continuous software engineering: an introduction. In: Bosch, J. (ed.) Continuous Software Engineering. HIS, pp. 3–13. Springer, Cham (2014). https://doi.org/10.1007/978-3-319-11283-1_1
23. Fitzgerald, B., Stol, K.-J.: Continuous software engineering: a roadmap and agenda. J. Syst. Softw. **123**, 176–189 (2017). https://doi.org/10.1016/j.jss.2015.06.063
24. Wüest, D., Fotrousi, F., Fricker, S.: Combining Monitoring and Autonomous Feedback Requests to Elicit Actionable Knowledge of System Use, pp. 209–225. Springer, Cham (2019)
25. Johanssen, J.O., Kleebaum, A., Bruegge, B., Paech, B.: How do practitioners capture and utilize user feedback during continuous software engineering? In: IEEE 27th International Requirements Engineering Conference (RE), pp. 153–164 (2019)
26. Stade, M., Fotrousi, F., Seyff, N., Albrecht, O.: Feedback gathering from an industrial point of view. In: IEEE 25th International Requirements Engineering Conference (RE), pp. 71–79 (2017)
27. Hege-René Hansen, A., Anders, I.M.: Super users and local developers: the organization of end-user development in an accounting company. J. Organ. End User Comput. (JOEUC) **18**(4), 1–21 (2006). https://doi.org/10.4018/joeuc.2006100101
28. McNeive, J.E.: Super users have great value in your organization. CIN: Computers, Informatics, Nursing. **27**(3), 136–139 (2009). https://doi.org/10.1097/01.ncn.0000336479.507 37.d8
29. Dittrich, Y., Bolmsten, J., Eriksson, J.: End user development and infrastructuring – sustaining organizational innovation capabilities. In: Paternò, F., Wulf, V. (eds.) New Perspectives in End-User Development. HIS, pp. 165–206. Springer, Cham (2017). https://doi.org/10.1007/ 978-3-319-60291-2_8
30. Torkilsheyggi, A., Hertzum, M.: Incomplete by design: a study of a design-in-use approach to systems implementation. Scandinavian J. Inf. Syst. **29** (2017)
31. Yin, R.K.: Case Study Research: Design and Methods. SAGE Publications (2009)
32. Gaver, B., Dunne, T., Pacenti, E.: Design: cultural probes. Interactions **6**(1), 21–29 (1999). https://doi.org/10.1145/291224.291235
33. Forbrig, P.: Does Continuous Requirements Engineering need Continuous Software Engineering? 3rd Workshop on Continuous Requirements Engineering. CEUR, Essen, (2017)
34. Cabitza, F., Simone, C.: "Drops Hollowing the Stone": Workarounds as Resources for Better Task-Artifact Fit, pp. 103–122. Springer, London (2013)
35. Agarwal, A., Gupta, S., Choudhury, T.: Continuous and integrated software development using DevOps. In: International Conference on Advances in Computing and Communication Engineering (ICACCE), pp. 290–293 (2018)

Design Decisions by Voice: The Next Step of Software Architecture Knowledge Management

Rafael Capilla[1]([⊠]) [iD], Rodi Jolak[2] [iD], Michel R. V. Chaudron[2] [iD],
and Carlos Carrillo[3] [iD]

[1] Rey Juan Carlos University, Madrid, Spain
rafael.capilla@urjc.es
[2] Chalmers and Gothenburg University, Gothenburg, Sweden
rodi.jolak@cse.gu.se, chaudron@chalmers.se
[3] Technical University of Madrid, Madrid, Spain
carlos.carrillo@upm.es

Abstract. Architectural Design Decisions (ADDs) capture the essence of relevant Architectural Knowledge (AK) and the underpinning rationale in order to produce well-designed software architectures. AK and design rationale might get lost if not captured at the same time when the architecture is discussed and modeled in early design phases. For years, this relevant knowledge has been captured using text templates and supported by a number of research tools. Nevertheless, as no commercial tool is still available combining AK capturing with UML notations to facilitate capturing the design decisions at the same time the architecture is modeled, is the major barrier to convince software architects and companies to invest in documenting the significant design decisions. As capturing AK using text templates requires an extra effort, we propose an approach to make the documentation process easier and reduce the effort thereof by using voice commands. In particular, we suggest an approach to: (i) capture ADDs using voice commands during design conversations, and (ii) link the captured ADDs to UML notations. Our approach integrates OctoUML, a modeling tool with voice commands for capturing design decisions by voice.

Keywords: Software architecture · Architectural knowledge · Design Decisions · Voice decisions · Knowledge capturing · UML

1 Introduction

It is well recognized by the software architecture community that documenting Architectural Design Decisions (ADDs) is extremely relevant to avoid knowledge vaporization [4]. For years, software architecture documentation has been focusing on documenting architecture models, design patterns, and the results

© IFIP International Federation for Information Processing 2020
Published by Springer Nature Switzerland AG 2020
R. Bernhaupt et al. (Eds.): HCSE 2020, LNCS 12481, pp. 166–177, 2020.
https://doi.org/10.1007/978-3-030-64266-2_10

of architecture evaluations. However, it is uncommon to find documented design decisions explicitly [10]. This is mainly because of the burden and cost of ADDs' capturing effort, as well as the lack of suitable tool-support [9]. Furthermore, capturing relevant Architectural Knowledge (AK) in Open Source Software (OSS) projects becomes more complex due to loosely coordinated software contributors who tend to code solutions without producing adequate documentation [7].

In a survey that we detail in Sect. 3, we find that software architecture experts and practitioners perceive capturing ADDs alongside other software artifacts as valuable. However, the poor flexibility, usability, and effectiveness of the majority of ADDs documentation tools is the main barrier to the adoption of these tools [6]. In order to facilitate the effectiveness of the AK-capturing process, we propose a novel approach that uses voice commands integrated with a modeling tool for capturing and management of Architecture Design Decisions by Voice, which is design decisions that are communicated by voice (ADDsV) during architecture design conversation. In this work in progress paper, we investigate the usefulness of "capturing ADDsV" through a survey with software architecture experts and practitioners, and we describe an approach to support: (i) Capturing ADDsV during early-phase design and modeling meetings, and (ii) Managing the captured ADDsV by linking these decisions to UML artifacts. The remainder of this article is as follows. Section 2 describes some related works and in Sect. 3 we outline our approach using a modified version of the OctoUML tool (https://github.com/Imarcus/OctoUML). In Sect. 4 we describe our first experiments and in Sect. 5 we provide the feedback collected from software architecture researchers and practitioners. In Sect. 6 we discuss some limitations of our approach and in Sect. 7 we discuss our conclusions and future research steps.

2 Related Work

Since 2004 architectural knowledge has become the next step [4] for documenting the design decisions and supported by the ISO/IEC 42010 standard [1]. There exist approaches suggesting a number of AK research tools for capturing and sharing the design decisions [6]. However, the diversity of these tools did not solve, in a satisfactory way, the duality of the AK capturing problem while software architects model an architecture [5], except two tools (i.e., AREL and ADMentor) that enable capturing design rationale with some modeling capabilities. In a survey described in [17], the authors study human aspects in software architecture decision-making such as collaborative group making, the role of agile practices in decision-making, and the facilities provided by several decision-making tools for capturing design rationale. However, the role of multimodal interfaces facilitating the tasks of capturing design decisions is not investigated by the authors.

Although some AK research tools offer some collaborative support for sharing the design decisions (e.g. WiKi tools like EAGLE [8]), only some recent tools (e.g. SAW [14], ASQ [18]) provide explicit support to achieve a consensus when stakeholders vote about decisions alternatives. As effective software design requires decision making and reasoning to solve the problem-solution co-evolution [16], we need to increase the ease of use of tools for capturing design decisions and modeling their architectures concurrently.

The use of multimodal interfaces for modeling architectures is now possible such as discussed in [13], where a prototype speech control system is used to enhance the interaction with UML tools. The approach described in [3] presents SketchLink, a tool to sketch diagrams in software engineering so designers can capture and annotate the diagrams and link these to code artifacts. Modern solutions like OctoUML [11] allow designers to interact combining touch screens and voice commands to depict architectural elements in a collaborative way [12]. Unfortunately, capturing design decisions and their rationale is not supported by OctoUML. Another work [20] envisions using video walls for collaborative decision making and capturing the decisions on the fly. However, the approach is not capable to extract the decisions from the voice files. Finally, a recent experience [15] suggests a similar approach to ours for capturing voice conversations during design meetings by using the KnoCap tool, with which designers can mark the most relevant fragments to be used at any time.

3   Approach

OctoUML [11] is a proof-of-concept open-source prototype that explores supporting software development teams by offering more human-centered interaction modalities in software development tools. In order to address the challenge for capturing design decision by voice and link these to UML artifacts we address the following research questions:

– RQ1 How useful is capturing ADDsV during collaborative design meetings?
– RQ2 How can design modeling tools be adapted to capture and manage ADDsV?

To this end, we use OctoUML, an interactive whiteboard software that supports touch and voice interaction, which can be used on standard PCs and tablets. Figure 1 shows the main interface of the tool.

The key features of OctoUML are summarized below:

– Supporting the creation and mixing of software models at different levels of formality – in particular sketches and formal 'geometric' models. This enables a smooth transition from design ideation to more formal design representations.
– Collaborative distributed development by offering a joint canvas where developers on different locations can draw and edit shared diagrams.
– Combining navigation in design and source code in a single view.

3.1   Voice Interaction

Current technology provides opportunities for more intuitive and efficient interaction with the software. One notorious challenge in software development has

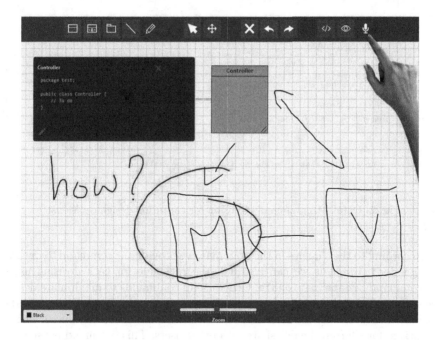

Fig. 1. Modeling an architecture with OctoUML using the touch interface.

been the production and maintenance of documentation, partly due to the old-fashion use of typing as the way to edit documents. In the last decade, mobile phones have pushed additional interaction modes, such as touch, voice, and gesture. We propose that these modalities can also be used to ease the work for software developers to enter and maintain documentation [11]. In particular, enabling voice-recording near the interactive whiteboard where design discussions take place, opens up new ways for registering design discussions, including design decisions and rationale. The OctoUML design environment supports interaction via voice commands by using the Sphinx4 voice recognition library [19].

3.2 OctoUML Grammar Extension

OctoUML provides a basic grammar (Java Speech Grammar Format) to define the voice commands the tool supports. In order to capture design decisions, we extended the grammar in the following way (See Fig. 2):

- We provide the ability to create a design decision that can be captured using voice.
- We support capturing the design rationale of the decision.
- We support replaying, changing (updating), and removing a decision by voice.
- We support sharing a decision with other users, which is useful in group decision making.

```
public <greet> = (name) (user | student | system | teacher| course |
          car | archivist | supervisor | detective | case
              | material | person | fact | photo | photograph
              | other | investigator | suspect | victim | task
              | subject | testimony | witness | personnel
              | agent | photographer | investigation | people | event | content |
     criminal | persons connected | persons associated | associated | collaborator |
     people connected | people associated | connected people | associated people |
     clue | class | package);
public <command> = (share) (decision);
public <command> = (create) (class | edge | package | design decision | rationale);
public <selection> = (choose) (draw | select | move | select decision | replay
decision | update decision | delete decision | show decision);
public <stop> = (stop naming);
```

Fig. 2. OctoUML grammar extension for capturing design decisions.

According to the changes in the grammar, we provide the command to create design decision, but we can also add the rationale for each decision using the command create rationale. Other useful commands to manipulate design decisions or rationale by voice are replay decision, update decision, delete decision, and show decision. We also created a separate command, share decision, for sharing the decisions with other users. This command is useful in distributed teams for group decision making.

3.3   Implementation with Sphinx

During the implementation, we integrated the OctoUML code with the CMUS-phinx library (https://cmusphinx.github.io/) used for controlling the voice. The graphical user interface is defined by the FXML (i.e. XML-based user interface markup language) created by Oracle Corporation, so in OctoUML we have two main files (i.e. classDiagramView.fxml, sequenceDiagramView.fxml), that we modified to include an icon supporting the voice management.

In order to include an icon to start the voice recording of the decisions, we used the abstract class *AbstractDiagramController.java*, so we recognize the voice commands based on the grammar. The problem, in this case, was that the microphone is an exclusive resource that can't be shared by other threads and once it recognizes a command, we must stop the recognition facility and start capturing the voice until the user presses the new icon to stop capturing the decisions. By the moment we cannot use a voice command to stop recording the decisions because we cannot know when a user finished describing a decision with the voice.

We also modified the class *voiceController* to add the new code supporting the changes in the grammar and avoid locking the microphone. Therefore, we implemented a new class named *RecordDDController* to manage the recording mode and capture voice decisions as WAV files. Once the microphone is unlocked and the record is finished, the class *RecordDDController* stores the voice file and replays the voice decision in the speakers. The recording mode finishes once the user clicks on the recording mode icon in the OctoUML smart touch screen releasing the resources.

Finally, we created another class, *RecordDDManagement* to assign a name to the voice file which stores the description of the design decision. The CMUSphinx4 package used for voice recognition and capturing also decodes the voice and translates this into a text string in case we need to display the decision on the screen. As a summary, the list of the classes we modified are the following:

- SpeechSourceProvider.java: allocates a new microphone each time it is required by the VoiceController class and to avoid locking the microphone which is managed by the RecordDDController class
- AbstractSpeechRecognizer.java: it allows access to the microphone enabling different operations
- LiveSpeechRecognizer.java: implements the method to unlock the microphone
- Microphone.java: is used to access the voice files

4   Capturing Voice Decisions

As a first experience based on the extension implemented in Sect. 3.3, we do a trial for capturing ADDsV. A decision and its rationale can be captured before or after the architecture is depicted using OctoUML's drawing tools. Figure 3 shows ADDsV capturing process. A user can interact with the tool by (1) activating the microphone (white button) to enter in "command mode". Then, the user-interface automatically switches into "voice recording" mode and starts (2) capturing the ADDsV using the "create design decision" command or capturing a rationale using "create rationale" command. Once the user finishes discussing the design decision or rationale, he/she interacts (3) with the screen by deactivating the microphone (red button). After that, the voice design decision or rationale is reproduced (4) so the user can know the last decision taken. The use of meaningful names for ADDsV is useful for searching, retrieving, or listing such decisions. Currently, the functionality used for naming decisions is implemented using the keyboard. This is because naming decisions can use symbolic names or a few short meaningful words. It turns out that using voice commands is not the easiest way for this step. One solution to this could be to train people to assign appropriate names. Once the decision is recorded, the tool automatically waits until the user gives a meaningful name to the decision (step 5). Once the user spells out the word "end", the tool stores (6) the ADDsV as *.wav* and *.txt* files.

5   Perception of Experts and Practitioners

We conducted a short survey with software architecture experts and practitioners. We asked them to answer 10 questions related to the usefulness of using voice for capturing architecture design decisions. We remark that this survey does not investigate the use and usability aspects of our prototype, but rather

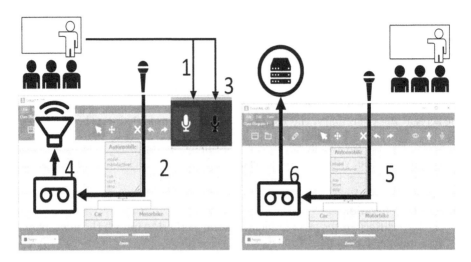

Fig. 3. Capturing design decisions by voice (left side), and giving a name to the recorded decision (right side). (Color figure online)

highlights: (i) to what extent it is important for practitioners capturing design decisions by voice that can be linked to software artifacts, and (ii) how this approach could be useful in agile software development approaches and collaborative decision-making activities. The results are shown in Fig. 4. We collected the data during October and November 2019, and we received 17 responses from 10 different countries in Europe, South America, and Canada. The age of the respondents varies between [27–67] years. The experience of the respondents in software architecture design ranges between [4–35] years, but most of them have between [6–9] years of experience in architecture design. The average age of the participants is 39.5 years and the average year of experience is 14 years.

From the responses of the subjects, we derived the following major findings.

1. Most of the respondents think that capturing architectural knowledge (AK) is valuable for software architecture design practice. This indicates the importance of our endeavor in capturing design decisions and AK via voice.
2. The respondents perceive that capturing decisions during modeling tasks is highly relevant for collaborative decision-making, especially for distributed teams. Sharing ADDsV is also perceived as valuable for developers. These results indicate that capturing and sharing design decisions of developers working in teams is still a challenging task that is not effectively supported by tools or practices.
3. Some respondents believe that capturing and linking ADDsV to architectural artifacts is important, but not as much as linking these decisions to a UML diagram. While we think that linking design decisions to the architecture and UML diagrams is important for traceability, it seems that some respondents prefer to use other diagrams than the UML to represent the architecture

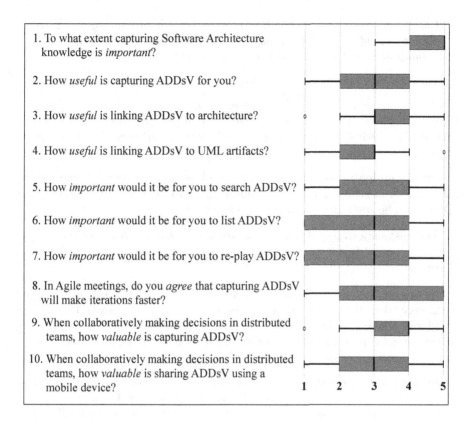

1. To what extent capturing Software Architecture knowledge is *important*?

2. How *useful* is capturing ADDsV for you?

3. How *useful* is linking ADDsV to architecture?

4. How *useful* is linking ADDsV to UML artifacts?

5. How *important* would it be for you to search ADDsV?

6. How *important* would it be for you to list ADDsV?

7. How *important* would it be for you to re-play ADDsV?

8. In Agile meetings, do you *agree* that capturing ADDsV will make iterations faster?

9. When collaboratively making decisions in distributed teams, how *valuable* is capturing ADDsV?

10. When collaboratively making decisions in distributed teams, how *valuable* is sharing ADDsV using a mobile device?

Fig. 4. Perception of practitioners capturing Architecture Design Decisions by Voice (ADDsV).

and, thus, indicated that the linking of ADDsV to UML diagrams is of less importance.

4. The respondents indicate that searching for, listing, and re-playing ADDsV are relevant and important matters, however, the diversity of the responses is wide. We think that this diversity in the responses is normal, as different users usually have different preferences of the features for the manipulation and interaction with the artifacts.

5. Many respondents believe it to be important to have ADDsV in agile meetings, as these decisions can be shared in a faster way than via documenting them. Again, this indicates the importance of our endeavor in capturing design decisions and AK via voice.

In addition to these findings, we performed a qualitative analysis of the personal opinions of the respondents. This analysis yielded some interesting issues: One subject indicated:

"I have never seen this in practice, so it is difficult to imagine how voice decisions would work. Perhaps you can consider transcribing the decisions automatically so that you also have them as text".

While another respondent expressed:

"Writing down decisions is favorable over voice decisions, because it forces the author into a certain thought process and proper formulation of her thoughts. Voice decisions may be easy to record, but that does not save much time in my opinion".

Our perception is that architects still think of documenting decisions as the main way to capture architecture knowledge, and they hardly perceive that ADDsV can be useful too. Another respondent said:

"The vast majority of decisions are not worthwhile to share; as the necessary context is not made explicit that allows the understanding of the decision".

We believe that decisions made for a specific software project are bounded by the context of the project, so all stakeholders should be aware of the context boundaries where decisions are meaningful for all of them. However, capturing the rationale by voice can help to make decisions more understandable.

Finally, one respondent mentioned:

"distributed teams collaborating over Jira or chat platforms (e.g. Slack) mostly document decisions in tickets. That approach works very well for them. I see the benefit of the tool, not to capture the decision itself, but rather for capturing alternatives and pro/con arguments of the decision".

We are in favor of capturing details as much as possible about the rationale of design decisions, including the pros and the cons of these decisions. ADDsV files can be augmented with more details on the pros and cons of the decisions. But overloading these files with extra details reduces the agility of the approach, as additional details on the pros and cons can be found in the detailed textual documentations.

From the qualitative analysis of the comments provided by the subjects interviewed we come up with the following issues. As capturing and documenting decisions by voice is a new practice for software architects our prototype plans to produce text strings of the voice decisions that can be documented in the traditional way, as searching for decisions in voice files could be complex. Also, the opinion expressed by one subject that voice decisions won't save much time could be partially true but in remote teams where users can use also their mobile phones to remotely capture a decision can ease the collaborative part in distributed teams, instead of having a UML tool to depict architecture artifacts. Therefore, capturing decisions more agile is not only a matter of time-saving. We agree that sharing a decision requires a context, but this can be added as an extension in the grammar. However, we believe all relevant stakeholders should know the context or specific project where decisions are made.

6   Limitations

Although this is an early experience for capturing design decisions by voice while modeling UML diagrams, our approach still has some limitations for practical use of the proposed solution. First, the proposed grammar can recognize commands for handling some decisions using voice, but the captured voice design decision is recorded as a voice stream, so currently, we cannot recognize pronounced sentences. One way to mitigate this factor is to integrate our solution with existing voice recognition software to provide extended capabilities. Second, extracting specific elements from the recorded voice is not possible at present, so we need to provide advanced capabilities to recognize concrete parts (e.g., the selection of a specific design pattern). Third, our current solution does not translate design decisions by voice to textual forms and does not provide mechanisms to manipulate these forms. However, this feature is planned for implementation in the future.

7   Conclusion and Research Challenges

Compared to previous approaches using text templates, we offer an approach that combines a multi-modal interface for capturing the relevant Architecture knowledge and depicting software architectures using the touch screen with voice for capturing the relevant AK. This approach provides an agile way that is suitable for agile development teams to capture design decisions in a non-intrusive way while designing or discussing an architecture.

We used a survey to assess the usefulness of capturing design decisions by voice during a collaborative architecture design meeting. The respondents perceived capturing design decisions by voice as useful and indicated the potential of our approach in supporting architecture knowledge management. From our initial experience, software architects need some training to capture design decisions by voice together with their rationale using concise sentences. In addition, we trust on the reliability of the survey as we asked experts in architectural knowledge and software architecture as well, even if we only got 17 responses.

Currently, the grammar for assigning names is a subset of the full English grammar, as most of the keywords are based on computer science terms. In this direction, there are some interesting experiences choosing a suitable NLP (natural language processing) dictionary for analyzing documents [2]. In addition, our approach goes beyond [15] as we use one single tool for architecture modeling as well as for capturing the design decisions by voice and not only capturing the voice in design meetings. Hence, software architects can model using a UML tool and capture the decisions at the same time they depict their architecture models.

Below, we provide a list of the research challenges that will guide the next steps of future work:

– Extend the grammar to support additional voice-based interaction functionality.

- Provide support for group-decision making.
- Support versioning of decisions to track history.
- Display voice decisions in the smart touch screen so users can easily find and replay the decisions linked to design artifacts.
- Explore the use of mobile devices for capturing voice in an agile way.
- Add more semantics to the decisions captured.

References

1. ISO/IEC 42010:2011, Systems & Software Engineering - Architecture Description. https://www.iso.org/standard/50508.html. Accessed 2019
2. Al Omran, F.N., Treude, C.: Choosing an NLP library for analyzing software documentation: a systematic literature review and a series of experiments. In: 14th Conference on Mining Software Repositories, pp. 187–197. IEEE Press (2017)
3. Baltes, S., Schmitz, P., Diehl, S.: Linking sketches and diagrams to source code artifacts. In: 22nd ACM SIGSOFT Symposium on Foundations of Software Engineering, pp. 743–746. ACM (2014)
4. Bosch, J.: Software architecture: the next step. In: Oquendo, F., Warboys, B.C., Morrison, R. (eds.) EWSA 2004. LNCS, vol. 3047, pp. 194–199. Springer, Heidelberg (2004). https://doi.org/10.1007/978-3-540-24769-2_14
5. Capilla, R.: Embedded design rationale in software architecture. In: 2009 Working IEEE/IFIP Conference on Software Architecture & European Conference on Software Architecture, pp. 305–308. IEEE (2009)
6. Capilla, R., Jansen, A., Tang, A., Avgeriou, P., Babar, M.A.: 10 years of software architecture knowledge management: practice and future. J. Syst. Softw. **116**, 191–205 (2016)
7. Ding, W., Liang, P., Tang, A., Van Vliet, H., Shahin, M.: How do open source communities document software architecture: An exploratory survey. In: 2014 19th International Conference on Engineering of Complex Computer Systems, pp. 136–145. IEEE (2014)
8. Farenhorst, R., Lago, P., Van Vliet, H.: Eagle: effective tool support for sharing architectural knowledge. Int. J. Cooper. Inf. Syst. **16**(3/4), 413–437 (2007)
9. Harrison, N.B., Avgeriou, P., Zdun, U.: Using patterns to capture architectural decisions. IEEE Softw. **24**(4), 38–45 (2007)
10. Jansen, A., Avgeriou, P., van der Ven, J.S.: Enriching software architecture documentation. J. Syst. Softw. **82**(8), 1232–1248 (2009)
11. Jolak, R., Vesin, B., Chaudron, M.R.V.: Using voice commands for UML modelling support on interactive whiteboards: insights and experiences. In: CIbSE, pp. 85–98 (2017)
12. Jolak, R., Wortmann, A., Chaudron, M.R.V., Rumpe, B.: Does distance still matter? revisiting collaborative distributed software design. IEEE Softw. **35**(6), 40–47 (2018)
13. Lahtinen, S., Peltonen, J.: Adding speech recognition support to UML tools. J. Visual Lang. Comput. **16**(1–2), 85–118 (2005)
14. Nowak, M., Pautasso, C.: Team situational awareness and architectural decision making with the software architecture warehouse. In: Drira, K. (ed.) ECSA 2013. LNCS, vol. 7957, pp. 146–161. Springer, Heidelberg (2013). https://doi.org/10.1007/978-3-642-39031-9_13

15. Soria, A.M., van der Hoek, A.: Collecting design knowledge through voice notes. In: Proceedings of the 12th International Workshop on Cooperative & Human Aspects of Software Engineering, pp. 33–36. IEEE (2019)

16. Tang, A., Aleti, A., Burge, J., van Vliet, H.: What makes software design effective? Des. Stud. **31**(6), 614–640 (2010)

17. Tang, A., Razavian, M., Paech, B., Hesse, T.: Human aspects in software architecture decision making: a literature review. In: 2017 IEEE International Conference on Software Architecture, ICSA 2017, Gothenburg, Sweden, April 3–7, 2017, pp. 107–116 (2017)

18. Triglianos, V., Pautasso, C., Bozzon, A., Hauff, C.: Inferring student attention with ASQ. In: Verbert, K., Sharples, M., Klobučar, T. (eds.) EC-TEL 2016. LNCS, vol. 9891, pp. 306–320. Springer, Cham (2016). https://doi.org/10.1007/978-3-319-45153-4_23

19. Walker, W., et al.: Sphinx-4: a flexible open source framework for speech recognition (2004)

20. van der Werf, J.M.E., de Feijter, R., Bex, F., Brinkkemper, S.: Facilitating collaborative decision making with the software architecture video wall. In: 2017 IEEE International Conference on Software Architecture Workshops (ICSAW), pp. 137–140. IEEE (2017)

Poster and Demos

Towards a Trustworthy Patient Home-Care Thanks to an Edge-Node Infrastructure

Carmelo Ardito[1], Tommaso Di Noia[1], Eugenio Di Sciascio[1],
Domenico Lofú[1,2](✉), Giulio Mallardi[1,2], Claudio Pomo[1],
and Felice Vitulano[2]

[1] Politecnico di Bari, Via E. Orabona 4, Bari 70125, Italy
{carmelo.ardito,tommaso.dinoia,eugenio.disciascio,giulio.mallardi,
claudio.pomo}@poliba.it
[2] Innovation Lab, Exprivia S.p.A., Via A. Olivetti 11, Molfetta 70056, Italy
{domenico.lofu,giulio.mallardi,felice.vitulano}@exprivia.com

Abstract. Ambient Assisted Living (AAL) promotes the assistance of a patient at home according to her/his Clinical Pathway, i.e., a set of diagnostic and therapeutic procedures related to the treatment of that specific patient. AAL is increasingly gaining momentum thanks to the Internet of Things (IoT). Edge-Computing would boost the AAL success, since this kind of architecture promotes a sort of distributed cloud computing at the edges of the IoT network, thus reducing latency and improving reliability. This poster paper focuses on the implementation, in a AAL system based on such an IoT-Edge-Computing coupled architecture, of an anomaly detection module able to detect deviations from the patient's Clinical Pathway (CP) and avoid processing of inconsistent or fake data, which could result in a serious life-threatening for a patient.

Keywords: Anomaly detection · Edge-computing · Smart healthcare

1 Introduction

It has been clear for several years now that, in order to reduce healthcare costs, it is important to leverage the possibilities offered by Ambient Assisted Living (AAL) for home care of patients. In addition, the recent COVID-19 emergency has also shown how, in order to mitigate the spread of the contagion, it is necessary to minimise access to hospital facilities by those chronically ill patients who can be monitored at home. And even COVID patients with mild symptoms can be cared for remotely, without the need to take up hospital places that can be allocated to more severe patients and without the risk of worsening their situation due to contact with the latter.

The adoption of Clinical Pathways CPs [7,14] would make AAL implementations much more effective, as it would allow remote monitoring of patient care

© IFIP International Federation for Information Processing 2020
Published by Springer Nature Switzerland AG 2020
R. Bernhaupt et al. (Eds.): HCSE 2020, LNCS 12481, pp. 181–189, 2020.
https://doi.org/10.1007/978-3-030-64266-2_11

and automate the reporting of critical events that deviate from the prescribed care, also thanks to the use of Machine Learning techniques. A CP consists of a set of diagnostic and therapeutic procedures. It can be considered as a process model characterized by two main phases: (i) some activities, or sub-processes, that can be managed by the personnel in the health structures; and (ii) some others that can be managed autonomously by the patient, in a sort of medical-unsupervised manner. The latter phase can be processed by an intelligent architecture able to deal with the specific clinical sub-path for the patient at home, also checking that is validated by a doctor or nurse, and guaranteeing its compliance with the actual medical indications specified in the clinical path.

AAL is becoming more and more successful thanks to the evolution of IoT technology and in particular of wearable devices. However, it must be considered that there are limits, mainly due to the latency of the network, that sometimes make the use of such solutions critical in the healthcare. The security of data being transmitted from sensors to the cloud is another area of concern, as their transmission could be affected either by technical problems or by malicious manipulations, in both cases resulting in life-threatening for the patient. Sensitive patient's information could also be sniffed.

In order to address these issues, the proposal in this poster paper consists of an architecture that couples IoT and Edge-Computing, which also implements a Clinical Path Anomaly Detection (CPAD) module able to detect deviations from the patient's CP.

Moreover, exploiting Edge-Computing in this approach, the privacy preserving requirements are embraced implicitly due to nature of this sort of distributed architecture.

1.1   A Usage Scenario

Suppose that a system based on the proposed system is used to monitor a patient's in-home care. The patient suffers from a particular pathology that, among other problems, causes high blood pressure. To be able to lower the pressure, the doctor has prescribed two pressure pills a day, one at 07.00 am and the other at 09.00 pm. The doctor's diagnosis and the prescriptions for the medications to be taken are part of the CP. The pills are in a smart container (e.g. RxCap[1]) which indicates the time at which a pill is taken. If the doctor has prescribed that the patient should only take the pill twice a day, the CP knows that the sensor that controls the opening of the container should only be opened (or closed) twice a day and the pill can only be taken twice. The sphygmomanometer worn by the patient, according to the pressure monitoring instructions of the CP, performs pressure monitoring 5 times a day: 06.00 am, 09.00 am, 03.00 pm, 05.00 pm, and 08.00 pm. If the value of the pressure measurement is not in the range indicated in the CP, the CPAD detects a *Specific Malfunction*. This generates a notification that informs the actors involved (doctor, patient and relatives) of this event, and the correction flows are then appropriately generated.

---

[1] https://rxcap.com/.

It is possible to know the behavior of each sensor because the hardware specifications and operating details (and also malfunctioning) are available. For example, the sphygmomanometer measures blood pressure at predefined intervals, as specified in the CP. The pressure measurement process takes 30 s. If the measurement process lasted only 10 s, it detects a *Hardware Malfunction*, which is due to several factors, e.g. low battery.

In the same scenario, an example of *System Hacking* is the following one: the doctor has prescribed two blood pressure pills a day. This information is codified in the CP, thus it is displayed on the patient's tablet or programmed in the pill dispenser. The system could be hacked so that the number of pills is increased to 4.

2 Related Work

With the advent of IoT, monitoring patients' care and their vital parameters has become easier thanks to wearable devices. Still, there are issues related to performances and security.

Weareable IoT devices are applied in crucial applications: monitoring vital signs, tracking indoor positions, or alerting for some crucial events [5]. Besides, with the advent of machine learning, these applications are becoming more and more sophisticated, requiring much computational power. Processes driven by such devices become time-consuming and harvest much computational power, thus also impacting on the battery life.

Low latency to send and receive critical data or high reliability to scale or replace these devices are the most critical constraints in the healthcare context. Standard cloud architectures to manage the network communications cannot be exploited. Indeed, cloud computing is not designed with these goals in mind, thus it doesn't fulfil these requirements [2].

The Multi-access Edge Computing (MEC) approach addresses this issue [16] [2]. MEC is defined as the ability to process and store data at the edge of the network, i.e., in the proximity of the data sources. By adopting this architecture, bottlenecks in healthcare systems can be significantly reduced thanks to the lower amount of data transferred to the cloud. MEC's advantage in a smart health environment is multifaceted, as it can provide short response time, decreased energy consumption for battery-operated devices, network bandwidth saving, secure transmission and data privacy [1].

Edge computing is a promising solution to mitigate this issue. It is distributed, thus sensible data are pre-processed on the edge of the network and obfuscated sensitive information of the patient are sent to a central server that needs only extracted features to perform related tasks.

However, these smart devices can also be subject to malfunctions and technical anomalies (intentional or unintentional). It is fundamental to detect in order to avoid serious life-threatening for a patient.

An anomaly detection system is proposed in [10]. It is based on the extraction of care-flow records that regularly capture medical behaviors in clinical processes, also identifying the anomalous ones. In order to monitor patient treatment and care behaviors in a variety of clinical settings, this approach requires an high-frequency detection rate of the care-flow records and a specific description of them.

Ahsanul Haque et al. [9] present a system for the detection of sensor anomalies in healthcare, able to distinguish real alarms from false alarms. The system is implemented in Java combined to WEKA framework. The system was tested on three real medical datasets. The value detected by a sensor is compared with the historical data, in order to detect suspicious variations. The experimental results show a Detection Rate (DR) of 100% and a low false-positive rate (FPR) for all the datasets.

Unfortunately, none of the solutions presented above fully meets the key requirements and challenges in the field of anomaly and attack detection in healthcare. The system proposed in this paper aims at offering a complete, autonomous, and effective architecture, which is also able to detect anomalies and cyber attacks in the healthcare domain.

3 System Architecture

The proposed system, thanks to the use of Bluetooth sensors, is able to monitor clinical parameters without the need of the physical presence of a healthcare professional. The system detects various clinical parameters (e.g., Blood Oxygen Level (OXI), Electrocardiogram (ECG), body temperature, etc.), processes captured data and generates the Clinical Pathway for the patient under treatment. This approach is a common strategy in this approach; like depicted in [2] [5] collecting remote data from these sensors will be more complex due to the heterogeneous devices involved in measurement of these parameters.

Figure 1 depicts a general overview of the system architecture for the continuous monitoring of a patient and safe management of his/her CP. Each smart device (e.g. headband, smartwatch) feeds the edge-node infrastructure with its specific data. Thanks to machine learning solutions and related e-health techniques, these data are used to monitor a patient and produce an efficient clinical path, give continuous feedback about health conditions to the doctor's control unit and enable interaction between doctor, patient, and his/her relatives.

The data management is a challenging aspect because of the ingestion of heterogeneous data with low latency and zero downtime, alongside the generation of a proper clinical Pathway based on patient history. These crucial aspects are linked to some other issues: one of the most critical is the anomaly detection.

The core of the architecture is a cluster of edge nodes that cooperate to perform a sort of Extract, transform, load (ETL) task. This cluster is intrinsically linked to the anomaly detection and it matches the constraints of MEC solution proposed by [16], which monitors the general task step by step. To guarantee efficient and robust communications between sensors and edge-node clusters (ENCs), at least two ENCs should be available in a neighborhood. Since this architecture inherits the spec of scalability from standard edge architecture, including new ENCs is almost effortless.

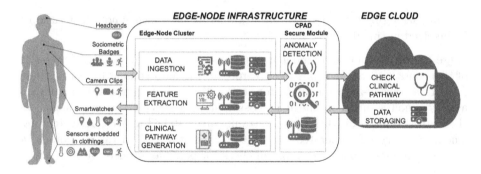

Fig. 1. The Proposed Architecture.

The main components of the architecture are described in the following.

Data Ingestion node. As stressed before, due to the massive employment of various smart devices, a data ingestion module orchestrates all data streams coming from these objects. This node is devoted to creating links between wearable medical devices and other modules belonging to the architecture. Data flows are injected into the Feature Extraction node for further specific elaborations and in the Clinical Path Anomaly Detection node to identify malformed data.

Feature Extraction node. One of the most critical issues to address is to guarantee the data privacy of each patient. For this reason, data flow coming from smart medical devices are processed at the edge of the network by this node. All vital sign data are analyzed to extract notable characteristics from the stream. These features are then injected into the Clinical Path Anomaly Detection module to be confident about the goodness of the detected data or to identify some troubles inside them.

Clinical Pathway Generation node. Among the goals of the system, the generation of a personalized clinical pathway is a crucial task. The approach adopted in Mallardi et al. [4] is growing up as the main instrument for the implementation of clinical guidelines and evidence-based medicine.

Thanks to this node, the system learns from patient's history and combine this knowledge with that provided by doctors, thus producing a tailored therapy. Also this node interacts with the Clinical Path Anomaly Detection module to identify possible issues.

The three nodes described above have their own suitable storage space on board to save data useful to exchange information to/from the CPAD, which is connected to the external edge cloud

Clinical Path Anomaly Detection (CPAD) module. The specific design of this module, which represents the main contribution here, is detailed in the next section. This module makes the system less prone to anomalous situations, such as: (i) a specific malfunction related to vital sign and the therapy specified in the clinical pathway, (ii) hardware fail situations like battery degradation, (iii) system hacking by the patient or data tampering by someone not authorized to be involved in this process.

Edge Cloud. With this component, it is possible to manage two specific aspects of this context. First, it is possible to store all the data coming from the single ENC in a privacy-aware manner. Recently, this kind of approach has emerged as a common solution in the IoT ecosystem with specific constraints, like in the health domain. In [16] these constraints are matched in MEC Architecture. Then, for every CP generated by the Clinical Pathway Generation module, a specific component performs a formal check for possible inconsistencies.

4   Clinical Path Anomaly Detection Secure Module

Anomaly detection is of pivotal interest not only in network intrusion detection [6], fraud detection in financial domain [3], air pollution [15], but also in the healthcare domain concerning medical diagnosis [17].

As stated in Sect. 3, sensors detect the vital parameters and send them at the ENC where the *Ingestion* node performs data orchestration. Then, the *Feature Extraction* node extracts key features. To check if data transmission is correct and that there have been no malfunctions (including system hacking), the proposed system is equipped with a module called *Clinical Path Anomaly Detection (CPAD)*. The CPAD module analyzes all the data transmitted from the devices monitoring the patient to the ENC and eventually notifies detected anomalies. Using specifically implemented machine learning techniques, the CPAD module manages the security issues that could occur during the data transmission process. In this context the anomaly could also consist of an attack to the monitoring of the patient's clinical parameters. The detected anomaly causes a dysfunction in the CP that in turn has a direct impact on the patient's health.

From a more technological perspective, the data collected in the *Ingestion* node can be seen as a queue and as organized into several sub-processes. Each sub-process represents the detection phase of a vital parameter from a single device worn by the patient. Thanks to the adoption of a recurrent sequential Long Short Term Memory (LSTM) autoencoder, the CPAD analyzes the various sub-processes of the chain to perform the detection of anomalies on the steps of the chain [11,12].

In particular, the advantage of using sequential LSTM autoencoders is two-fold: (i) taking advantage of the dimensionality reduction and extraction capabilities of the autoencoder to efficiently perform the data reconstruction process, and then detect the anomaly and (ii) using LSTM networks to manage the sequential nature of the data detected by the sensors.

The difference between a regular and recurrent autoencoders may be summarised as it follows: regular autoencoders work on sequential data by fixing the data size, usually by padding all sequences with zero vectors to the length of the longest sequence [13]. In contrast, the recurrent autoencoders that were adopted in this proposal can compress variable-length sequences into fixed-length representations [8]. Therefore, they can generalize dependencies between nearby frames to other positions in the sequence.

In this way, the CPAD Module is able to define whether or not the patient's CP is correct. Otherwise, a specific machine learning algorithm adjusts the CPs according to the data currently detected. The CPAD Module is able to detect three types of anomalies:

1. **Specific Malfunction**: it indicates a specific system malfunction. The module can detect whether the parameters that are transmitted from wearable devices to the edge node are reliable or not. It is also able to monitor whether the actions to be performed are those as per the CP.
2. **Hardware Malfunction**: it indicates a hardware malfunction. The module can detect the battery-charge status of the devices and the malfunctioning of the detection probes and patches. It also detects transmission errors at the Bluetooth protocol level.
3. **System Hacking**: it indicates system hacking. The module can detect if someone is trying to hack the system and if the user is trying to trick them.

5   Discussion and Conclusion

The main contribution of this position paper is about the Edge-Node architecture and its capability of detecting different kinds of anomalies in the healthcare domain, which could be useful in particular for patient assisted at home. This approach exploits a novel machine learning technique, implemented in the CPAD module, that encapsulates two layers of LSTM into an Autoencoder structure. Indeed, the overall idea is to detect and keep track of anomaly situations with respect to the clinical history of a patient.

In order to deeply assess that this design correctly meets all the constraints of this kind of scenario, it is mandatory a set of studies addressing the system performances from two different points of view. The former is to evaluate the anomaly detection performances of the CPAD module. The first challenging step here is the collection and annotation of data from a large number of patients with different diseases. The following step is to evaluate the CPAD module with these real data to measure the system's performance in terms of the traditional metrics, like precision.

An interesting factor to address for future development is a module that acts as an "explainer". The explanation of artificial intelligence is a critical aspect in all the system that supports human decisions, and also this scenario could be examined from this point of view. This aspect represents a conjunction of different spheres: from the classical side of philosophical details to human-computer interaction. An extensive scientific literature corpus supports the importance of the explanation in this kind of systems. It could be fascinating to examine this aspect in the proposed approach to measure how various actors of the domain perceive system decisions.

This aspect is strictly linked to the users' trustability in the system. This is particular important in the healthcare domain, since it involves crucial aspects of people's life. For example, suppose that a patient is used to take a pill to control blood pressure twice a day. If some vital parameters involved in his/her pathology go out of a determined range, the Clinical Pathway Generator module could proactively react and change the pathway, asking the patient to take one more pill. How could the patient be serene that the modification does not depend on a malfunction? It is interesting to explore how visual explanations can improve system trustability. Nevertheless, such smart devices could have a peculiar trustability, eventually equipped with some hardware extensions. For instance, it could be beneficial to monitor some situations in which they could be hacked, unintentionally or not, by the patient. Considering the pill dispenser, by counting the number of times it is opened, it keeps track of the number of pills that the patient takes. But what does it happen if the patient picks a pill from the dispenser, but she does not actually take it because of dementia? The pill dispenser could be equipped with a micro-camera that captures arm and hand movement to check the correctness of the action. As a further example, If the patient has a pedometer and his CP prescribes that he could take a certain amount of steps per day, he may give his device to someone else, or to his dog, who achieves the goal for him. A machine learning algorithm could discover the lie based on the patient's historical data, pathology, or speed.

References

1. Abdellatif, A.A., Khafagy, M.G., Mohamed, A., Chiasserini, C.: EEG-based transceiver design with data decomposition for healthcare IoT applications. IEEE Internet Things J. **5**(5), 3569–3579 (2018)
2. Abdellatif, A.A., Mohamed, A., Chiasserini, C.F., Tlili, M., Erbad, A.: Edge computing for smart health: Context-aware approaches, opportunities, and challenges. IEEE Network **33**(3), 196–203 (2019)
3. Ahmed, M., Mahmood, A.N., Islam, M.R.: A survey of anomaly detection techniques in financial domain. Future Gener. Comput. Syst. **55**, 278–288 (2016)
4. Ardito, C., Bellifemine, F., Di Noia, T., Lofù, D., Mallardi, G.: A proposal of case-based approach to clinical pathway modeling support. In: Proceedings of the IEEE Conference on Evolving and Adaptive Intelligent Systems (EAIS 2020) (2020)
5. Awad, A., Mohamed, A., Chiasserini, C., El-Fouly, T.M.: Distributed in-network processing and resource optimization over mobile-health systems. J. Netw. Comput. Appl. **82**, 65–76 (2017)
6. Bhuyan, M.H., Bhattacharyya, D.K., Kalita, J.K.: Network anomaly detection: methods, systems and tools. IEEE Commun. Surv. Tutorials **16**, 303–336 (2013)
7. Cappelletti, P.: Pdta e medicina di laboratorio. La Rivista Italiana della Medicina di Laboratorio-Italian Journal of Laboratory Medicine (2017)
8. Fabius, O., van Amersfoort, J.R., Kingma, D.P.: Variational recurrent auto-encoders. In: Bengio, Y., LeCun, Y. (eds.) 3rd International Conference on Learning Representations, ICLR 2015, San Diego, CA, USA, May 7–9, 2015, Workshop Track Proceedings (2015)
9. Haque, S.A., Rahman, M., Aziz, S.M.: Sensor anomaly detection in wireless sensor networks for healthcare. Sensors **15**(4), 8764–8786 (2015)
10. Huang, Z., Lu, X., Duan, H.: Anomaly detection in clinical processes. In: AMIA Annual Symposium Proceedings (2012)

11. Leung, K., Leckie, C.: Unsupervised anomaly detection in network intrusion detection using clusters. In: Proceedings of the 28th Australasian Conference on Computer Science, Vol. 38, pp. 333–342 (2005)
12. Meidan, Y., et al.: N-baiot-network-based detection of IoT botnet attacks using deep autoencoders. IEEE Pervasive Comput. **17**(3), 12–22 (2018)
13. Sakurada, M., Yairi, T.: Anomaly detection using autoencoders with nonlinear dimensionality reduction. In: Proceedings of the MLSDA 2014 2nd Workshop on Machine Learning for Sensory Data Analysis (2014)
14. Schrijvers, G., van Hoorn, A., Huiskes, N.: The care pathway: concepts and theories: an introduction. Int. J. Integrated Care (2012)
15. Shaadan, N., Jemain, A.A., Latif, M.T., Deni, S.M.: Anomaly detection and assessment of pm10 functional data at several locations in the Klang valley, Malaysia. Atmos. Pollut. Res. **6**(2), 365–375 (2015)
16. Taleb, T., Samdanis, K., Mada, B., Flinck, H., Dutta, S., Sabella, D.: On multi-access edge computing: a survey of the emerging 5G network edge cloud architecture and orchestration. IEEE Commun. Surv. Tutorials **19**(3), 1657–1681 (2017)
17. Wong, W.K., Moore, A.W., Cooper, G.F., Wagner, M.M.: Bayesian network anomaly pattern detection for disease outbreaks. In: Proceedings of the 20th International Conference on Machine Learning (ICML-03), pp. 808–815 (2003)

Paying the Pink Tax on a Blue Dress - Exploring Gender-Based Price-Premiums in Fashion Recommendations

Alexander Brand[(⊠)] 📵 and Tom Gross 📵

Human-Computer Interaction Group, University of Bamberg, Kapuzinerstr. 16,
96047 Bamberg, Germany
hci@uni-bamberg.de

Abstract. In the field of Human-Computer Interaction there is considerable awareness on diversity and inclusion. At the same time topics such as gender and race have become more prominent recently. One aspect that has received little attention, however, is the possible reproduction of real-world socio-demographic inequality structures through recommendation systems in fashion. To investigate gender-specific differences in recommender systems, we utilise data from Amazon and use quantile regressions to calculate what price differences exist for the recommended products concerning the primary product. Our results show a bias in recommended pricing premiums about addressed gender. While a higher price in comparison to the viewed product is charged for all genders, product recommendations for women generally show a higher premium than those for men (about 5% more at the median, ceteris paribus). This can be influenced by the starting price and the popularity of the product, i.e. the sales ranking.

Keywords: GenderIT · Gender price gap · Recommendation bias

1 Motivation

Product recommendations are a relevant part of the shopping experience when buying clothes virtually [1]. The possibility to access similarly presented products in addition to the directly found items and to compare them simply and playfully offers advantages for users as well as for suppliers [2]. Sellers can present a wider range of products and potential buyers get better insights. In this respect, it is central for a good user experience that recommendations represent balanced alternatives. However, the question arises whether the underlying recommendation systems work in a non-discriminatory way as desired. From an HCI perspective this is especially important, because such factors undermine the idea of building systems that are equally accessible and usable for all. Here, aspects like gender [3, 4] and race [5] are becoming more and more part of the discourse and shape the thinking about what is socially expected when designing software. Accordingly, research on discriminatory patterns in established shops is necessary to learn about potential sources of bias and where to start when trying to minimise it,

© IFIP International Federation for Information Processing 2020
Published by Springer Nature Switzerland AG 2020
R. Bernhaupt et al. (Eds.): HCSE 2020, LNCS 12481, pp. 190–198, 2020.
https://doi.org/10.1007/978-3-030-64266-2_12

when engineering new software. One factor that has become prominent in recent years is the so-called "pink tax" [6–9], i.e. the fact that products for women as consumers have higher prices than their male equivalents. This factor is observed especially with popular products [10]. For example, a study by the consumer advice centre in Hamburg, Germany, showed that they found such patterns in online stores like Douglas and dm (drug store chains) [11]. This raises the question of whether recommendations on such sites also follow or even reinforce such pricing patterns or counteract this trend. In this article, we use a large product data set from Amazon [12, 13] to investigate to what extent such tendencies can be identified for the clothing industry. Our evaluation uses quantile regression models [14] to take into account the wide dispersion of the price premium and to obtain adequate estimates for the parameters. In this context we address the following research questions:

Q1) How do price differences of recommendations to clothes differ according to the gender addressed?

Q2) How does the interplay between addressed gender and popularity vary in terms of price?

Q3) How does the interplay between addressed gender and original price vary in terms of price?

2 Related Work

Concerning the effects of gender-oriented pricing, Stevens et al. [8] show that despite the awareness of unequal treatment about prices, women are willing to buy them if the product signals sufficient affection. A comprehensive report on the extent of differences is provided by An der Heiden und Wersig [11] who find considerable differences in services such as haircutting. Here, only 11% of all providers would offer men and women the same prices for short haircuts. Also for clothes, specific offers like professional cleaning 68% would charge different prices. The authors provide similar results for the German market as previous studies on price differences for the USA and UK [15, 16]. Concerning possible bias in recommender systems, Ekstrand et al. [17] show for the online book market that recommendations can have a gender bias, but differences depending on the underlying algorithm have to be taken into account. In principle, however, recommender systems could also help to counteract filter bubbles and not support them, as the work of Nguyen et al. shows [18]. Such an effect is particularly relevant when personalised recommendations are considered, as these recommendations are of particular importance, also in comparison to recommendations closer to the people, such as "other customers also bought", as considered in this study. In relation to more general approaches, the branch of the investigation of fairness in recommender systems [19], which methodically deals with the reduction of bias has emerged. Depending on the area, bias can refer to socio-demographic characteristics [20] as well as undesirable patterns due to strong differences in popularity [21]. Possible approaches are punishing the corresponding model parameters if the bias is too strong [19]. While these approaches include a variety of areas of application the authors are not aware of any in-depth statistical analysis of gender bias for the field of fashion, which is especially interesting because pricing itself is analysed quite often [22–25].

3   Theoretical Background

Pink Tax describes a circumstance, which assumes that a similar or the same product is offered with different prices for men and women. Often products for women are priced higher than those for men [10]. In addition to a price component, this is also reflected in the product range—for instance, when the choice of products for women is smaller [7]. A combination of signalling [10] and role theory [26, 27] can be used as a justification for the perceived use. Looking at signalling, it can be explained that the products offered are interpreted by the female buyers in such a way that the annotations made to the products give the impression of a gender connotation of the product [10]. Consequently, the purchase of pink products or objects "for Her", as an example, illusorily illustrates the affiliation to the group of "real" women [13]. Consequently, the use of a gender-addressed object represents an act of legitimation of personal sexuality [10]. Duesterhaus et al. conclude that correspondingly larger price differences should be found for publicly visible aspects such as hairstyles and feminine clothing [10]. Furthermore, when considering gender pricing, the specific role and public display of women [28] in the social and working environment must be taken into account. For example, the fear of potential disadvantages that may arise from the inadequate use of gender-specific, reputable clothing may encourage purchasing decisions for correspondingly gender-addressed products [10]. This can be applied to the consideration of additional recommendations in a way that the alternatives to a product define a range of acceptable alternatives. These are legitimised by the fact that the alternatives showed are either similar in nature, compatible, or serve the same purpose. Since the alternatives define a price range, they indicate which range of prices is acceptable for a given item. According to the expectations regarding the individual prices, products, which address women, should also show a right-shifted distribution of the prices of the recommended products. If these are popular products, there should also be a larger price difference, because it would be expected that these products would be used to meet social expectations and would therefore be bought at higher premiums. Consequently, a larger price premium can be expected for products addressed to women. Additionally, due to gender pricing for more everyday products, a larger difference should be found for more frequently demanded goods, i.e. in this case more popular items. In this respect, the following hypotheses are to be tested:

H1) Products for women have more expensive recommendations than products for men.

H2) The price difference is influenced by the popularity of the product.

H3) The price difference is influenced by the price of the product.

4   Methods

For the evaluation, Amazon product data was used because the recommendations are presented explicitly and separately based on the current product under consideration. For the analyses, the recommender system data of UC San Diego [12, 13] with 1,503,384 products was used, which include data such as a description of the item, price, product categories, brand, sales rank, and alternative clothing items recommended for the product. We calculated for all products the ratio from the average of the prices of the recommended products and the displayed products and named the result "Price Premium". In this respect, the target value is a variable that has the value range $[0, +\infty]$. Values >1 indicate a more expensive recommendation, while values <1 mean that the recommended products are cheaper than the selected product. Besides, information on the products was extracted from the stored product categories. Since clothing for young adults and children can also have other rules for consumption [29], only the categories "Women" and "Men" were used as indicators for the gender assignment of the products. Due to non-normality ($p < 0.001$, Shapiro-Wilk-Tests), non-parametric methods were chosen. To test the hypotheses, quantile regression models were used, which on the one hand allow to relax the underlying distribution assumptions and on the other hand are robust against outliers and thus are often applied in pricing research [14, 30–32]. For the calculation, interaction effects between the addressed gender and the sales rank were taken into account. Furthermore, the price of the original product and interactions of the original price with the addressed gender were considered in the modelling to test for general pricing effects. In this respect the unrestricted model can be written as:

$$Q_\tau(Premium_i) = \beta_0(\tau) + \beta_1(\tau)Gender + \beta_2(\tau)Rank \\ + \beta_3(\tau)Gender * Rank + \beta_4(\tau)Price + \beta_5(\tau)Gender * Price + \varepsilon \quad (1)$$

Where τ is considered for the values 0.1–0.9 and $\beta_0(\tau)$, $\beta_1(\tau)$, ... , $\beta_5(\tau)$ are calculated accordingly as the result of a minimization problem for the estimated value of τ.

5 Results

Regarding the used variables we observe a high dispersion in Price, Price Premiums, and Ranking with a high right skewness. The mean price is around 34\$ and the mean price premium is around 1.28 which indicates a surplus of about 28% for recommendations. Regarding the addressed gender we observe 244908 products for women and 140117 products for men. The descriptive analysis of the variables addressed gender, sales rank, price and average recommended price show bivariate relationships of varying strength and direction. If we look at possible differences according to gender, significant differences between the addressed genders can be seen for both the price and the price difference between product and recommendation. A Mann-Whitney U test shows that the median of products for women ($Mn = 22$) surpass those for men ($Mn = 21.6$) on a significant level ($W = 3649143244$, $p = 0.0004$). The same is observable for the distribution of the price premiums. Accordingly, a Mann-Whitney U test shows that female products ($Mn = 1$) surpass products, which address men ($Mn = 0.988$) on a significant level ($W = 2622305840$, $p < 2.2e-16$). The usage of quantile regression lines reveals a negative relationship in the graphical representation of ranks against premiums. It is important to note here that this effect can only be differentiated for ranks >100 and that the sample contains too few products addressed to women. Otherwise the pure plotting of the observations does not show a clear direction when ignoring the addressed gender.

Testwise, we observe the same effect as in Fig. 1 (right side). Our calculations using spearman rank correlation tests indicate that there is a significant relationship between the premium and the sales rank ($r_s = .13$, $p < .001$) (Fig. 2).

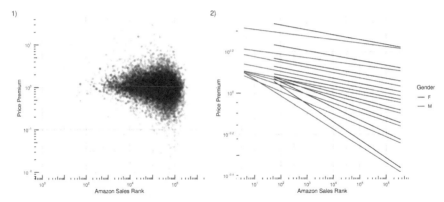

Fig. 1. Relationship between (Sales) Rank and Price Premiums. Left side displays the distribution of observations on a log-log scale to account for high dispersion. Right side shows the results of gender-facetted quantile regression smoothening. The lines symbolise the 10% quantiles within a gender (F = Female, M = Male), which are displayed in different colours.

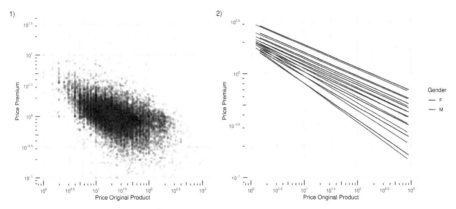

Fig. 2. Relationship between Price and Price Premiums. Left side displays the distribution of observations on a log-log scale to account for high dispersion. Right side shows the results of gender-facetted quantile regression smoothening (F = Female, M = Male) like Fig. 1.

Looking at the regression model the available number of observations for the test variables differ highly, which leads to a usable sample of 150919 observations for the model. For $\tau = 0.5$ (median), a significant effect on the parameter "For Men" ($\beta = -0.014$, $p < 0.001$) can be observed. Considering the other variables, continues to increase and finally has a value of $\beta = -0.053$ ($p < 0.001$).

This means higher prices for female targeting products ceteris paribus. A positive significant effect ($p < 0.001$) can be shown for the interaction with the starting price, which has an effect of $\beta = -0.0004$, which shows a dependency of the gender effect in relation to the original product price. Looking at the variable Sales Rank (1000s) a negative significant relationship ($\beta = -0.001$, $p < 0.001$) can be observed. This means unpopular products tend to have lower gendered differences in price premiums ceteris paribus. A similar picture is shown when the calculation is carried out for all values of τ. Here, for all considered values of the parameter "For Men", an effect significantly different from 0 is shown concerning the difference between the product and recommended products. A similar effect can be observed for price and rank. A more differentiated effect can be determined for the interaction terms. Here significant positive effect can be seen for larger values of τ. This can be interpreted to mean that for very high price differences, other variables (e.g. discounts) may be more important. In order to check the influence of brands, the average brand prices and the quantiles of the average prices of the brands were checked. Here, no relevant differences were found about the parameters. In summary, the results indicate a higher price premium for female targeting products, which depends on the original price and the popularity (Fig. 3).

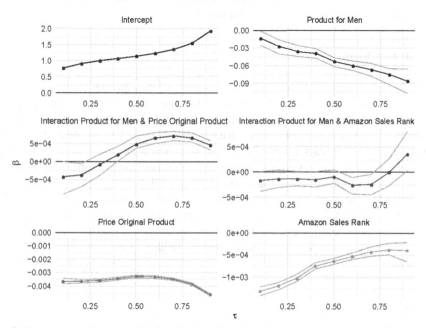

Fig. 3. Parameter estimations of β for the unrestricted model (see methods section) for given τ. The area around the estimates shows the 95% confidence band.

6   Discussion

Our results show a significant difference in the prices of recommendations depending on whether the product is addressed to men or women. The effect is slightly determined by the starting price and the popularity of the product. However, there are large differences in the quantiles of the distribution of the premium. While smaller and medium price differences according to gender are rather little influenced by the other variables considered, these factors show an influence on the gender difference, especially for higher-priced and less popular products. In this respect, the addressed gender seems to make a difference, but this is not suitable to explain extreme differences such as >78% (90%-quantile) premium alone. Following H2, interactions have to be considered here. In this respect, the argument of a broadly observable pricing strategy differentiated according to gender show that even in the case of a large provider, corresponding discriminatory structures can still be found. Another effect is that the coefficients are not much lower for popular products, which shows that such effects are not only relevant for fringe group interests, but also meet the casual shopper. One aspect which is put forward here in defence is that products for women are not directly comparable to products for men, as there might be differences in quality or products might not be comparable due to other characteristics. In this case, the algorithm used already constitutes a space of products that can be considered as comparable. Additionally, for clothing that is mass-produced there should not normally be any major differences in production costs [11] and as checked before, the effect is not affected much by the chosen brand.

7 Limitations

We showed that fashion recommendation systems have the potential to reproduce sexist pricing strategies. Further research is needed with respect to recommendation algorithms [33–35]. Especially the consideration of the different brands suggests very different gender orientation bases, even if recommendations also include clothes outside the considered label [36]. The data set used here offers little comparable meta information about the products and buying behaviour. Further research should explore other relevant background factors in greater depth and compare between different suppliers. Besides, the focus was only on items of clothing that were explicitly identified by Amazon as for men or women. Here, image recognition and natural language processing methods can help to classify the target groups more precisely to further increase the number of cases on the one hand and to reduce potential selective failures due to designation errors on the other.

References

1. Kotouza, M.T., Tsarouchis, S., Kyprianidis, A.C., Chrysopoulos, A.C., Mitkas, P.A.: Towards fashion recommendation: an AI system for clothing data retrieval and analysis. In: Maglogiannis, I., Iliadis, L., Pimenidis, E. (eds.) AIAI 2020. IAICT, vol. 584, pp. 433–444. Springer, Cham (2020). https://doi.org/10.1007/978-3-030-49186-4_36
2. Senecal, S., Nantel, J.: The influence of online product recommendations on consumers' online choices. J. Retail. **80**, 159–169 (2004). %@ 0022-4359
3. Bardzell, S.: Feminist HCI: taking stock and outlining an agenda for design, pp. 1301–1310 (2010)
4. Stumpf, S., et al.: Gender-inclusive HCI research and design: a conceptual review. Found. Trends® Hum.–Comput. Interact. **13**, 1–69 (2020)
5. Schlesinger, A., Edwards, W.K., Grinter, R.E.: Intersectional HCI: Engaging identity through gender, race, and class, pp. 5412–5427 (2017)
6. Jacobsen, K.A.: Rolling back the "Pink Tax": dim prospects for eliminating gender-based price discrimination in the sale of consumer goods and services. Calif. West. Law Rev. **54**, 2 (2018)

7. Lafferty, M.: The pink tax: the persistence of gender price disparity. Midwest J. Undergr. Res. **11**, 56–72 (2019)
8. Stevens, J.L., Shanahan, K.J.: Structured abstract: anger, willingness, or clueless? Understanding why women pay a pink tax on the products they consume. In: Stieler, M. (ed.) Creating Marketing Magic and Innovative Future Marketing Trends. DMSPAMS, pp. 571–575. Springer, Cham (2017). https://doi.org/10.1007/978-3-319-45596-9_108
9. Yazıcıoğlu, A.E.: Pink Tax and the Law: Discriminating Against Women Consumers. Routledge, Abingdon (2018)
10. Duesterhaus, M., Grauerholz, L., Weichsel, R., Guittar, N.A.: The cost of doing femininity: gendered disparities in pricing of personal care products and services. Gend. Issues **28**, 175–191 (2011). https://doi.org/10.1007/s12147-011-9106-3
11. An der Heiden, I., Wersig, M.: Preisdifferenzierung nach Geschlecht in Deutschland (2017)
12. McAuley, J., Targett, C., Shi, Q., Van Den Hengel, A.: Image-based recommendations on styles and substitutes, pp. 43–52 (2015)
13. He, R., McAuley, J.: Ups and downs: modeling the visual evolution of fashion trends with one-class collaborative filtering (2016)
14. Koenker, R., Hallock, K.F.: Quantile regression. J. Econ. Perspect. **15**, 143–156 (2001)
15. Liston-Heyes, C., Neokleous, E.: Gender-based pricing in the hairdressing industry. J. Consum. Policy **23**, 107–126 (2000). https://doi.org/10.1023/A:1006492207450
16. Whittelsey, F.C.: Why women pay more: how to avoid marketplace perils (1993)
17. Ekstrand, M.D., Tian, M., Kazi, M.R.I., Mehrpouyan, H., Kluver, D.: Exploring author gender in book rating and recommendation. In: Proceedings of the 12th ACM Conference on Recommender Systems, pp. 242–250 (2018)
18. Nguyen, T.T., Hui, P.-M., Harper, F.M., Terveen, L., Konstan, J.A.: Exploring the filter bubble: the effect of using recommender systems on content diversity (2014)
19. Islam, R., Keya, K.N., Pan, S., Foulds, J.: Mitigating demographic biases in social media-based recommender systems. In: KDD (Social Impact Track) (2019)
20. Kamishima, T., Akaho, S.: Considerations on recommendation independence for a find-good-items task (2017)
21. Abdollahpouri, H.: Popularity Bias in Ranking and Recommendation (2019)
22. Archak, N., Ghose, A., Ipeirotis, P.G.: Deriving the pricing power of product features by mining consumer reviews. Manag. Sci. **57**, 1485–1509 (2011)
23. Lee, K., Lee, Y.S., Nam, Y.: A novel approach of making better recommendations by revealing hidden desires and information curation for users of internet of things. Multimed. Tools Appl. **78**(3), 3183–3201 (2018). https://doi.org/10.1007/s11042-018-6084-4
24. Schoinas, I.: Product Recommendation System (2019)
25. Zheng, Y., Gao, C., He, X., Li, Y., Jin, D.: Price-aware recommendation with graph convolutional networks, pp. 133–144. IEEE (2020)
26. Goffman, E.: Gender display. In: Goffman, E. (ed.) Gender Advertisements. COMMCU, pp. 1–9. Springer, London (1976). https://doi.org/10.1007/978-1-349-16079-2_1
27. Beckmann, C., Gross, T.: Social computing—Bridging the gap between the social and the technical. In: Meiselwitz, G. (ed.) SCSM 2014. LNCS, vol. 8531, pp. 25–36. Springer, Cham (2014). https://doi.org/10.1007/978-3-319-07632-4_3
28. West, C., Zimmerman, D.H.: Doing gender. Gend. Soc. **1**, 125–151 (1987). %@ 0891-2432
29. Darian, J.C.: Parent-child decision making in children's clothing stores. Int. J. Retail Distrib. Manag. **26**, 421–428 (1998). %@ 0959-0552
30. Chen, C.W.S., Li, M., Nguyen, N.T.H., Sriboonchitta, S.: On asymmetric market model with heteroskedasticity and quantile regression. Comput. Econ. **49**, 155–174 (2017). https://doi.org/10.1007/s10614-015-9550-3
31. Hung, W.-T., Shang, J.-K., Wang, F.-C.: Pricing determinants in the hotel industry: quantile regression analysis. Int. J. Hosp. Manag. **29**, 378–384 (2010)

32. Mak, S., Choy, L., Ho, W.: Quantile regression estimates of Hong Kong real estate prices. Urban Stud. **47**, 2461–2472 (2010)
33. Gross, T.: Group recommender systems in tourism: from predictions to decisions. In: Neidhardt, J., Fesenmaier, D., Kuflik, T., Woerndl, W. (eds.) Proceedings of the 2nd Workshop on Recommenders in Tourism - RecTour 2017 - Co-Located with the 11th ACM Conference on Recommender Systems - RecSys 2017, Como, Italien, 27 August, CEUR Workshop Proceedings, Aachen, Deutschland, vol. 1906, pp. 40–42 (2017)
34. Beckmann, C., Gross, T.: Towards increased utility of and satisfaction with group recommender systems. In: Berkovsky, S., Herder, E., Lops, P., Santos, O.C. (eds.) Extended Proceedings of the 21st Conference on User Modelling, Adaptation, and Personalisation - UMAP 2013, Rome, Italy, 10–14 June, CEUR Workshop Proceedings, Aachen, Germany, vol. 997, pp. 3–5 (2013)
35. Beckmann, C., Gross, T.: AGReMo: providing ad-hoc groups with on-demand recommendations on mobile devices. In: Dittmar, A., Forbrig, P. (eds.) Proceedings of the European Conference on Cognitive Ergonomics - ECCE 2011, Rostock, Germany, 24–26 August, pp. 179–183. ACM, New York (2011)
36. Lieven, T., Grohmann, B., Herrmann, A., Landwehr, J.R., Van Tilburg, M.: The effect of brand gender on brand equity. Psychol. Mark. **31**, 371–385 (2014). %@ 0742-6046

Wearable Touchscreens to Integrate Augmented Reality and Tablets for Work Instructions?

Jan Van den Bergh$^{(\boxtimes)}$ (ID) and Florian Heller (ID)

Expertise Centre for Digital Media Diepenbeek,
Hasselt University - tUL - Flanders Make, Hasselt, Belgium
{jan.bergh,florian.heller}@uhasselt.be

Abstract. Manual assembly in high variety - low volume production is challenging for the operators as there might be small changes from one product to the next. The operators receive adapted instruction sets to be aware of these small differences, currently either printed or presented on a computer terminal. Augmented Reality (AR) is considered the future of work instruction display as it promises hands-free interaction, but interacting with AR interfaces can be problematic in production environments.

In this paper, we report on an exploratory study where we compare tablet interaction with three different ways of touch interaction for AR glasses: on the table, on the glasses, and the lower arm. While keeping the instructions the same in all conditions, we measured how placement affects the overall workload while performing an assembly task. Results indicate that combining additional wearable touch input with AR glasses is at least a promising direction for future research and, at best, an enabler for more widespread AR usage in manual assembly.

Keywords: Work instructions · Augmented reality · Tablet · User-centered design · Assembly · End-user feedback

1 Introduction

Despite all automation achieved in manufacturing, a large part of the work is still performed by manual assembly operators, called just operators from now on. Especially in high variety, low volume production, they perform the majority of the work. In many cases, different models are assembled on the same line in mixed-model assembly systems (MMAS). This poses challenges for operators regarding cognitive load as these models might only differ in small details. Operators, thus, increasingly get (digital) work instructions that guide them during the assembly. However, given the challenging environment that a production line is, how can the operators interact best with these instructions.

J. V. den Bergh and F. Heller—Both authors contributed equally.

Wearables—computing devices worn at specific places on the body (e.g., arms, legs, belt) or head—have been described as promising to support operators in their tasks [7,8,10], as, e.g., head-mounted displays can superimpose information directly onto the assembly [1]. The issue of presenting the work instructions at the *right time* and offering a feedback channel for the operators to flag potential defects in the instructions [4] makes an input capability for the AR interface a necessity. Body-based touch input can be given under various circumstances, such as standing, sitting, or kneeling [12]. This paper discusses an exploratory study on how operators can interact with work instructions on the shop floor. As the work environment is likely to interfere with voice input and gestures, we focus on touch interaction, which is already supported by several such devices. We ran an experiment to evaluate the impact of the touch input location on the perceived workload while performing a primary assembly task. We presented the instructions on a tablet and an AR headset, and tested touch input on the tablet, the headset, or the lower arm.

2   Related Work

Augmented reality is frequently realized through HMDs. Koelle et al. investigated user attitudes towards these glasses and recommended being task-focused and using a least capabilities approach [6]. In the case of operators, this implies that if they are not expected to contribute pictures or videos, HMDs without a camera may be recommended. People have concerns about being recorded and may not even notice indicator LEDs when present, as shown in earlier research with laptops [9].

While gesture interaction with an HMD without a camera is limited, such interaction may not be desirable anyway [13]. Also, other research found that hand gestures that can be detected by such a camera may not be desirable; e.g., Hsieh et al. [5] found in their experiment on a gesture system for use in public space (using gloves) that most people naturally performed the gestures roughly around the lower torso. Most participants considered the gestures appropriate for use in the workplace (and other public conditions).

Nonetheless, a recent survey of 12 augmented reality glasses [11] showed that all but one have a camera built-in, although it can only take pictures on some devices. Control options mostly include a limited set of buttons and/or a touchpad on the glasses or a wired handheld device. Many reviewed AR glasses also offer voice or gesture control. Taking these studies together may imply that using other input than that offered by the devices may need to be explored. All devices should have this possibility as all glasses in the survey by Syberfeldt et al. [11] provide wireless connectivity options, which could be used to provide these alternative means of interaction.

3   Alternative Touch Interactions

To assess the potential of new multimodal interaction techniques on assembly lines, we performed an experiment where we compared various placements of

Fig. 1. Left: the assembly instructions are shown with a minimal navigation interface that allows to go to the next/previous step, give feedback on the current step, and get additional help. Middle: The feedback menu allows to record audio, to flag an unclear description or an unclear picture, and to activate the camera with zoom (right).

visual output and touch input and their impact on the perceived workload. Visualizing assembly instructions on a screen, for example, is robust and straightforward, yet cumbersome for the worker if the assembly area is large and she has to carry the tablet with her, for example. Moving the visualization to an AR headset is promising as it allows the worker to look at the instructions at all times if needed. The instructions can also be laid over the real-world components to provide an even more seamless experience [1]. Our goal is to provide a robust touch input surface with basic control of the worker's interface.

We evaluated how the visualization of the instructions (Fig. 1) and the placement of the control interface affects the perceived workload while assembling components. We wanted to investigate the effect of instruction placement (AR or tablet) and control (tablet, forearm, or head) on workload and performance.

3.1   Interface Description

Figure 1 shows the user interface, as shown on the tablet or the AR-headset. The instructions take up most of the screen with the feedback and navigation controls placed vertically on the right side. Feedback regarding the current instruction step can be given at different levels of granularity: to draw attention to a specific step in the instructions, the user can flag that step by pressing the topmost button. This button is intended for fast interaction if the problem is obvious, or the user is unable to provide more information due to time constraints, situational disability, or limited motivation. The light-bulb button leads to the submenu where the user can provide more detailed information, such as adding dedicated flags for *unclear description* or *unclear image*, or an audio recording or a picture. These options would enable motivated operators to provide richer input during assembly.

We implemented our interface in Unity and ran it on an HTC Nexus 9 as a tablet and a Microsoft Hololens as AR glasses. Our wearable device was a 2.8-inch touchscreen (Robopeak RPUSBDISP) attached to a Raspberry PI Zero W running Raspbian, and the control interface was implemented using Python and PyQt. The control interface sent its commands to the visualization application using OSC messages.

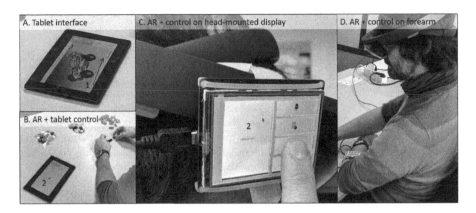

Fig. 2. Experiment conditions used in the experiment (A.-D.). We added explicit feedback instructions (1) and AR interface minimization button (2).

3.2 Experimental Setup and Procedure

Similar to the experiment by Funk et al. [2], participants had to assemble LEGO Models according to given instructions. To level the difficulty of the assembly, we used models from the LEGO Racers Tiny Turbos series (8642 (hereafter referred to as *Red*), 8644 (*Yellow*), 8657 (*Blue*), 8658 (*Black*)). The models had between nine and 11 instruction steps, with the number of parts to be added in a single step ranging from one to seven (M = 3.1, SD = 1.6) and the total number of pieces to assemble ranging from 27 (*Black*) to 38 (*Red*) (M = 32, SD = 4.5). All instruction sets contain a phase where the assembled model has to be flipped around to add pieces to the bottom side.

We defined four conditions, shown in Fig. 2. We used the tablet as a baseline condition (A). In the remaining cases, we visualized the instructions on the AR-headset and ran the control interface on a tablet (B), and a wearable device fixed to the glasses (C), or the participant's lower non-dominant arm (D).

Due to the limited display resolution and field-of-view (FOV) of the AR-headset, the instructions covered a large part of the visible area. Participants could, therefore, minimize the instructions to the upper left corner of the FOV using a dedicated button in the control interface (Fig. 2, 2). We deliberately did not fix the instructions to a particular physical location in the AR conditions, as this would basically mimic a dedicated screen at that position, which we already covered by the tablet condition.

We added requests to press specific buttons on the control interface to some of the instruction steps to simulate workers giving feedback (Fig. 2, 1). This allows the participant to decide whether to react to this request immediately or finish the assembly of the components first and provides the same amount of triggers to all participants.

The order of the conditions and the order of the models to be assembled was randomized using Latin squares. After each condition, we asked the participants

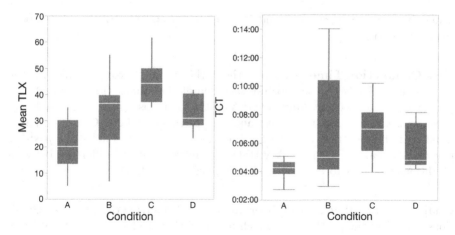

Fig. 3. Left: Mean RTLX by condition Right: Mean task completion time in minutes by condition (Fig. 2). Both graphs indicate mean, quartiles, and whiskers. The only significant difference was between condition C and the other conditions for both workload (RTLX) and completion time.

to fill out a pen-and-paper NASA TLX workload assessment questionnaire. We used the raw scores, frequently referred to as RTLX method [3].

3.3 Results

We recruited 10 participants (all male, mean age 31.1 years, SD = 6.4) from our lab. We removed one trial for the *blue* and one for the *black* model from quantitative analysis, as the task completion times deviated more than two standard deviations from the mean.

Workload. The mean TLX scores are reported in Fig. 3. We ran a repeated-measures ANOVA on the mean TLX scores with *condition* and *model* as fixed effects. *User* was modeled as random effect and the TLX scores were normally distributed. *Condition* had a significant effect on the average workload ($F_{3,30.03} = 10.32, p < .0001$). A *post-hoc* Tukey HSD-test showed that the workload in condition C (AR glasses and interaction on glasses) was significantly higher than in all other conditions ($p < 0.039$), but there was no significant difference between the other pairs. The type of model to be assembled did not have a significant effect on the workload ($F_{3,30.03} = 2.75, p = .0603$)

We ran a repeated-measures ANOVA on the mean TLX subscale ratings with *condition* as fixed effect and *user* as random effect. Pairwise *post-hoc* comparisons were made using Tukey HSD tests. We can observe the difficulties with condition C on the individual subscales of the TLX questionnaire. *Condition* had a significant effect on *Mental Demand* ($F_{3,33} = 5.5984, p = .0032$) and *Frustration* ($F_{3,33} = 6.3473, p = .0016$). Only condition C was significantly more mentally demanding than conditions A and B ($p < .0444$) and frustrating ($p = .0007$) than condition A.

Task Completion Time. Similar to the workload, just having the tablet al.one (condition A) leads to the shortest task completion times (Fig. 3 right). We performed a repeated-measures ANOVA on the log-transformed task completion times with *condition* as fixed effect and *user* as random effect. Condition had a significant effect on task completion time ($F_{3,33.01} = 3.3, p = .0323$). A *post-hoc* pairwise comparison with a Tukey HSD-test showed only the difference between conditions C and A to be statistically significant ($p = .032$).

Qualitative Feedback and Observations. After having completed all conditions, we asked the participants which interface they preferred, and seven chose tablet only without the AR glasses. They justified their choice with the well-known look-and-feel and that they could place it at a fixed position of their choice, making it easy to reach. One participant mentioned that he would prefer this interface even more than the original paper instructions because he does not have to look for the step he was at when he shifted his attention to the construction. Three participants said they preferred the combination of AR-Headset and the arm-worn wearable because the instructions are always in the field-of-view

One major issue with the AR-visualization was the Microsoft HoloLens that we used. When justifying their choice for the tablet visualization, participants complained about the weight and the visual quality. This includes the low physical resolution and color depth, but also the low contrast and the fact that it is obstructing the view in general. Six of the seven participants who opted for the tablet as preferred interface mentioned one of the AR-based combinations as second choice with high chances of moving to first choice if the headset was more comfortable.

From the seven participants that opted for the AR visualization as a second choice, five also discussed which control interface they would like to use along with it. Three mentioned the wearable on the arm as of their interest and a request to make it more polished as they did not like the hardware's prototype appearance.

Overall, participants had trouble with the red model's instructions in the AR conditions because it contains many dark pieces that are difficult to perceive with the HoloLens due to low contrast. Two participants had one non-critical piece left over after assembling the *red* model which they forgot in step five of the assembly. With this model, most of the participants had to return a few steps, but all were successful in recovering from that mistake.

We observed that during simple assembly steps, participants overlooked feedback instructions. Participants quickly grasped which pieces were to assemble and how, and then hit the *next* button while returning to the instructions. In a real-world setting, the trigger to give feedback will not be external as in this experiment, but intrinsic to the worker. However, it indicates that additional information needs to be prominent to grab attention from the primary task.

3.4 Discussion

In this experiment, we gained insights on how AR visualization and various control interfaces influence how people perceive work on an assembly task. The assembly task we had the users perform was constrained to a small space in front of the user, which allowed them to place the tablet right next to the components and leave it there. This may not always be possible in practice; the components might be located on shelves from which the user has to collect them before the assembly. In some cases, the workspace is much larger than a desk, requiring movement. There might not be free space to place the tablet next to the working area. These factors might tip the preference more towards an AR headset or wearable displays that are more mobile and leave the hands free (most of the time).Nevertheless, more light-weight headsets with a good visual quality are required for a tool that can be worn throughout an 8-h shift.

The screen placement only had a minor impact on both workload and task completion time compared to the placement of the feedback control panel. Once we move from a very local assembly task to larger items, this input device needs to be carried around, making the wearable control panel much more interesting. This also opens possible workarounds for the problem of the heavy headset, such as a combined input and output on a small touchscreen attached to the lower arm. To visualize assembly instructions, the screen needs to be bigger than the control interface. Smartphones or small tablets are already used to visualize instructions, and a similar size may be appropriate.

Some aspects of the experiment limit generalizability of the results. Given the exploratory character, we opted for a limited amount of participants. This means an experiment with a larger sample size is needed. This experiment is preferably also carried out with assembly operators and AR glasses, rather than an AR headset.

On the practical level, we would pay more attention to the limited contrast of AR devices as it might affect readability more than visible on a regular screen. Ideally, the devices in the different conditions also have a similar level of refinement. Possible changes in the presentation include presenting the instructions on the wearable controller and making it easy to put it on a table. This could create a hybrid between the tablet and AR glasses.

4 Conclusion

We studied where assembly instructions should be presented and how interaction with a minimal feedback interface affects workload. Most participants preferred the tablet solution, but they also stated that a more comfortable AR setup, especially with wearable touch-interaction, might be preferred.

Wearable, easily removable, touch controllers, possibly integrating display of instructions in combination with less bulky AR glasses, seem promising. The latter are already available [11]. Before definitive conclusions can be drawn on which interface technologies are best suited in such settings, more refined prototypes and evaluation with a large group of operators are still needed.

Acknowledgements. The work has been funded by the FlandersMake project OperatorKnowledge (grant number: HBC.2017.0395). The committee of ethics of Ghent University has approved the study (approval 2018/0439).

References

1. Barfield, W. (ed.): Fundamentals of Wearable Computers and Augmented Reality. CRC Press, Boca Raton (2015). https://doi.org/10.1201/b18703
2. Funk, M., Lischke, L., Mayer, S., Shirazi, A.S., Schmidt, A.: Teach me how! interactive assembly instructions using demonstration and in-situ projection, pp. 49–73. Springer Singapore, Singapore (2018). https://doi.org/10.1007/978-981-10-6404-3_4
3. Hart, S.G.: Nasa-task load index (nasa-tlx); 20 years later. In: Proceedings of the Human Factors and Ergonomics Society Annual Meeting, vol. 50, pp. 904–908. Sage publications Sage CA: Los Angeles, CA (2006)
4. Haug, A.: Work instruction quality in industrial management. Int. J. Ind. Ergon. **50**, 170–177 (2015). https://doi.org/10.1016/j.ergon.2015.09.015
5. Hsi eh, Y.T., Jylhä, A., Orso, V., Gamberini, L., Jacucci, G.: Designing a willing-to-use-in-public hand gestural interaction technique for smart glasses. In: CHI 2016, pp. 4203–4215. ACM, New York, NY, USA (2016). https://doi.org/10.1145/2858036.2858436
6. Koelle, M., Kranz, M., Möller, A.: Don't look at me that way!: understanding user attitudes towards data glasses usage. In: MobileHCI 2015, pp. 362–372. ACM, New York, NY, USA (2015). https://doi.org/10.1145/2785830.2785842
7. Kong, Xiang T.R., Luo, Hao., Huang, George Q., Yang, Xuan: Industrial wearable system: the human-centric empowering technology in industry 4.0. J. Intell. Manuf. **30**(8), 2853–2869 (2018). https://doi.org/10.1007/s10845-018-1416-9
8. Lukowicz, P., Timm-Giel, A., Lawo, M., Herzog, O.: WearIT@work: toward real-world industrial wearable computing. IEEE Pervasive Comput. **6**(4), 8–13 (2007). https://doi.org/10.1109/MPRV.2007.89
9. Portnoff, R.S., Lee, L.N., Egelman, S., Mishra, P., Leung, D., Wagner, D.: Somebody's watching me?: assessing the effectiveness of webcam indicator lights. In: CHI '15, pp. 1649–1658. ACM, New York, NY, USA (2015). https://doi.org/10.1145/2702123.2702164
10. Stanford, V.: Wearable computing goes live in industry. IEEE Pervasive Comput. **1**(4), 14–19 (2002). https://doi.org/10.1109/MPRV.2002.1158274
11. Syberfeldt, A., Danielsson, O., Gustavsson, P.: Augmented reality smart glasses in the smart factory: product evaluation guidelines and review of available products. IEEE Access **5**, 9118–9130 (2017). https://doi.org/10.1109/ACCESS.2017.2703952
12. Thomas, B., Grimmer, K., Zucco, J., Milanese, S.: Where does the mouse go? an investigation into the placement of a body-attached touchpad mouse for wearable computers. Pers. Ubiquit. Comput. **6**(2), 97–112 (2002). https://doi.org/10.1007/s007790200009
13. Werrlich, S., Nguyen, P.A., Daniel, A.D., Yanez, C.E.F., Lorber, C., Notni, G.: Design recommendations for HMD-based assembly training tasks. In: SmartObjects@ CHI, pp. 58–68 (2018)

ProConAR: A Tool Support
for Model-Based AR Product
Configuration

Sebastian Gottschalk[1(✉)], Enes Yigitbas[1], Eugen Schmidt[2],
and Gregor Engels[1]

[1] Software Innovation Lab, Paderborn University, Paderborn, Germany
{sebastian.gottschalk,enes.yigitbas,gregor.engels}@uni-paderborn.de
[2] Paderborn University, Paderborn, Germany
eschmidt@mail.uni-paderborn.de

Abstract. Mobile shopping apps have been using Augmented Reality
(AR) in the last years to place their products in the environment of the
customer. While this is possible with atomic 3D objects, there is still a
lack in the runtime configuration of 3D object compositions based on user
needs and environmental constraints. For this, we previously developed
an approach for model-based AR-assisted product configuration based on
the concept of Dynamic Software Product Lines. In this demonstration
paper, we present the corresponding tool support ProConAR in the form
of a Product Modeler and a Product Configurator. While the Product
Modeler is an Angular web app that splits products (e.g. table) up into
atomic parts (e.g. tabletop, table legs, funnier) and saves it within a
configuration model, the Product Configurator is an Android client that
uses the configuration model to place different product configurations
within the environment of the customer. We show technical details of
our ready to use tool-chain ProConAR by describing its implementation
and usage as well as pointing out future research directions.

Keywords: Product configuration · Augmented Reality ·
Model-based · Tool support

1 Introduction

In the last years, Apple and Google have pushed the topic of Augmented Reality (AR) in mobile apps within their mobile ecosystems. One area of focus is
mobile shopping [3], where AR can support the decision process of the customer
with additional product information, direct placement of products in the environment, and a greater product choice [4]. Examples for these mobile apps are

This work was partially supported by the German Research Foundation (DFG) within
the Collaborative Research Center "On-The-Fly Computing" (CRC 901, Project Number: 160364472SFB901).

the placing of an atomic product in the environment as in IKEA Place app[1], the configuration of products like windows in the VEKA Configurator AR app[2], or the placement of multiple products in an environment as recently announced by Amazon[3]. While these approaches focus on simple placements, they neglect the runtime configuration of 3D object compositions based on user needs and environmental constraints.

To improve this configuration process, we previously presented a model-based AR-assisted product configuration [6] that uses the concept of Dynamic Software Product Lines (DSPLs) [2]. The approach consists of a *Design Stage* and a *Runtime Stage*. At the *Design Stage*, we use the concepts of feature models and reuseable assets from Software Product Lines (SPLs) [1] to split the product representation and its possible configurations from the corresponding 3D objects. Out of both, we export a configuration model that is used at runtime. At the *Runtime Stage*, we import the configuration model and use the MAPE-K architecture [7] to monitor the user needs in the form of user inputs, the actual product configuration, and the environment. Based on the measured inputs, we configure possible product configurations within the environment.

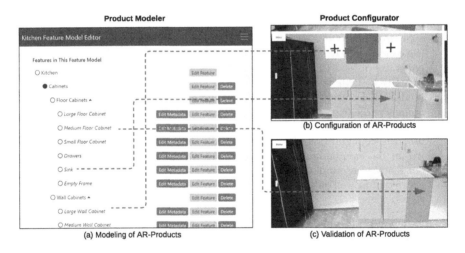

Fig. 1. ProConAR consists of a *Product Modeler* used by the *Developer* and a *Product Configurator* used by the *User*

In contrast to our research paper [6], in this demonstration paper we focus on the technical implementation of the corresponding tool ProConAR and point our

[1] IKEA Place at Apple's AppStore: https://apps.apple.com/us/app/ikea-place/id1279244498.

[2] VEKA Configurator AR at Apple's AppStore: https://apps.apple.com/us/app/vμ-configurator-ar/id1450934980.

[3] Announcement of Amazon: https://techcrunch.com/2020/08/25/amazon-rolls-out-a-new-ar-shopping-feature-for-viewing-multiple-items-at-once/.

future research directions. ProConAR, as shown in Fig. 1, consists of a *Product Modeler* and a *Product Configurator*. The *Product Modeler*, which is used at the *Design Stage*, is an Angular web app based on an existing feature model editor in [5]. It can be used to create feature models of possible product configurations (see Fig. 1 (a) for a developed kitchen model). Moreover, for each feature, a 3D object together with additional attributes can be saved. The created configuration model can be exported for the *Product Configurator*. The *Product Configurator*, which is used at the *Runtime Stage*, is an Android client based on the Unity Engine[4]. It imports the configuration model and uses the information to configure products within the environment (see Fig. 1 (b) for kitchen configuration in the environment). Moreover, it adapts the product configuration to the user needs, the product requirements, and the environmental constraints (see Fig. 1 (c) for validation of the product in the environment).

The rest of the paper is structured as follows: Sect. 2 provides the solution architecture of ProConAR in the form of a component diagram. Section 3 shows technical details in the modeling of the product, the transfer of the assets from the *Product Modeler* to the *Product Configurator*, and the configuration of the product. Finally, in Sect. 4 we conclude our paper and point out future research directions.

2 Solution Architecture

In this section, we provide a solution architecture for ProConAR based on a component-based architecture as shown in Fig. 2. The solution is divided into the *Design Stage*, which consists of the *Product Modeler* and the *Asset Modeler*, and the *Runtime Stage*, which consists of the *Product Configurator*.

In the *Design Stage*, the configuration parts of the products are modeled through a *Feature Model Editor* together with the attributes for additional product information as presented in [6]. Moreover, the assets for the configuration parts are made available with the *Asset Model Exporter* which is an external graphic modeling tool. Both, the *Feature Model* and *Assets*, are connected so that each feature can consist of an asset with a specific type (e.g. product, part of product, texture) and positioning (e.g. left slot, right slot, upper slot) to other features. Next, both are serialized through the *Asset Binder* to create a single *Asset Feature Bundle* which can be transferred to the *Product Configurator*. By choosing the *Asset Feature Bundle* as a loose coupling between both stages, the tools of each stage can be exchanged independently.

In the *Runtime Stage*, the *Asset Manager* is used to deserialize the *Asset Feature Bundle* into components. Here, we use the *Feature Model* to store all possible configurations, the *Configuration Model* to store the actual product configuration, the *User Model* to store the user needs and the *Environment Model* to store the environmental constraints. While the *Assets* can be directly used in the *Configurator Manager*, the *Features* need to be analyzed by the

---

[4] Unity Engine: http://www.unity.com.

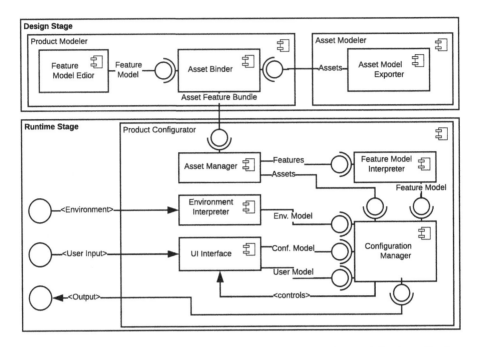

Fig. 2. Component overview of the developed *Product Modeler* and *Product Configurator* together with the external *Asset Modeler*

Feature Modeler Interpreter to derive the *Feature Model*. Moreover, the *Configuration Manager*, whose activities are based on the MAPE-K architecture and explained in [6], receives the requirements of the user, the configuration, and the environment during the runtime. While the *User Input* of the *UI Interface* can be directly restricted to use the *Configuration Model* and *User Model*, the *Environment* needs to be analyzed by the *Environment Interpreter* to derive the *Environment Model*. This is done by analyzing the images of the camera. With all these requirements the *Configuration Manager* can control the *UI Interface* and provide the configuration to the *Output*.

3   Technical Implementation

In this section, we present the technical implementation of the *Product Modeler*[5] and the *Product Configurator*[6]. Both tools are built on top of well-accepted development techniques to allow the reusing for other researchers. The *Product Modeler* is built on an Angular web app and can run directly in the web browser.

---

[5] Source Code of the Product Modeler: https://github.com/sebastiangtts/feature-modeler.
[6] Source Code of the Product Configurator: https://github.com/sebastiangtts/ar-product-configurator.

Moreover, we use an existing feature modeler [5] to cover all possible feature restrictions and dependencies. The *Product Configurator* is built on ARCore, the AR SDK of Android. Moreover, we use the Unity SDK that provides solutions for most interactions with the environment like detecting obstacles or modifying 3D mesh models. For the transfer between both tools, we use the assets bundling mechanism of Unity by using an *Importer Script* for the feature model, stored as JSON file, and the assets in the form of 3D meshes, stored as FBX files, and textures, stored as PNG files.

In the following, we are focusing on the steps of product modeling, the transfer of product configurations, and the product configuration. While this demonstration paper just roughly goes through the whole process of ProConAR, the detailed description of the installation and usage is provided within the repositories.

3.1 Step 1: Product Modeling

In the first step of our process, we have to define the products which we want to configure in the environment. For that we need to design the parts of our product in the *Asset Manager* and model the possible product configurations within the *Product Modeler* as shown in Fig. 3.

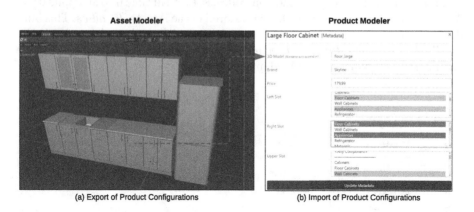

(a) Export of Product Configurations   (b) Import of Product Configurations

Fig. 3. Creating of products with the *Asset Modeler* and modeling them with the *Product Modeler*

At first, we use an *Asset Manager* like Blender[7] or AutoDesk[8] to separate the different product parts from each other and create a single model for each part (e.g. fridge of a kitchen). Moreover, we separate the 3D mesh as FBX from the texture as PNG to allow a reusing of the texture for different meshes. After that, we store both within our Unity product in the *Assets/Inputs* folder so that we can reference them with the corresponding *Importer Script*.

---

[7] Homepage of Blender: https://www.blender.org.
[8] Homepage of AutoDesk: https://www.autodesk.com.

Next, we have to model the possible product configurations within our *Product Configurator*. For that, we create a new feature model that adds multiple features that can have the type of wrapper, product-part, or textures. While wrapper features are just used for structuring the model itself, the product-part and texture features contain corresponding 3D mesh files or images. These files are referenced in the assets folder of the importer by choosing the same naming. For each feature of type product-part, we can set a brand, a price, and slots for left, right, and upper positioning. After adding all features to the feature model, we can export the model as a JSON file and store it within the *Assets/Inputs* folder so that it is useable within the *Importer Script*.

3.2   Step 2: Transfer of the Product Configuration

In the second step, we need to transfer the product configuration from the *Product Modeler* to the *Product Configurator*. The transfer process is shown in Fig. 4. In the last step, we have already shown the design and modeling of the product and its transfer to the *Importer Script*. This script is written for the Unity Game Engine and imports all files from the *Assets/Inputs* folder. After validating the files (e.g. looking if all references of the feature model are inside the folder), it bundles the JSON with the 3D meshes and textures by using the asset bundling[9] which is a build-in technique of Unity to load non-code assets at runtime into an application. After the bundling process, the DB file is stored in the *Assets/Bundles*. This bundle can be uploaded to a web server, for which we used GitHub, and downloaded by the *Product Configurator*. The *Product Configurator* downloads the asset bundle and interprets it which is described in the next step.

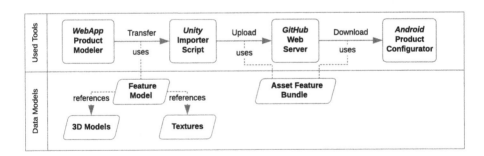

Fig. 4. Transfer of the product configuration from the *Product Modeler* to the *Product Configurator* by using the *Feature Asset Bundle*

---

[9] Asset Bundling of Unity: https://docs.unity3d.com/Manual/AssetBundlesIntro.html.

3.3   Step 3: Configuration of Products

In the last step, we need to configure the product out of the asset file as shown in Fig. 5. In the beginning, the app loads the file from the webserver and splits into the JSON feature model and the assets in the form of 3D meshes and textures. After that, the app deserializes the JSON with an external library[10] and builds an internal structure of the model to validate violations at runtime.

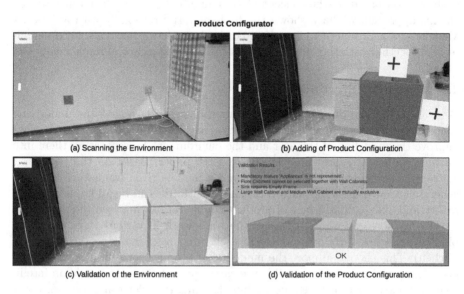

Fig. 5. Configuration of the product by scanning the environment, adding product parts and validating the product configuration

After that, the customer can scan the environment to detect horizontal surfaces on which the product parts will appear standing and vertical surfaces that will provide spatial boundaries of the environment (see Fig. 5 (a)). After that, the customer can tap on the environment and select the first product part he wants to add to the environment (see Fig. 5 (b)). From this point, the customer clicks on the plus buttons next to the placed product parts to extend the configuration and is informed with visual hints if an error (e.g. two stoves in one kitchen) duo to the placement has occurred (see Fig. 5 (c)). Moreover, the configurator validates at runtime if constraints of the underlying feature model or the user needs are violated. For that, we have developed our own feature model interpreter script. At the end of the configuration (see Fig. 5 (d)), the configurator check also violations which can not be displayed during the runtime.

---

[10] Unity-Library for JSON Interpretations: https://assetstore.unity.com/packages/ \discretionary-tools/input-management/json-net-for-unity-11347.

4   Conclusion and Outlook

Mobile shopping apps have been used Augmented Reality (AR) in the last years to place their products in the environment of the customer. While this is possible with atomic 3D objects, there is still a lack in the runtime configuration of 3D object compositions based on user needs and environmental constraints. For this, we previously developed an approach for model-based AR-assisted product configuration based on the concept of Dynamic Software Product Lines. Based on this approach, we have shown the tool-support ProConAR with a Product Modeler and a Product Configurator. For both, we have shown a solution architecture together with the most important parts of the technical implementation.

4.1   Research Directions

We want to extend our approach and our tool support so that the underlying concepts can be used domain-independent across VR and AR apps. For that, we improve the modeling of the user and the environment by separating them into distinct models as represented in our research paper. Based on that, we want to transfer our model-based approach into a model-driven framework that can generate code for different platforms. These platforms can be all kinds of mixed reality and allow a fluid usage of product configurations between the platforms.

Furthermore, we want to extend the framework in various ways: First, we plan to configure parts of products in each other (e.g. changing the grips of a kitchen). This should support the modeling of product configuration with finer granularity and extend the possible use cases. Second, we want to add an intelligent obstacle detection based on machine learning (e.g. detecting sockets, water connections). This should improve the constraints space of the possible product configurations with the environment. Third, we add support for collaborative product configuration (e.g. changings of the product configuration by the customer and the kitchen salesman). This will allow a multi-user experience in the configuration of products by taking also a product validation based on different user feedback into account.

References

1. Apel, S., Batory, D., Kästner, C., Saake, G.: Feature-Oriented Software Product Lines. Springer, Heidelberg (2013). https://doi.org/10.1007/978-3-642-37521-7
2. Capilla, R., Bosch, J., Trinidad, P., Ruiz-Cortés, A., Hinchey, M.: An overview of dynamic software product line architectures and techniques: observations from research and industry. J. Syst. Softw. **91**, 3–23 (2014)
3. Chatzopoulos, D., Bermejo, C., Huang, Z., Hui, P.: Mobile augmented reality survey: from where we are to where we go. IEEE Access **5**, 6917–6950 (2017)
4. Dacko, S.G.: Enabling smart retail settings via mobile augmented reality shopping apps. Technol. Forecast. Soc. Chang. **124**, 243–256 (2017)
5. Gottschalk, S., Rittmeier, F., Engels, G.: Hypothesis-driven adaptation of business models based on product line engineering. In: Proceedings of the 22nd Conference on Business Informatics (CBI). IEEE (2020)

6. Gottschalk, S., Yigitbas, E., Schmidt, E., Engels, G.: Model-based product configuration in augmented reality applications. In: Human-Centered Software Engineering. Springer (2020)
7. Kephart, J.O., Chess, D.M.: The vision of autonomic computing. Computer **36**(1), 41–50 (2003)

Augmented and Virtual Reality Object Repository for Rapid Prototyping

Ivan Jovanovikj$^{(\boxtimes)}$ ⓘ, Enes Yigitbas ⓘ, Stefan Sauer ⓘ, and Gregor Engels ⓘ

Department of Computer Science, Paderborn University, Paderborn, Germany
{ivan.jovanovikj,enes.yigitbas,stefan.sauer,gregor.engels}@upb.de

Abstract. Augmented Reality (AR) and Virtual Reality (VR) are technologies on the rise and as their market grows, speeding up the process of developing new ideas becomes even more important. In achieving rapid development, rapid prototyping plays a very important role. To support rapid prototyping, this demo paper presents an approach that relies on an object repository. It enables scanning, editing, storing and publishing of virtual objects that can be reused in different augmented and virtual reality applications. To show the benefits of the approach, an exemplary scenario is illustrated by prototyping an interior design application.

Keywords: Augmented Reality · Virtual Reality · Object repository · Rapid prototyping

1 Introduction

Augmented Reality (AR) and Virtual Reality (VR) have received grown interest by customers and media. The worldwide spending is predicted to over 20 billion USD in 2020[1] and up to 192 billion USD in the following three years[2]. Hence, the rapid development of new applications becomes even more important. Therefore, software designers and engineers should be able to quickly build AR/VR prototypes. However, developing such prototypes is not an easy task as the existing tools and SDKs are often highly technical and as such require much up-front learning effort [2,5]. Additionally, they are platform-dependent, making platform evaluations more complex. To support the designers in reusing existing objects in multiple prototypes and to gain a quick look at how the application might look and work, a large collection of different kinds of objects is needed. A fast way of building such a collection is translating physical objects into virtual ones. To speed up the prototyping of AR and VR applications, we combine an object repository with prototyping mechanisms. Therefore, in this demo paper, we present *AVROsitory* which is an **A**ugmented and **V**irtual **R**eality **O**bject Repo**sitory**. Our approach utilizes the strengths of both object repositories and prototyping tools and comprises three main components: server (with an object repository), mobile client, and a web client component, as shown in Fig. 1.

---

[1] idc.com https://bit.ly/3cI02HT.

[2] statista.com https://bit.ly/3jgLX6x.

R. Bernhaupt et al. (Eds.): HCSE 2020, LNCS 12481, pp. 216–224, 2020.
https://doi.org/10.1007/978-3-030-64266-2_15

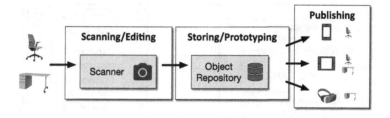

Fig. 1. Overview of the solution idea

The *Scanning/Editing* component is a mobile client which enables the designers to add new objects or edit existing ones. The real-world physical objects can be scanned and transferred into digital objects via Photogrammetry [1]. It is also possible to scan physical objects with a smartphone and add them to the repository as virtual objects. Photogrammetry offers a quick solution for creating mock-ups, that can be used for prototypes, but as final AR/VR objects too. The *Storing/Prototyping* component, i.e., server, is a an object repository which enables reusability by providing a tagging system to classify the objects, thus allowing a quick search on existing objects. Furthermore, objects can be also classified by the level of detail quality so that depending on the usage scenario an object with a suitable quality can be provided. While in some cases an object must be in great detail, the same might be used in the background somewhere else, requiring less detail and fewer resources. Business logic can be also added to objects with a specific task by using the logic templates. Finally, the *Publishing* component is a web client which provides a mechanism (Unity Scripted Importer) to Unity IDE. As a result, a reusable Unity object (prefab) is added to the project's assets in Unity and it can be used for developing AR/VR prototypes or AR/VR applications. Furthermore, it provides also an option for creating custom importers for other IDEs.

The rest of the paper is structured as follows: In Sect. 2, the architecture of the repository is presented. To show the feasibility of our approach, in Sect. 3, we present an application example where the developed repository was used in a prototyping scenario. In Sect. 4, we briefly discuss the related work and in the end, Sect. 5 concludes the work and gives an outlook on future work.

2   Solution Concept

In this section, we present the solution concept which builds upon an object repository for prototyping and development of AR/VR applications. As shown in Fig. 2, our solution consists of three main components. The central component is the server which contains the object repository.

Before explaining the object repository, we shortly discuss the different types of supported objects. An *object* is defined as a 2D or 3D graphical model with optional business logic. It can depict small single real-world items as well as entire

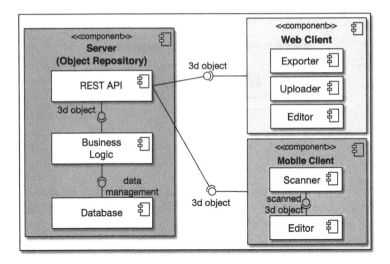

Fig. 2. Solution architecture: a central server application with a web interface and an Android client.

rooms. The business logic is rather basic as it does not contain any application-specific context. For example, an object representing a button would contain only a basic on-click listener without specific behavior. By evaluating existing AR applications publicly available, we classified the objects based on the user interaction into *non-interactive*, *click/touch-triggered*, and *range-triggered*. A *non-interactive* object entails no business logic, e.g., a decorative object. On the contrary, a *click/touch-triggered* entails a business logic, e.g., a UI button. Finally, a *range-triggered* object is triggered according to a user's distance, e.g., a descriptive text appears when a user is in a given range. The object repository includes business logic for these object classes in terms of logic templates only, that can be written by the repository users, extending the existing solutions to their needs. So, the object repository stores graphics, business logic, and metadata. The objects are accessible via a REST-API which means that data is stored as entities, which can be retrieved, updated, and deleted via HTTP requests. The entities consist of metadata and binaries. Whereas the metadata is stored in a database, the binary objects are stored in the server's file system. The binary objects include original graphics, as well as converted binaries in formats distributed via the REST-API. The second component of the object repository is a mobile application which is the main client for designers. A mobile application was chosen, because of the wide availability of smartphones today, which makes prototyping easier and quicker. As the object repository is based on a server that offers an API, other client applications that run on Microsoft's HoloLens[3], or photogrammetry equipment, e.g., tablets, can be added later on. The mobile client supports multiple tasks. As the client application synchronizes with the

---

[3] www.microsoft.com/hololens.

server, the users can display and browse the repository everywhere. This enables the users to preview their objects in their current environment. Furthermore, multiple objects can be combined into one composition thus allowing more complex mock-ups. The mobile client also enables users to create new objects and upload them to the server. The user can use photogrammetry and chroma-keying to create 3D and 2D graphics respectively. The objects can then be extended with metadata, like tags and quality levels. The last component is a web client that has similar functions to the mobile client, except that it does not allow any kind of scanning. However, it allows existing graphics to be uploaded. Its main purpose is to enable exporting objects to an IDE.

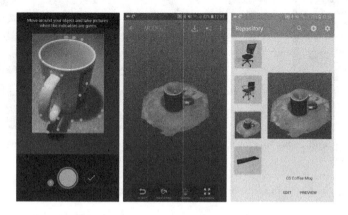

Fig. 3. Scanning of a coffee mug: Defining photogrammetry key points marked in green (left and middle); The imported object in the repository (right). (Color figure online)

3   Application Example

This section presents an exemplary prototyping scenario of an interior design application. The application should enable users to decorate an empty office desk, to make design choices. Therefore, the application enables them to augment their desk with decorations and items from a catalog in the AR application. To achieve this, we firstly scan physical objects from an existing, real office desk and add them to the repository. These objects are then previewed, provided with business logic, if necessary, and in the further development process, replaced by high-quality 3D models. At the beginning, we have two 3D models of office chairs and one of a keyboard. Then, the three objects are added, all of them in good quality without any logic (classes). We begin by determining which catalog items we want to provide with our application. For simplicity, we support a basic set of coffee mugs, keyboard, monitor, and chairs. As our repository already contains chairs and a keyboard, we want to add models of coffee mugs and a monitor. The coffee mugs are scanned with photogrammetry, as shown in Fig. 3.

As *AVROsitory* does not include an integrated photogrammetry solution, we use Scann3D[4], a third-party tool. As we are in an early development phase, it is sufficient for our monitor model to be two-dimensional. Therefore, we are using the build-in object creation by taking a photo. We also provide metadata for the object, as shown in Fig. 4a, for further reuse.

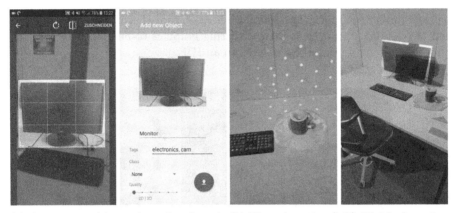

(a) Cropping and importing of a photo in the repository

(b) Plane detection (left); Finished preview with simulated shadow (right)

Fig. 4. Cropping, importing, and previewing of repository objects

So far, we have all objects in our repository that we need. We can thus proceed to test how our application would look like, when the user previews the decoration. To do that, we create a composition of our repository objects (the screenshot on the right in Fig. 4b). To enable interaction with the objects, we firstly sketch a button prototype on a board and we add it to the repository by simply taking a picture, as shown in the screenshots in Fig. 5. After minor editing, the button can be used in the example application. To really test the added objects, the programmers create a prototypical application using the objects. Firstly, they import the objects into Unity using the *AVROsitory* web client and add some business logic to our buttons, as shown in Fig. 6.

As the development is going on, we design high-quality models for our furniture, and we add these models to our repository as high-quality versions of our prototyping objects. Also, more buttons are needed and for this purpose, we can reuse the existing button logic in the repository. As we now have higher quality objects, we can replace the mock-ups in the actual application, as shown in Fig. 7.

---

[4] Scann3D by SmartMobileVision. Paid application. Not related to this work.

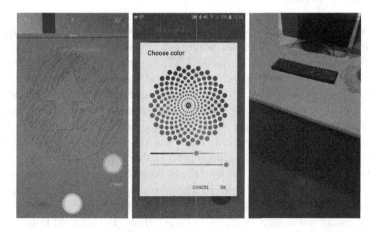

Fig. 5. Taking a picture in front of a monochromatic background (left) and using chroma keying to get a transparent background (middle and right).

Fig. 6. Using the web client (left) to export our objects into Unity (right)

Fig. 7. Adding some button logic in the button script (left); object composition in Unity with better quality (right).

4   Related Work

AR and VR applications are widely spread in various application domains (e.g., health [6], education [8], etc.). As described in previous work (e.g., [3,7]), the prototyping and development of AR and VR applications is a cumbersome and challenging task. Multiple research projects and commercial tools are trying to make AR/VR application prototyping and development easier, quicker and overall more accessible. One can roughly categorize them into two types: repositories and authoring tools. Unity Asset Store[5] and Google Poly[6] are both repositories, albeit they serve different purposes. Poly is a sharing platform for digital art, mostly 3D models and its sole purpose is to enable designers to browse through the catalog and look for useful models. Unity Asset Store, on the other hand, distributes assets, whereby assets refer to whole components of programs, including art, audio and business logic. Furthermore, Unity Asset Store is neither limited to AR/VR assets nor does it specifically target them. In contrast, Poly is focused on AR/VR development, although it is not necessarily limited to these applications. So, object and asset repositories enable user to share and re-use their content over multiple projects. Nonetheless, they come with some pitfalls. If a repository is too restrictive, Poly for example, then its use is limited as it only allows plain 3D objects with no logic. Unity Asset Store contains almost every type of component that can be made in Unity Engine, which is why it is time-consuming to find an asset that fits your needs. Then, there are authoring tools, like DART [4] and ProtoAR [5], both of them targeting AR. They do not provide content in terms of 3D objects, but rather support the prototyping and/or development of applications. While DART is based on Macromedia Director and thus acts as a development environment, ProtoAR serves as a prototyping tool only. As it only simulates AR functionality, ProtoAR does not fully support development. DART assist prototyping with its ability to record sensor data and play them back outside of the targeted environment. In contrast to ProtoAR, DART stronger supports development. DART's approach, however, is inflexible, because it ties the development to a specific tool for the whole process, from design prototyping to actual implementation. This approach might have been useful in the early 2000s, because of limited AR framework, today, however, it is too restrictive. The approach of ProtoAR, a tool for prototyping only, seems more appropriate. Designers can use ProtoAR to create mock-ups for their UI design, while developers can work with a tool set of their own choice. While this is more flexible, it does mean the designers cannot extend their prototype gradually, as at one point they have to switch their tool set.

Therefore, our solution, combines both approaches. It is an object repository, providing AR/VR specific objects, that can be used in any development environment. These objects also contain templates for logic, thus assisting the developers when prototyping or developing. This can be combined with a tool set for designers to create digital mock-ups from paper and previewing their

---

[5] https://assetstore.unity.com/.
[6] https://poly.google.com/.

design on an actual AR/VR device. The repository can be accessed via REST API, therefore the supported IDEs and devices can be extended.

5   Conclusion and Future Work

In this demo paper, we presented our approach for object round-tripping which supports the rapid prototyping of AR/VR applications. Designers can add new objects to the repository by using existing graphics or by creating new ones by taking pictures or via photogrammetry. Objects can be classified to support their reusability. Metadata, graphics, and business logic are stored separately, enabling easier and independent editing. Additionally, this enables storing each of those units to be stored either as a database for metadata or the file system for binary objects. With the case study, we have shown an exemplary use of the object repository and how the designers can benefit from the different provided features. While the concept is promising, several topics can be addressed by subsequent research. As the object repository is designed with extensibility in mind, using a platform-independent REST-API for all central functionalities, the approach can be extended to a variety of client devices. For example, a dedicated photogrammetry scanner or AR devices, like Microsoft's HoloLens can be added. They may increase the object quality without increasing the workload significantly. Additionally, the repository can be extended by object recognition to enable automatic tagging of objects.

Acknowledgements. We would like to thank our student Niklas Junge who helped implementing the presented approach.

References

1. Foster, S., Halbstein, D.: Integrating 3D Modeling, Photogrammetry and Design. SCS. Springer, London (2014). https://doi.org/10.1007/978-1-4471-6329-9
2. Gandy, M., MacIntyre, B.: Designer's augmented reality toolkit, ten years later: implications for new media authoring tools. In: Proceedings of the 27th Annual ACM Symposium on User Interface Software and Technology, UIST 2014, pp. 627–636. ACM (2014)
3. Krings, S., Yigitbas, E., Jovanovikj, I., Sauer, S., Engels, G.: Development framework for context-aware augmented reality applications. In: ACM SIGCHI Symposium on Engineering Interactive Computing Systems, EICS 2020, pp. 9:1–9:6. ACM (2020)
4. MacIntyre, B., Gandy, M., Dow, S., Bolter, J.D.: DART: the designer's augmented reality toolkit. https://ael.gatech.edu/dart/
5. Nebeling, M., Nebeling, J., Yu, A., Rumble, R.: ProtoAR: rapid physical-digital prototyping of mobile augmented reality applications. In: Proceedings of the 2018 CHI Conference on Human Factors in Computing Systems, CHI 2018, pp. 353:1–353:12. ACM (2018)
6. Yigitbas, E., Heindörfer, J., Engels, G.: A context-aware virtual reality first aid training application. In: Proceedings of Mensch und Computer 2019, pp. 885–888. GI/ACM (2019)

7. Yigitbas, E., Jovanovikj, I., Sauer, S., Engels, G.: On the development of context-aware augmented reality applications. In: Abdelnour Nocera, J., et al. (eds.) INTERACT 2019. LNCS, vol. 11930, pp. 107–120. Springer, Cham (2020). https://doi.org/10.1007/978-3-030-46540-7_11
8. Yigitbas, E., Tejedor, C.B., Engels, G.: Experiencing and programming the ENIAC in VR. In: Mensch und Computer 2020, pp. 505–506. ACM (2020)

Author Index

Printed in the United States
By Bookmasters